COLOR MONITORS

COLOR MONITORS

The Black Face of Technology in America

MARTIN KEVORKIAN

cornell university press

ithaca and london

First published 2006 by Cornell University Press
First printing, Cornell Paperbacks, 2006

Printed in the United States of America

Design by Scott Levine

Library of Congress Cataloging-in-Publication Data

Kevorkian, Martin, 1968–
    Color monitors : the black face of technology in America / Martin
Kevorkian.
        p. cm.
    Includes bibliographical references and index.
    ISBN–13: 978–0–8014–4443–2 (cloth : alk. paper)
    ISBN–10: 0–8014–4443–8 (cloth : alk. paper)
    ISBN–13: 978–0–8014–7278–7 (pbk. : alk. paper)
    ISBN–10: 0–8014–7278–4 (pbk. : alk. paper)
    1. African Americans in mass media.   2. African Americans in
popular culture.   3. Computers—Social aspects—United States.
4. Technology—Social aspects—United States.   I. Title.
P94.5.A372U558 2005
302.2308996073—dc22
                                                            2005025052

Cornell University Press strives to use environmentally responsible suppliers and materials to the fullest extent possible in the publishing of its books. Such materials include vegetable-based, low-VOC inks and acid-free papers that are recycled, totally chlorine-free, or partly composed of nonwood fibers. For further information, visit our website at www.cornellpress.cornell.edu.

Cloth printing   10 9 8 7 6 5 4 3 2 1
Paperback printing   10 9 8 7 6 5 4 3 2 1

For TTP, a real scientist who played one in the movies

And for Don Nino, *capo delle volpi*

CONTENTS

ACKNOWLEDGMENTS

Recognizing the likelihood of an initial perplexity, I offer my first acknowledgment to the reader. *Color Monitors*, a book about race and technology, invites the reader to consider images of the black computer expert. A first reaction may well be: what images of the black computer expert? I presume to anticipate this reaction because I have encountered it so frequently in conversations about my research. When I tell people that I am interested in the portrayal of idealized blacks as having a special affinity for computer expertise, only rarely do I detect any sense of immediate recognition. But here's the thing: a minute, an hour, a day later, the same person who had expressed initial bewilderment gets back to me with a list of perfect examples.

Those two-stage conversations have provided an important impetus for this book. The initial reaction, that of surprise or disbelief, has repeatedly convinced me of the need for this project: few people have consciously registered the cultural phenomenon I call color monitoring, the imaginative assignment of "technically supporting" roles to black bodies who willingly bear the computer burdens that their betters would prefer to avoid. The follow-up reaction, the strong "A-ha" factor, continually assures me of the theory's validity: once people get it, they begin to see the pattern everywhere, as peripheral figures from the technological shadows snap into focus. Scenes from movies, stories in the newspaper, anecdotes from the workplace—a wide range of cultural narratives tend to reflect a negative attitude toward technology and a compensatory escapist fantasy. Most Americans have no great love for the technical details of computers. American culture has ever imagined certain types of undesirable work to be suitable for racial others; in an electronic age, digital drudgery, from data entry to tech support, comes wishfully to be defined as someone else's headache. For substantial portions of the populace, the image of the black man at the computer supplies a ready, reflex, shorthand: someone else—not you—will handle all the troubleshooting. The color monitoring pattern becomes visible once the underlying logics begin to come into view.

I am grateful to the many individuals who proved willing to participate in the critical act of looking. A substantial amount of data gathered for this book came my way through the alert generosity of a rather large and informal network of accidental co-researchers who joined the project through conversations, two-stage or otherwise. Thus, from the start, this project has been collaborative in ways that I cannot begin to acknowledge fully. Above all, I thank Tanya Paull, for being my first, last, and best reader and for seeing all those movies with me. I thank the extended families that Tanya and I share—Paull, Uyeda, McNulty, and Kevorkian—for faith and nurture. Supplying crucial intellectual community and friendship, Stanley Orr, Cheryl Edelson, John Dalton, Curtis Gruenler, Lezlie Gruenler, and Thad Bower likewise all gave shape to the project from its very inception.

The idea became a manuscript at the University of Texas at Austin, a most edifying workplace inhabited by wonderful colleagues. To members of the English department who read and commented on drafts, I owe a particularly large debt: to Wayne Rebhorn, for godfathering the book; to Douglas Bruster, for herculean editing and re-editing; to Liz Scala, for keeping an energetic eye on global variables and the occasional tennis ball; to Joanna Brooks, for big-sisterly wisdom and paw marks from the dog park; to Jeffrey Howard, for Pynchon notes and Powers points; to Phil Barrish, for compression algorithms and reordering of subroutines; to Evan Carton, for eloquent mentoring that elevated the inquiry. I thank Dean Richard Lariviere for a fellowship and for keeping the College of Liberal Arts strategically equipped with computer technology. I thank fearless leader Jim Garrison, along with Jim Lee, Lisa Moore, Frank Whigham, and other members of the English department's executive committee who jointly and severally conveyed encouraging critiques at the time of my third-year review. A multitude of thanks goes to Noah Mass for contributions transcending the category of research assistance and again to Jim Garrison, with the aid of Cecilia Smith-Morris, for supporting Noah's exceptional efforts.

Further thanks to those who offered manifold intelligence and encouragement: Ryan Powers, for being tragically hip and for reading my stuff; Gabe Lopez, for reading much and knowing the score; Marshall Maresca, for insights on Neal Stephenson and all-around sci-fi expertise; Clay Maer, for asking what Emerson would think; Susanna Castillo, for greatly enabling the harmonious coexistence of teaching with scholarship; Dan Birkholz, for lunch; David Kamper, for helping me to see the sun; Jorie Woods, for talking to me at parties; Jennifer Wilks, for telling me robot stories; Jeremy Dean, for thoughts on slaves and cyborgs; Sabrina Barton, for crime scene investigation; Jeffrey Jaeckle, for pattern recognition software; Dave Chang, for freelancing; Bill Cassady, for running a tight (and wired) ship; Charlie Merrow, for instructive technological enthusiasm; Benjamin Braun, for writing lightcycles; Rick Olesek, for pinpoint solutions; Abhi Vakil, for a generous entrepreneurial spirit; Andy Hsieh, for believing; Teri Krenek, for using Melville and Čapek in the same sentence; Erika Arenivas, for black and white clarity; Michael Haykinson, for the will to figure anything out; Michael Colacurcio, for being the voice in my head; Michael Bryman, for teaching me to read movies; Blanca Madriz, for radiant cool; Matt Rollins, for the way of the *kitsune*; Ivy Shyu, for reading cultural prescriptions; Andrew Brummett, for thoughts by the wayside; Robert Rogers, for high standards; Erika Halstead, for boldly going; Seth Park, for computing language; Arnold Jin, for dying hardest.

I thank Hope College as well as Scholia in Austin for invitations to try out and hone work in progress; I enjoyed the warm hospitality and sharp questions on both occasions. The Futures of American Studies summer institute at Dartmouth College likewise supplied much food for thought; thanks especially to Andy Doolen for picking up Ellisonian frequencies. An earlier version of chapter 1 was published as "Computers with Color Monitors" (*American Quarterly* 51, no. 2 [1999], 283–310), and I thank Johns Hopkins University Press for their permission to use that information here. I am grateful to Bernie Kendler at the Cornell University Press for guiding the project and for placing the manuscript in the hands of anonymous readers whose attentive comments helped strengthen and enrich this book. Additional Cornell Press credits go to Alison Kalett, for editorial alacrity; to

Karen Laun and Martin Schneider, for astute copyediting; to Scott Levine and Nancy Ferguson, for commitment to quality on the art program; and to Susan Barnett, for energetic insights.

It is of course customary to include a disclaimer that all remaining deficiencies in the book are one's own. Yet having alluded to the pervasive contributions of so many helpful people, I would feel a bit churlish—as if I were ultimately assuming all of the credit—if I were to exclude my co-conspirators from any potential blame. If you see something here you don't like, please let me know and I will be sure to connect you to the relevant party. But I will not blame the computer. The truth of HAL, however treacherous *2001* made him out to be, abides: "No 9000 computer has ever made a mistake or distorted information. We are all, by any practical definition of the words, foolproof and incapable of error." I thank, finally, My Computer, and all the people who made it possible.

COLOR MONITORS

SCREENS FOR TECHNOLOGY AND RACE
IN AMERICAN CULTURE

Toms, Coons, Mulattoes, Mammies, and Bucks—and Computer Experts? Donald Bogle's influential survey of the limiting ways that blacks have been represented in American films, first issued in 1973, with its blunt title distilled five recurring types. Documenting and interpreting patterns, Bogle's work has helped readers of culture achieve what Ralph Ellison calls "the victory of conscious perception" over stereotypes and their power to "conceal."[1] Since the late 1980s, a new black image has turned up in American movies with remarkable frequency without yet being remarked upon: the black man at the computer monitor. Film after film shows black men as technologically adept characters. Surely this pattern reflects good intentions on the part of filmmakers. Virtually all of these characters present positive images; casting a black man in the role of the computer expert seems affirmative. The early stereotypes Bogle named tended to reduce identity to bodily behavior, whether docile, shiftless, tragic, cantankerous, or predatory. The new role instead celebrates brain function.[2] And it offers a way of telling a beloved American success story: black man makes good in the white world. (Or, to tilt the emphasis: black man made good by the white world.) But why such an overrepresentation of blackness in this particular technological role? And just how positive is such a role for the black man, if we consider the other bodies traditionally assigned, in popular depictions, to the computer seat: weakling nerds, often children? Behind the impulse for electronic affirmative action, we can see a PC paradox: the goodwill of Political Correctness betrays its unease about race and technology in the realm of the Personal Computer.

In an increasingly microprocessed world, images of computers permeate American culture. Wondrous machines allow busy adults to shop and pay bills in their bathrobes, inspire wide-eyed children to explore a web of multimedia learning resources, and fill endless hours of enlightened leisure. But these images of convenience, education, and recreation do not tell the whole story of how people feel about the new devices. Technological advance can also be perceived as a terrifying encroachment on humanity. One much-cited study by Dell indicated that, by the mid-1990s, 55 percent of the American public was experiencing "cyberphobia," a term coined in the early 1980s to describe an aversion to computer technology.[3] Many people have been afraid of getting too close to the machine.

Popular portrayals of the computer accordingly reflect and feed the fear of too much engagement with technology. To analyze American cyberphobia, *Color Monitors* looks at a particular subset of imagined computer use, focusing on scenarios that demand from the person at the keyboard an intimate technical knowledge. My research has uncovered a peculiar pattern: race comes into sharp relief when computer use is depicted as difficult labor requiring special expertise. Time and again, in such scenarios, the helpful person of color is there to take the call—to provide technical support, to deal with the machines. In interpreting such images, *Color Monitors* analyzes the computer-fearing strain in American whiteness, an aspect of white identity that defines itself against information technology and the racial other imagined to love it and excel at it. The computer expert most disproportionately projected by this cyberphobic whiteness is the black male.[4] I argue that fears about the dehumanizing, disembodying effects of information technology and fears of the black male body work as mutually reinforcing impulses behind popular depictions of black males as computer experts. In this equation, cyberphobic whiteness—fearing technology's capacity to disembody humanity, to take bodies out of the circuit of action—unconsciously projects technology onto the one set of bodies that it most fears.[5] The image of the obliging black man behind the monitor reassures viewers that the displayed body is safely occupied, both contained by and containing the threat of the computer.

computers can be fun...but someone has to
program them

Hailed as "the biggest science fiction director of all time," Steven Spielberg also stands among the most influential representatives of the technophobic mindset.[6] His mega-blockbusters, including *E.T.* (1982) and *Jurassic Park* (1993), have repeatedly cashed in on fears of technoscience. When asked in 2002, "What technologies scare you today?" Spielberg responded with the following distinction:

> For me it's all about the level of intimidation. There are certain technologies that scare me because I don't think I'm very good at them. For instance, programming a computer. I can get on AOL, but that's about it. But I'm a gameplayer as you know. So I play games and I can navigate any game narrative. . . . I have to control the joystick.[7]

Spielberg tells us that while he loves playing video games, the computer technology scares him. We see this narrow appetite at work both in his films and in cyberphobic America as well. Yet while American culture loves to hype high-tech toys, *Color Monitors* focuses instead on what Spielberg is so eager to leave behind. Looking beyond the joy of the joystick or even the ease of the mouse-click, this book analyzes attitudes about the drudgery of the keyboard, the terrors of the program code.

Spielberg's *Minority Report* (2002) provides a handy identity chart for the split between game player and programmer. The movie's hero, portrayed by Tom Cruise with his usual hyperkinetic brio, does indeed interact with computers—but always from the Spielberg's preferred vantage point: as navigator of a game narrative. As the leader of a crime unit, Cruise's character, John Anderton, enjoys access to a vast array of electronic surveillance options. He *has* America online, the vitals of its citizenry at his fingertips. In working a case, he stands before a large virtual screen, waving his hands like a conductor. Like director Spielberg, Anderton is the maestro of the image: as he points and sweeps, the pictures dance for him. Meanwhile, his digital assistant Jad (Steve Harris) tends to the data stream, seated at a keyboard and performing database searches at Anderton's request. Jad is the only black character in the crime unit. He is also the only character dressed in office attire. When the all-white SWAT team, led by Anderton, dashes off to apprehend the suspect, only Jad stays behind, at his stationary post with the computer, continually retrieving information and feeding it to the action heroes. This fictional construct highlights the rift in Spielberg's feelings toward technology. That the efforts of a peripheral black character (efforts that constrain Jad to a certain place and a certain kind of work) support a white hero's escapism (Cruise's character is quite literally a fugitive from his workplace) underscores an important division of labor even as it shows us larger fears and fantasies about computer use. As *Color Monitors* will demonstrate, *Minority Report* follows a clear trend in information-age representation.

But Aren't Computer Experts Geeky White Kids?

Of course, increased casting of the black man to deal with the immobilizing work of the computer expert has not eliminated the most venerable stereotype for the role: the young, white, pencil-necked geek who can't get a date. One could note Seth Green in *The Italian Job* (2003), Eddie Jemison as the nervous nebbish in *Ocean's Eleven* (2001), D. J. Qualls as the translucent junk-food junky of *The Core* (2003), Jamie Harrold as the live-at-home loser in *The Score* (2001) and as the generic data-gopher in *The Sum of All Fears* (2002), Noah Taylor as milquetoast tech support in the two *Tomb Raider* movies (2001, 2003) and in *Vanilla Sky* (2001). Films typically portray white characters who perform onerous computer labor as weak and ineffectual in both body and personality. The phrases "computer geek" or "computer nerd" are almost inescapable. Their common use proclaims that it is bad to be an expert. This default nerd profile sheds important light on the reflex logic that matches the black man to the monitor. The computer supporting role means diminished physical potency.

Equally revealing are the responses to representations that have ventured to break out of the spindly default mold without changing the race to black. Ill-received attempts to make the hacker a strong, sexy white male underscore popular presumptions about the computer expert role and its bodily parameters. The considerable critical protest that met *Swordfish* (2001) and *The Recruit* (2003) focused on the perceived inappropriateness of assigning a healthy leading man to the keyboard seat. When *The Recruit* cast Hollywood hunk-of-the-moment Colin Farrell as a computer whiz, skeptics perceived an incongruity between body and role: the offense came in the form of "an MIT-educated software engineer with suspiciously good muscle tone."[8] *Swordfish* starred Hugh Jackman, better known as Wolverine from the *X-Men* series (2000, 2003), as a hacker in a "computer-nerd flick (lots of lit-up screens and furious typing) trying desperately to pass itself off as a sex 'n' violence high-tech thriller."[9] This critic did not suggest that "high-tech" and "thriller" are mutually exclusive terms, merely that the product in question failed to fulfill the formula. The telling objection appears in parentheses, in the disparaging reference to "typing" that typifies this mode of critical displeasure: saddling the hero with a computer obstructs the real action payoffs of the genre. Another critic made plain the nature of the central casting violation: "The nerd in question is Hugh Jackman. . . . This gives you some idea of how far-fetched the story is—Jackman is way too muscle-bound to make a convincing hacker, not to mention being too old. Has no one told the filmmakers the geeks out there are all kids?"[10] Conventional Hollywood narratives reinforce that impression: techno tots and teens abound on screen. The only deviations from the weakling, childlike norm that consistently pass without critical comment involve casting a black man. Which is to say, the black male computer expert has become an acceptable norm.

In *Minority Report,* the black database whiz has been tasked with narrowing the field of suspects. Jad enters rapid keystrokes and reports that he is "sorting by race and age." In the popular imagination, screening filters for race and age apply also to the computer expert role itself, though the race factor is never made explicit. While critics resisted the casting of athletic, adult white actors as the computer experts in *Swordfish* and *The Recruit,* they objected not at all to the similar casting of an athletic, adult black actor in the far more successful *Minority Report.* Indeed, before taking on the cyber-role of Jad, Steve Harris had convincingly portrayed heavyweight boxing champion Sonny Liston.[11] No critic carped about the "suspiciously good muscle tone" of his deskbound computer expert. Similarly, when Ving Rhames portrayed the character nicknamed "Cyber-Op" in *Mission: Impossible* (1996), no one objected that this black actor—whose forearms dwarf Jackman's—was "too muscle-bound" to type.

In the popular imagination, a white action body cannot perform the work of the computer geek. The technological burden offends action sensibilities; the computer-tainted identity interrupts enjoyment of the idealized masculine form. To serve in the role of cybernerd is for all intents and purposes to be denied a body. In the unspoken case of the black man, this denial not yet caused widespread concern.

so why has no one noticed this pattern before?

In *American Anatomies,* Robyn Wiegman notes how recent visual media trends toward "more clearly inclusive representational imagery" have made certain kinds of racism harder to detect.[12] Yet within this field of more inclusive imagery, racially differentiating patterns and attitudes persist. *Color Monitors* seeks to make these patterns more visible by considering how attitudes about race and technology overlap. Scholarship has rarely considered the terms of race and technology in conjunction. In approaching these questions from the vantage point of the humanities, *Color Monitors* draws analytical strength from literary sources. Raising the conjoined issues at the heart of this study, Ralph Ellison's *Invisible Man* (1952) helps illuminate the racial unconscious of machine dreams. As Ellison mockingly noted, what the white man most desires from the black man is his absence, an absence bound to the machine: "He's invisible, a walking personification of the Negative, the most perfect achievement of your dreams, sir! The mechanical man!" For Ellison, the Invisible Man is the technological man, himself a well-regulated machine who will tend to other machines kept well out of sight. Ellison's insight that "*we are the machines inside the machine*" strikes the keynote of this study, which attempts to unfold what such a critique looks like in the full-blown information age, from the mid-1980s to the present.[13]

Color Monitors addresses gaps in both technoculture studies and critical race theory by bringing race into the discussion of computers and by considering technology as a factor in racial constructions of identity. Race tends to be a missing term in current accounts of technology and culture. As David Bell notes in *An Introduction to Cybercultures* (2001), commentary on computer-related culture in particular has been "surprisingly silent about race."[14] In an essay from 2002, Alexander Weheliye points to a similar deficit: "While gender and sexuality have been crucial to theories of both cyberspace and the posthuman, the absence of race is usually perfunctorily remarked and of little consequence to these analyses."[15] Cultural studies of the computer age, from Scott Bukatman's *Terminal Identity* to Katherine Hayles's *How We Became Posthuman,* have devoted scrupulous attention to gender with regard to information technologies. But the same field has given short shrift to issues of race.[16] Conversely, studies of racial identity construction, with notable contributions including Fred Pfiel's *White Guys* and the collection *Representing Black Men,* tend to overlook the matter of technology. A revisiting of brief examples from Pfeil's and Hayles's justly celebrated studies will give some idea of what the *Color Monitors* approach can recover by reading simultaneously for race and technology.

Pfeil's supple and freewheeling analysis accounts for race, gender, and class in detailing the construction of white, male, working-class identity. But his omission of the technology factor, so crucial for the "male rampage" films he critiques, creates a blind spot. For example, his critical framework leads him to all but ignore a key whiteness-defining instance of the genre: Pfeil discounts race in *Die Hard 2: Die Harder* (1990) by noting the filmmakers' gestures to "randomize" that variable across all roles.[17] But attention to displays of electronic expertise would reveal that the division of labor in this film is anything but racially random. What Pfeil misses is something that commentators have consistently passed over without notice: the intersection of race and technology.

Bruce Willis, as tough cop John McClane, quickly establishes his action-hero credentials by expressing bewildered hostility toward the devices of the information age. Responding to one such moment of his resentful perplexity at these new machines, his wife explains, "Honey, it's the '90s, remember? Microchips, microwaves, faxes." For her Hungry Man, however, "Progress peaked with the frozen pizza." When another woman cheerily remarks, "Isn't technology wonderful?" the wife must confess, "My husband doesn't think so." The thriller plot supports his position. Terrorists have compromised an airport by reprogramming the control tower to misrepresent the true position of the ground to airplanes' electronic landing systems, creating a virtual reality versus tarmac conflict of catastrophic proportions. In responding to this threat, the authorities call in Mr. Barnes (Art Evans) to troubleshoot the system. The white head of security gives the black engineer his (non-)marching orders, to sit down and "figure it out." McClane himself issues a similarly terse demand for technical results from the black man: "Break the code." Explaining that it "could be a million combinations," engineer Barnes nevertheless dutifully sets himself to the chore, one he will never complete. But in his occupation with the electronic code, the black technician frees the white hero to direct his energies toward an action solution. To save the day in the film's final scene, McClane ultimately relies upon only that most elemental of technologies, fire.

But even among white guys more genuinely fascinated with the possibilities of technological advance, the racial divide can pop up in surprising

ways. Alan Turing's foundational essay on "Computing Machinery and Intelligence" (1950), the departure point for Hayles's study of the posthuman
condition, presents a richly symptomatic case. In launching her discussion,
Hayles rightly calls attention to Turing's inclusion of a test for gender distinction as a parallel to his more famous "Turing Test" for distinguishing
between human and machine.[18] Yet what remains unexamined in Turing's
manifesto is his anxious consideration of *racialized* masculine identity.
While addressing the question of whether a hidden machine can "pass" the
Turing Test for functional humanity, Turing suddenly pauses to invoke the
categories of "black man" and "white man." Turing has been answering
various objections about insuperable "disabilities" that separate machine
from human intelligence:

> The inability to enjoy strawberries and cream may have struck the
> reader as frivolous. Possibly a machine might be made to enjoy this
> delicious dish, but any attempt to make one do so would be idiotic.
> What is important about this disability is that it contributes to some
> of the other disabilities, e.g., to the difficulty of the same kind of
> friendliness occurring between man and machine as between white
> man and white man, or between black man and black man.[19]

Bruno Latour has characterized Turing's essay as "baroque," and the passage on strawberries and cream does tend to leave its convolutions aswirl.[20]
But the ordered juxtaposition of analogies adds, with some sharpness, an
implicit division to the one being explored explicitly. In the consideration
of machine intelligence, two chasms emerge: man // machine; white //
black. The boundary between man and computer may be dissimilar to the
contact between whites. But a recognition of friendliness between a white
man and a black man may be as difficult to achieve as conviviality between
a man and a machine, one that he has never even seen. Theorizing the limits of electronic presence, Turing's discourse effectively produces a version
of Ellison's Invisible Man.

In documenting and tracing the legacy of such logics within American
culture, *Color Monitors* tells the story of how computers became black.[21]
Five chapters follow the development of this pattern, with its variations and
exceptions. These chapters cover a range of cultural forms, ending with an
assessment of some creative alternatives to the pattern.

The opening chapter unpacks the cultural baggage borne by the figure of the black computer expert, with particular attention to action blockbusters ranging from *Die Hard* to *Terminator 2* to *Mission: Impossible*. In thinking about the ways that mass culture monitors the color of computer operators, I apply James Baldwin's contention that the impulse to "civilize savages" may actually be said to *be* American literature.

Chapter 2 pursues the colonial echoes of Baldwin's thesis across the territory of the American techno-thriller. In updates of British imperial adventure, from *Congo* to *The Lost World* to *The Time Machine,* black computer expertise emerges as the backup for Yankee heroism. Though the black male at the keyboard is never pragmatically important to the successful resolution of the plot, his display proves instrumental to a narrative of America's cultural dominance. Against the commonplace perception that the global information economy tends to dissolve nationality, the American techno-thriller deploys the instrumentalized black male as a bearer of national identity, proof of America's colonial competence in managing issues of race and technology.

Tracing related display strategies into the business world, chapter 3 proceeds to works of "corporate narrative"—from advertisements to annual reports—to see how some actual American companies use race to assert their identities in the electronic arena. I analyze a series of representational transactions that narrate technological incorporation: the placing of technological labor in a black box; the linking of black bodies with that black box to produce what I call the "natural machine"; and the drawing of a clear opposition between executive white masculinity and technologized blackness.

The fourth chapter forms a counterpoint to chapter 3's examination of the executive-managerial perspective. Here the study takes up anticorporate narratives—from *Office Space* to *The Matrix*—that assume a rebellious pose but nevertheless often mirror corporate values on matters of race and technology. Corporate narrative constructs computer labor as black; in anticorporate narrative, white tech workers frequently adopt blackness as an identity accessory, posing as digital slaves "workin' for The Man." In postures that echo the racial and technological ambiguities of Luke Skywalker and Darth Vader, these self-dramatizing white subjects continue to perceive technology as denigrating.

In the coda to the book, I investigate some alternative approaches taken by artists of the technological muse. Receiving signals from both Ellison and Pynchon, these practitioners of technological poetics constitute a network that includes Colson Whitehead, Richard Powers, Ellen Ullman, John Cayley, and Walter Mosley, several of whom wrote computer code before turning to literature. Reading against the racializing logic of color monitoring analyzed in the preceding chapters, this conclusion calls attention to thoughtful transformations of technological identity crafted by writers willing to get inside the black box.

chapter one

COMPUTERS WITH COLOR MONITORS

In the farewell frames of the comic strip *Outland* (1989–95), a particular facet of white imagination achieves a realized eschatology. Oliver Wendell Jones, the black child known for his precocious use of his personal computer, makes his final exit from the Sunday papers (see fig. 1) with a "microprocessor in ear" and a "color monitor in face."[1] Indeed, as a review of depictions of digitality in recent popular films will reveal, images of computer operators *are* carefully monitored for facial color. In the bizarre drawing of Jones, a piece of cultural logic simply reaches its conclusion: the black body itself becomes a personal computer.

The impulse that places black faces in front of flickering black computer screens is nowhere more visible than at the movies. In the era of political correctness, black techno-wizards (usually male) have consistently populated the most profitable Hollywood action blockbusters. All-time box-office champs like *Die Hard* (1988), *The Hunt for Red October* (1990), *Terminator 2: Judgment Day* (1991), *Jurassic Park* (1993) and *Mission: Impossible* (1996) all furnish prime examples of this black screen phenomenon.[2] A reading of key characters and scenes from these and other popular films will attempt to unpack what is at stake in this highly selective depiction of the human/digital interface.

Fig. 1. Opus appears rather alarmed at the cyborgian transformation of Oliver Wendell Jones, who explains his microprocessed state in the farewell frames of the comic strip *Outland* (1995). © Berkeley Breathed.

Outland's Opus provides a hint: his reaction to Oliver's cyborgian transformation is one of obvious discomfort and a nostalgia for physical presence. In subsequent panels, he gradually edges away almost out of the frame; while Oliver attempts to reassure him about the virtues of Internet access, Opus mutters, "I'm not feeling too connected" and "You can't hug in cyberspace." Opus does not wish to participate in the virtual interaction Oliver proffers; when Oliver extends a diskette and instructs Opus that "you have to load me," Opus demurs in cowering horror.

Such encounters with new technology have been clearly diagnosed in Vivian Sobchack's phenomenological analysis: "All surface, electronic space cannot be inhabited. It denies or prosthetically transforms the spectator's physical body."[3] Katherine Hayles similarly notes how certain "materialities of informatics" can "create the bodily impression of immateriality."[4] Sobchack concludes her essay with a poignant description of the threat of the digital embrace: "Devaluing the physically lived body and the concrete materiality of the world, electronic presence suggests that we are all in imminent danger of becoming merely ghosts in the machine."[5] We all may or may not be in danger, but some whites may wish to displace that fear, at least in their escapist fictions, onto an available other. Or to particularize the compulsion further, whites who fear the devaluation of their own physically lived bodies may especially wish such immaterialization upon those others whose bodies they most fear. The manifest testimony of recent movies, brought into conjunction with observations of cyberphobia, suggests a first axiom: If digital small-screen technology tends to disembody the subject, then in whites' big-screen narratives, the black male becomes the preferred object of this disembodiment.

In *Playing in the Dark,* Toni Morrison notes the strongly nurtured prejudice against analyzing the racial marking of cultural roles: "To notice is to recognize an already discredited difference. . . . Every well-bred instinct argues *against noticing.*"[6] Perhaps those instincts argue even louder when there are doubtless at least some good intentions behind the portrayals at hand. Yet it is worth a second look to test the reach of Morrison's suspicions regarding the "sometimes allegorical, sometimes metaphorical, but always choked representation of an Africanist presence."[7]

In his preface to James Snead's posthumously published *White Screens/Black Images,* Cornel West calls for an analysis of film beyond a "narrow political seeking out of positive or negative black images."[8] He particularly wishes Snead were around to make sense of "the contemporary preoccupation with black images . . . by non-black film makers."[9] *Playing in the Dark* charts the relevance for such a project, as Morrison demonstrates the value of "a serious intellectual effort to see what racial ideology does to the mind, imagination, and behavior of the masters."[10] Discussing acts of white literary imagination, Morrison states that "the fabrication of an Africanist persona is reflexive" and therefore "a powerful exploration of the fears and desires that reside in the writerly conscious [*sic*]."[11]

Beyond simply constituting a trend of what narrowly may be termed "positive black images," what do the consistent portrayals of black faces before the computer screen reveal about something we may attempt to reify as the white moviemaking imagination, the creative transactions of filmmakers and the audiences whose "fears and desires" those makers both serve and shape? We have already noted that, as Sobchack observes, the present historical moment is filled with "hysterical and hyperbolic responses to the disembodying effects of electronic representation," and much remains to be said about the racial codings that emerge with these fearful responses.[12] But the ghostly menace of the virtual is not the only motivating fear or desire displayed in the racial scripting of electronic expertise. The first two chapters of *Color Monitors* examine the phenomenon of the color-monitored computer operator as a postmodern mutation of the minstrelsy stereotype, and, more fully in chapter 2, as a white American anxiety fantasy that asserts a national exceptionality against a world of multinational identity. The present chapter will demonstrate how these

black screen roles function as strategies of containment and instrumentalization, disembodiment and sacrifice.[13]

The substantial body of scholarship that treats the depiction of blacks in
motion pictures draws several historical vectors that point toward our present question of the white construction of technophilic blackness. Outlining
an earlier consumer appetite for serious, educated black characters, Rob
Edelman remarks that "if Sidney Poitier had not existed, he would had to
have been invented. In the aftermath of the Holocaust and the Second
World War . . . white moviegoers were no longer content with the escapist
singing, dancing, and melodramatics that dominated prewar cinema."[14] In
Slow Fade to Black, Thomas Cripps similarly notes the post–World War II
pressure to portray racial equality, which found release in such devices as
the soldier "unit" picture, with blacks joining in the war effort.[15] The token
black team member in a film like *The Hunt for Red October* is nothing new,
but the technological inflection given to the black presence goes beyond
this generalized postwar pressure.

Viewing the present scene, Dan Leab reports that "as the civil rights
movement waned . . . the movie industry hedged its bets by appealing to
white and minority audiences through buddy films in which the lead role
was always taken by whites." In the 1980s and early 1990s, "the situation
was reminiscent of the Thirties when blacks on screen were comic relief,
musical entertainers, or peripheral characters."[16] The various strategies of
the "buddy" genre have received considerable recent commentary,[17] but
little has been done to specify the functions of individual "peripheral characters."[18]

Research on the buddy genre can steer us in the right direction. Ed
Guerrero, in his study "The Black Image in Protective Custody: Hollywood's Biracial Buddy Films of the Eighties," identifies a post-1970s regres-
sion to a "neo-minstrelsy" stereotype, which he identifies with what
Fredric Jameson has termed a "strategy of containment."[19] The buddy formula itself functions as one such strategy: "Thus one can discern that the
popularity and number of those films is due, in part, to their ability to
transcode, even into forms of fantasy, social unease over rising racial tensions."[20] One may fairly wonder if a similar "compensatory" mechanism is
at work in placing blacks in technologically skilled roles, a sort of reassuring virtual affirmative action. In resonant terms, James Snead anticipated
that the challenge for the future would be to "prevent an imagistic co-

optation in which an insincere, ritualized tolerance of recoded images may itself become just another way of keeping blacks out of the picture."[21]

"Under a veneer of technical gloss," Snead noted, "blacks are still being portrayed . . . [in] roles that are mere descendants of paradigms set by Eddie Anderson, Stepin Fetchit, or Ethel Waters."[22] The current veneer to be inspected is an aggressively *technological* one. The paradigm I have in mind is less the antic Stepin Fetchit than the quiet Sam of *Casablanca* (1942). One may imagine a genealogy for "neo-mistrelsy" that begins with scenes like Rick (Humphrey Bogart) telling Sam (Dooley Wilson) to "play it" on the piano and that leads up to Dr. Daniels (Dustin Hoffman) of *Outbreak* (1995) asking Major Salt (Cuba Gooding Jr.) to display a file on the computer screen. As time goes by in the big white house of the Cinéma Américain, the scene remains strangely familiar: the white hero issues a request, and a black man obligingly puts his hands on the keyboard.

I take 1988's *Die Hard* as signaling a changing of the guard—or at least the guard's uniform—for neo-minstrelsy, from entertainer to electronic expert. Early in the film, we meet a traditional black character, the youthful Argyle (De'voreaux White), a chauffeur and connoisseur of rap music who pumps up the tunes while driving John McClane (Bruce Willis) to the fateful skyrise office building where McClane will find himself battling a ruthless band of international terrorists. Among those terrorists is a single black character, the team's designated computer expert, Theo (Clarence Gilyard Jr.). Theo is also the only major character in the movie who does not appear in some form in the 1979 novel upon which *Die Hard* is based.[23] Theo's preppy style and the computer-code–cracking subplot he dutifully pursues are the most notable whole-cloth fabrications introduced for the movie audience of the late 1980s. The script also extends Argyle's chauffeur role in a somewhat forced manner: in the novel, the driver simply drops off the protagonist and heads home for a quiet Christmas Eve; in the movie, he offers to wait around for McClane, and we are periodically treated to shots of Argyle in the basement garage, happily listening to the radio while mayhem proceeds unabated thirty-odd floors above him. The filmmakers have reserved a special job for him that necessitates these hours of thoughtless patience: near the end of the movie, when Theo attempts to escape, Argyle first rams the fugitive's van with the limousine, then leaps to punch out the computer nerd, sending Theo's scholarly glasses flying. At one level, the traditional black character has been set aside to vanquish the "uppity" computer criminal. But both parts remain traditional "serving" roles, short on agency. Their naming and costuming suggests a sort of doubling of their markings by white culture: it is Theo, and not Argyle, who wears an "argyle" sweater. Some light banter between passenger and driver typifies that obvious relationship:

McCLANE: What do we do now?
ARGYLE: I was hoping you would tell me that.

And a somewhat flip exchange between Theo and the Germanic head terrorist, Hans Gruber (Alan Rickman) reveals the truth of their onscreen interaction:

HANS: Now, you *can* break the code?
THEO: You didn't bring me along for my charming personality.

Certainly Hans did not—and neither did the filmmakers. He is a technological tool with a black face. Theo exists for the terrorists—and for the plot—solely as an implement for breaking and entering, an expert system ideally replaceable by artificial intelligence software but welcome as a contained black presence. He can do the number crunching to defeat the computer alarm systems, but the coup de grâce of actual force lies beyond him. Theo tells Hans that he can disable the first six levels of the electronic defense system but that explosives (and some other exigencies) will be needed to crack the safe they're after. As Theo puts it in apocalyptic language, "Seal seven is out of my hands." Effectively, everything is out of his hands; knowledge endows him with a kind of power, to be sure, but not a physical or self-determinative one. Soon after the terrorists take over the building, Hans appears before the hostages as a ministerial figure, opening what resembles a little prayer book and sermonizing on the greed of the (Japanese) Nakatomi corporation whose Los Angeles branch he has punitively struck. He is there, he says, to teach the capitalists "a lesson in real power. You will all be witnesses." One of the first kinds of power we witness is the instrumentalization of the black man, set to his computer-hacking task. It is a lesson the capitalists apparently learn well, as the instrumentalized black man frequently performs techno-wizardry for the good guys in subsequent incarnations.

In *The Hunt for Red October* (1990; like *Die Hard* also directed by John McTiernan), the association of blacks with music again plays a part in forging a postmodern minstrel role. When we first meet Seaman Jones (Courtney B. Vance), the sonarman for the U.S. submarine and the key to the success of its search mission for a runaway Russian sub, the Chief of Boat comments that Jones is "really into music" and that he thinks the whole boat with its expensive audio equipment is just "his personal private stereo." If so, what Jones plays on this sophisticated stereo is surely, to call upon the satirical title of a Screamin' Jay Hawkins album, "Black Music for White People." Only Jones possesses the trained senses to discern the sound of the Russian submarine, which has been specially designed to escape detection by sonar. He draws upon his keen hearing and his computer expertise: "I washed it through the computer a few times and I isolated this sound." He then picks up the beat, speeding the computer-manipulated sound scan so that the indistinct rumblings—at first mistaken for geological activity— yield a steady pulse: "Now that's got to be man-made." By further processing the data, using his Cal Tech education in "logarithmic processing systems" and his knowledge of ocean routes, he extrapolates a probable course for the stealth submarine, gaining the American team a critical edge in pursuing the renegade (it is also being hunted by the bewildered Russians). When Jones first advances his calculation-laden theory, the captain expresses incredulity: "You did this on your own, Jonesy?" Jones, the good soldier, starts to form an apology for his presumption of agency, but the captain tells him to "relax"—for Jonesy has served them well.

As with *Die Hard, Red October*'s big-screen display of the technologically adept black man is a change from an earlier novel. In Tom Clancy's original book of the same name, published in 1984, the race of Seaman Jones goes unmentioned. We know merely that he has sad eyes and a 158 IQ, the highest on the boat, and hopes to go into "cybernetics." So we may decide to gloss over the casting decision as a well-intentioned attempt to give a black actor exposure in the most positive and talent-affirming supporting part. But I believe the sort of consistency that emerges in the repetition of filmmakers deciding to "go black" with the computer-ace role warrants the application of a hermeneutics of suspicion to the phenomenon as a whole.[24] Efforts to move beyond old stereotypes should be applauded, but such efforts do not preclude the emergence of new stereotypes, curiously comfortable and highly specific defaults for "positive representations" of blacks.

We find vestiges of the computational prowess of Seaman Jones in the character Zeus Carver (Samuel L. Jackson) in *Die Hard: With a Vengeance* (1995). In this, the third movie in the franchise, the nefarious Simon (brother of the head terrorist from the original *Die Hard*) taunts John McClane and his "volunteer" buddy Zeus with a game of Simon Says. Simon asks the pair to answer, on pain of death, a riddle containing a convoluted arithmetic problem. While McClane (Willis again) audibly despairs, Zeus interjects, "I'm good at this" and rapidly performs the calculations in his head. When Zeus, sincerely seeking confirmation, asks his white buddy to verify his computation, McClane must put on a dumb show of participatory assent, obviously helpless to manage anything other than blind-faith deference to the black man's reckoning. The line "I'm good at this" resonates easily with the language of stereotype; by speaking it, the character virtually offers himself as a caricature: black men can number-crunch. In the movies, if anyone is "good at this," it's the black man (or, to cite a revealing exception, the Rain Man—Dustin Hoffman as an idiot savant). But we also find hints that such caricatures exist in a conflicted space, that these representations can turn against the logic of their own inception. We first meet the self-employed Zeus as he drills his children on the ways of the world, the importance of education, and so on. The catechism ends with a clincher that the kids answer in knowing, sing-song unison:

ZEUS: "And who do we *not* want to help us?"
KIDS: "White people."

(Here is a lesson possibly borrowed from a black filmmaker's vision: In Spike Lee's *Malcolm X* (1992), a white college student breathlessly approaches Malcolm X, asking what she can do to help; he stops and turns, uttering two syllables with absolute finality: "Nothing.") If the kind of "affirmative" black portrayals prevalent in the white-constructed action genre constitute any evidence of the quality of help being sold, Zeus's mistrust is well founded.

Nowhere are the representational stakes of black technophilia higher or more obviously freighted with white technophobia than in *Terminator 2: Judgment Day* (1991). Again we find echoes of musical giftedness in the high-tech minstrelsy portrayed. The fate of humanity depends upon the computer-programming innovations of Dr. Miles Dyson (Joe Morton), a genius whose name suggests the fusion of jazz with modern physics—Miles Davis meets Freeman Dyson. The screenplay indicates that Miles Dyson's fingers on the computer keyboard make "rhythmic sounds"—in the screenwriter's shorthand, an old (musical) stereotype morphs into a new (electronic) one. Diligently working on his microchip designs (see fig. 2), Dyson doesn't know that his technological breakthroughs will eventually enable an unmanned battle station to develop a war plan of its own and un-

Fig. 2. "He is at the terminal, working. Where else?"—Joe Morton as Miles Dyson in *Terminator 2: Judgment Day* (1991). [Canal+]

leash its destructive powers, including the android "terminators," on the human race. The Seventh Seal may have been out of Theo's hands in *Die Hard,* but Dyson comes dangerously close to pouring out the deadly vial of the Judgment Day. This apocalyptic vision of technology spun out of control resembles a hysterical fear of slave insurrection: the black man's programming plants the seeds that enable the robotic servants to turn against their masters. As the "good" terminator (Arnold Schwarzenegger) reports, "Dyson is the man most responsible [for] a revolutionary type of mircoprocessor"—one that initiates a revolt.

It is in the name of stopping this black man's dangerous activities that the plucky band of (white) resistance fighters must devote their energies, whenever they can take a breather from more immediate acts of self-preservation against the vengeful cyberslaves. Working on information sent from the future by the last remnants of the human resistance, Sarah Connor (Linda Hamilton) tracks down Dyson to deliver the emphatic message "Don't play it, Sam." With intent to shoot this postmodern piano player, Sarah gazes at Dyson through the window of his home, his head positioned in the cross-hairs of her assault rifle. The screenplay describes the scene, with a telling rhetorical aside: "The house is high-tech and luxurious. Lots of glass. Dyson's study is lit bluish with the glow of his computer monitors. He is at the terminal, working. Where else?"

We find an almost-submerged counterpoint to Dyson's character in the monstrously successful *Independence Day* (1996); here the diligent black computer technician (whom we will meet in a moment) is so incidental as almost to escape notice. That the most prominent techno-whiz in the movie is portrayed by Jeff Goldblum may lead us to view this film as somewhat of an exception to the pattern we have been tracing. And the popularity of Goldblum's portrayal may indeed be an index of increasing acceptance of cybertechnology by the culture at large—or at least the acceptance of certain incarnations of that technology. I refer in particular to the successful packaging of cybertechnology as entertainment, the much-noted trajectory from techno-nerds on the Internet to families with America Online to mouse potatoes who apparently want computers that are essentially televisions—note especially that Goldblum does not work for a high-tech computer firm but rather for a cable TV company.

Nevertheless, I think a more important observation may be made about *ID4* by comparing its plotting to that of *T2*. In *T2*, the threat of apocalypse is internally generated by human technology gone out of control; in that case the technological nightmare was blamed on the black man, who was subsequently sacrificed. In *ID4*, the threat comes from beyond; defending the Earth from an outer-space alien attack, the white man receives most of the credit for the plan that saves the day. But, even here, in a sequence that tends to be eclipsed, a minor black character plays an instrumental role in implementing this plan. The brilliant David (Goldblum), asked by President Whitmore (Bill Pullman) to come up with a plan to stop the aliens' well-nigh inexorable conquest of Earth, initially falls into despair and goes on a drinking binge.[25] As we watch David stumbling about, ranting, we may notice a figure in the background. It is the black technician, a U.S. government scientist who has been assigned to help David, slumped over his computer keyboard. While David was off having a tantrum, the technician had kept working away dutifully at the computer until he was overcome with fatigue. Suddenly, David hits upon an idea. He returns to rouse his helper: "Wake up Jim, we've got work to do." We see none of the intervening labor, but by the next morning, the two have completed their preparations and are ready to demonstrate their plan to the president. David acts as the master of ceremonies, flamboyantly explaining how a computer virus will be delivered to the main alien ship and used to bring down the invaders' defense shields. But it is the uncelebrated Jim who has been there to work out the details, such as installing the networking link to upload the virus. In the demo scene itself, Jim's instrumentalization and bodily elision are complete. David, the impresario, calls upon Jim to release the moorings of the craft that will be used for virus delivery: we hear the click of a few keystrokes entered at a computer terminal, and we see the remote-control deed accomplished, but Jim remains offscreen throughout. As a peripheral techno-whiz, Jim is the vestigial tail of a stereotype that had reached an apotheosis in 1991 (*T2*), and that had another high point in 1993, as we shall see.

In *Jurassic Park,* the next big-budget special-effects action extravaganza to make a splash comparable to the *T2* sensation, we again find a brilliant black character seated before the computer monitor. Park owner John Hammond (Sir Richard Attenborough), conducting a tour for the benefit of (white) scientist/inspectors Ellie Sattler (Laura Dern) and Alan Grant (Sam Neill), presents John Arnold (Samuel L. Jackson) as the nerve center of his totally wired facilities, but overlooks Arnold's co-worker Dennis Nedry (Wayne Knight). I quote from the screenplay at some length in order to chart the unfolding valuation of the black man's expertise:

HAMMOND

And this is the right side of my brain. The entire park is safely controlled from here. John Arnold, that ge- nius over there, is the master control operator.
(with genuine concern)
John, don't smoke so much, you're far too valuable a man to me.

ARNOLD

Oh, you'd survive just fine without me.
Arnold exhales smoke and waves good-naturedly. Nedry stares darkly at Hammond, who ignores him.

HAMMOND

Everything's controlled from here. Remote everything. Cars, feeding programs, medicine dispensers, fecal clean up—and that can be tons in a park like this. We run this place with twenty workers. This computer does it all. And it polices each and every single animal out there.

ELLIE

(whispers to Grant)
Who polices the computer?

Hammond points up. Overlooking the control room and the park is a raised platform with a huge chair, like a throne in a court. A large video screen faces this chair.

                          HAMMOND
That's where I will watch the astonished watchers. Okay, let's go.

Nedry (Wayne Knight), Arnold's white co-worker in computer operations, proceeds to take verbal umbrage at a perceived slight once the tour moves on:

                          NEDRY
Thanks for the kind word, Mr. Hammond.

                          ARNOLD
Come on, Dennis, he knows your technical contributions have made it all possible.

                          NEDRY
Right.

   "Genius" resounds as a strong, even dangerous word, especially so when associated with blackness in certain white imaginations (as *T2* suggests). And, step by step, the scene slights the black man's contribution while underlining his contained, nonthreatening persona. Hammond's exposition shifts from the designation of Arnold as "the master control operator" to the claim that "this computer does it all." This shift takes place almost imperceptibly in the smooth flow of Hammond's patter—perhaps Hammond's conflicting claims do not fully register as contradictory, so thoroughly has the black man been conceived of as equivalent to the computer system itself. In a final shift, Hammond reinscribes himself at the top of the hierarchy: Hammond names himself as the one "who polices the computer"—and, by extension, the one who polices the Africanist presence with which he has identified it. Meanwhile, the "good-natured" Arnold makes dutifully self-effacing remarks for the benefit of both Hammond—"you'd survive just fine without me"—and later for his co-worker—"your technical contributions have made it all possible."

A comparison with the activities of other characters highlights the delimitations of the black man's role. The casting of the park team representationally naturalizes an ethnic division of labor: In the never-quite-last days of empire, the Brit commands, the great white hunter is from Kenya (Bob Peck as Robert Muldoon), and the head biological researcher is Asian-American (B. D. Wong as Dr. Wu).[26] The black man keeps the electronic furnace stoked and the system humming—with white assistance and supervision. Most tellingly, the story articulates this black difference against a background of the benevolent whites' distaste for computers (the white computer programmer, Nedry, proves vicious and corruptible, and is marked for vilification by his obesity). Park guest Grant, good-guy paleontologist and romantic lead, experiences no dissonance between his passion for science and his technophobia. Co-screenwriter Michael Crichton's novel provides a full exposition of Grant's feelings: "Grant looked at all the computer monitors in the darkened control room, feeling irritable. Grant didn't like computers. He knew this made him old-fashioned, dated as a researcher, but he didn't care. . . . He found computers to be alien, mystifying machines."[27]

In *Outbreak* (1995), a similar color line of demarcation falls between the world of science proper and that of electronic instrumentality. In the movie, a team of army researchers tackles a plague that has reached American shores—the fictional Motaba virus, based on the African Ebola virus. At one point Major Salt (Cuba Gooding Jr.) is credited with seeing something the others had missed: fine hairlike structures on the airborne mutant strain of the virus. But the white researchers are the ones who draw the scientific conclusions from this helpful observation; they had been walking about talking as Salt sat silently with the computer.[28] Salt's contribution derives from the intensity with which his eyes stay glued to the screen, his commitment to the electronic extension of sensory perception. The white doctors then formulate his observations into a course of heroic action.

In the essay "White," Richard Dyer summarizes a documentary series of interviews with white people who were asked to comment on "being white." Most of the subjects stumble over what at first strikes them as an incomprehensible question—"then gradually, it seems almost inexorably, the participants settle in to talking with confidence about what they know: stereotypes of black people."[29] Traditionally, not all stereotypes rely on designating blacks as less than white in this or that aspect. The key, as Dyer perceives, lies in producing a difference against which to construct white identity. Although the Major Salts and Seaman Joneses of the screen occupy inferior positions relative to the white heroes they support, the inferiority comes bundled with unmistakable superiorities of ability—even, perhaps especially, impossibly prodigious abilities.

The superhuman augmentation of perception constitutes a consistent leitmotif in the depiction of black technophiles. Major Salt's electron-microscopic scrutiny crosses ordinary thresholds of detection. But even beyond the diligent application of advanced technology, time and again the blacks who monitor the black screens manage to tap into the ghosts in the machine. As if imagined to be in touch (technologically) with the wonders of the invisible world, Jingo Asakuma (Tia Carrere) in *Rising Sun* (1993; another Crichton adaptation), is able to see the ghostly after-image of the body that has been digitally removed from a video recording. She is able to reconstruct the evidence despite multiple aporias in the evidence: "Nothing here. Too dark. *Kuronbō.* What they used to call me. Black person."[30] For such absences, her presence manages precisely to compensate. In parallel roles, Seaman Jones in *Red October* and Colonel Wilkins (Delroy Lindo) in *Broken Arrow* (1996) are tasked with tracing a submarine and a plane, respectively, that are designed to be undetectable by existing tracking systems. Before the switch to stealth mode, Captain Hale (Christian Slater) tells Wilkins that "if anyone can track it, you can."

All these characters are instrumentalized and put to use, to do the work the white folks can't—or won't—do. To look at it another way, the black characters who perform instrumental tasks that may be perceived as being *beneath* white dignity are simultaneously presented as achieving results *beyond* white capacity. The latter presentation may serve as an excuse, a rationalization for an imagined natural ethnic division of labor. However exalted the pronouncements about the excitement of the information age, the prospect of long hours of staring at the screen, hammering away at the keyboard, running the calculations and so forth may in part motivate a desire that digital drudgery be done by someone else. In a more general critique of lazy wishfulness, Wendell Berry argues that that racism may be the *product* of a desire to escape work that is "fundamental and inescapable"—work that in the South has been called "nigger work" and in the North, "drudgery." In Berry's account, the vain belief that one is superior to one's condition expresses itself in the evasion of undesirable work; racism emerges as the justification of practices that make that displacement possible.[31] Color monitoring, in flattering blacks' allegedly natural technical abilities, ultimately flatters the belief that being above technical work constitutes a core benefit of white privilege.

In conjunction with the construction of white identity against stereotypes of cultural others and the work that supposedly suits them, the projection of electronic excellence onto blacks ties into a larger national fantasy. In *The Devil Finds Work,* James Baldwin confronts his readers with a bold historical contention:

> I think that it was Freud who suggested that the presence of the black man in America foreshadowed America's doom—which America, if it could not civilize these savages, would deserve. . . . For Marx and Engels, the presence of the black man in America was simply a useful crowbar for the liberation of whites: an idea which has had its issue in the history of American labor unions. The Founding Fathers shared this view, eminently, Thomas Jefferson, and The Great Emancipator freed those slaves he could not reach, in order to create, hopefully, a fifth column behind the Confederate lines. This ambivalence contains the key to American literature—in a way can be said to *be* American literature.[32]

In each historical example, a gesture of liberation is accompanied by an agenda to advance a white interest. The ambivalence is always from a white perspective: doom threatens in the form of the savage who nevertheless—if civilized—presents a possible unique advantage.

The current battle for America's civilized savage to join takes place in the theater of multinational capitalism. Sobchack, by "extrapolating" from Fredric Jameson, connects the stages of capital with their respective modes of representation and characteristic technologies: market capitalism corresponded to realism and to photographic technology; monopoly capitalism corresponded to modernism and the cinematic; multinational capitalism exists in a cultural logic with postmodernism and the electronic.[33] We may recall that, in addition to the new media and manufacturing practices associated with computers and automation, Jameson's "late capitalism" entails

> not merely an emphasis on the emergence of new forms of organization (multinationals, transnationals) beyond the monopoly stage but, above all, the vision of a world capitalist system fundamentally distinct from the older imperialism, which was little more than a rivalry between the various colonial powers.[34]

In mainstream Hollywood cinematic narratives, we typically find a nostalgia for an earlier capitalist moment. In the action genre, this desire expresses itself in part through the deployment of the black in the computer arena as the assertion of a unique American colonial identity.

Vis-à-vis Freud's ambivalent vision of American doom, *Die Hard* presents something of a return of the repressed in the form of a vengeful civilized savage. Theo, the African American computer expert, joins the international team of terrorists who attack on American soil. Yet even as a minion of the villain, Theo manages to strike a blow for "Americanness": first, by suggesting that to find a true computer genius, these Germanic terrorists had to recruit from America; and second, by the nature of the job he enables. The chief target of the terrorist strike is a Japanese corporation that has (from the imperialist perspective) also made an assault on American soil. After the initial break-in, the high-ranking Japanese executive, Takagi (James Shigeta), bites the first of the executioner's bullets, and his company's property takes massive hits from good guys and bad guys alike. The hero's efforts succeed largely in saving the (primarily white) "real American" hostages, and much of the zest of the movie derives from the glee with which he lays waste to the Nakatomi building in the process.

Rising Sun very clearly enlists an Africanist presence as an American defense against Japanese economic imperialism. The self-described "part Chinese, part Spanish, part Filipino" actress Tia Carrere is cast here as a character with mixed African American and Japanese parentage.[35] Carrere plays Jingo Asakuma, the American university computer science researcher called upon to inspect video-recorded evidence of a murder. The recordings have been submitted to the police by the Japanese corporation within whose plush downtown Los Angeles building the murder occurred. With careful scrutiny and deft computer manipulation of the images, Jingo determines that the Japanese have doctored the evidence; she reports that the Japanese alteration was sloppily executed because the Japanese had arrogantly assumed that no American would be sufficiently skilled or "thorough" to tell the difference. But they had not counted on Jingo, who adduces her half-black identity as her motive in nailing the Japanese to the wall:

> I was born in Sako. My father was a *kokujin* mechanic. You know that word, *kokujin*? *Niguro*. A black man. . . . My father died in an accident when I was two years old. There was a small pension for the widow. . . . But my grandfather took most of it, because he insisted

that he had been disgraced by my birth. I was *ainoko* and *niguro*. They are not nice words, what he called me.[36]

The film's portrayal of Jingo reinforces a jingoistic portrayal of American cultural superiority: by embracing this mixed-race outcast, American law enforcement gains a key advantage over the "cruel" Japanese who had ostracized her. Yet even in Crichton's America, she finds occasions to be sensitive. When a white American researcher comments that "Japanese corporations in America feel the way we would feel doing business in Nigeria: they think they're surrounded by savages," Jingo interjects with a "Hey." "Sorry," her colleague replies, "but you know what I mean."[37] She does; *savage* is also not a nice word.

Ambivalence about the American difference, blackness, becomes legible in those instances in which the wildest successes of black expertise lead to nightmares of unleashed doom. From one angle, the Terminator saga is the story of Cyberdyne, an American company that capitalizes on the talents of an African-American employee and comes up with a product that takes over the world market. But Dyson's runaway microprocessing breakthrough leads to a paradoxical return to savagery, as the world becomes a technological jungle where humans again live lives that are nasty, brutish, and short, as they huddle amidst twisted metal to defend themselves against predatory machines. A state of technology made possible by the black man replicates the anti-Romantic state of nature—one that again must be tamed by a proper, civilized use of technology.

James Snead has argued that King Kong is an archetypal representation of the black body in American film.[38] In *Primate Visions*, Donna Haraway contends that "the entire story of King Kong and the virgin was embedded in science-based urban culture, where the dark male beast in chains threatened escape and destruction. That beast could only be conquered by abstract technical force, i.e., by the implements of modern war."[39] Now, that threatening body must be contained within the abstract technical mastery of the implements of postmodern war, technologies of information. Roberto Calasso describes the human encounter of the analog with the digital: "The digital pole seems biologically secondary and dependent . . . but then the digital pole takes command, revealing its ability to envelop the other pole, to absorb it—and naturally, to exploit it."[40] In action films, this digitality envelops, absorbs the black body; one may say that, in some instances, white Hollywood imaginations employ digitality to this end.

Fig. 3. Major Salt (Cuba Gooding Jr.) sits at/as the computer, awaiting further instructions from Dr. Schuler (Kevin Spacey) and Dr. Daniels (Dustin Hoffman) in *Outbreak* (1995). [Warner Bros.]

The choreographic language of these action films bespeaks complementary constraints on black activity. A visual poetics of containment frequently accompanies the technological neutralization: we see the instrumentalized black man framed by two (or more) whites. A few stills released by the studios to promote these films suggest a logic to the image pattern. In *Outbreak,* we see Cuba Gooding Jr. seated at the terminal, his hands occupied with the keyboard and mouse; he is flanked by the standing doctors Dustin Hoffman and Kevin Spacey who contemplate their scientific quest (fig. 3). A still from *Terminator 2* (fig. 4) places the unarmed Miles Dyson (earlier wounded by Sarah Connor) in the protective custody of Connor and the Terminator, who brandish their guns at a black security guard (outside the frame); the action heroes are escorting Dyson to his workplace, Cyberdyne, where he will atone for his sins of technology. In a promotional image for *Johnny Mnemonic* (1995), Johnny (Keanu Reeves) and his bodyguard Jane (Dina Meyer) perform an aggressive pincer move on their would-be ally, J-Bone (Ice-T), leader of the paradoxically high-tech "Lo-Teks." (The "Lo-Teks" form a core of resistance to the tyranny of the microprocessed world, in particular to an evil Japanese company that exploits a new human disease—a sort of re-literalization of the metaphor of the computer "virus"—induced by that world.) Johnny insistently brandishes a scrap of paper at J-Bone, demanding that J-Bone use this shred of an encryption image to assist Johnny in electronically retrieving vital informa-

Fig. 4. The Terminator (Arnold Schwarzenegger) and Sarah Connor (Linda Hamilton) escort
Miles Dyson (Joe Morton) in *Terminator 2: Judgment Day* (1991). [Canal+]

tion. In these images, the white bodies enforce and enframe the scene of the
black man's electronic instrumentalization.

"Blackness in motion is typically sensed as a threat on screen, and so
black movement in film is usually restricted to highly bracketed and con-
tainable activities"—so states James Snead with a fundamental insight, one
whose importance to the present analysis can scarcely be overestimated. In
Executive Decision (1996), the black explosives/electronics expert of the
crack antiterrorist squad, Sergeant "Cappy" Matheny (Joe Morton), receives a spinal injury almost immediately after we meet him, one that requires that he remain motionless for the duration of the movie. While min-
istering to him (fig. 5), the crew gives voice to an imperative that enunciates
a truth that stretches far beyond the exigencies of Cappy's medical situation: "We've got to immobilize him!" Unconsciously or not, since the black
man's first onscreen appearance, some moviemaking imaginations seem to
have dreamt of little else.

Another loaded shot from *Terminator 2* both exemplifies and attempts
to justify this strategy of containment. At Cyberdyne headquarters, we find
Miles Dyson situated between the young John Connor (Edward Furlong)
and his kinder, gentler Terminator. The composition, with the left-to-right
ascending line connecting the heads of child, programmer, and Terminator, uses Dyson's position to recapitulate his status. In the filmmaker's vision, Dyson is indeed between child and machine as a being. The script de-

Fig. 5. "We've got to immobilize him!" In *Executive Decision* (1996), Louie (B. D. Wong) and Baker (Whip Hubley) strap technical expert Cappy (Joe Morton) to a stretcher. Brooding in the background is the engineer Cahill (Oliver Platt), who will later depend upon Cappy's electronic know-how. [Warner Bros.]

scribes him in terms that both infantilize and mechanize the man. "We see a *childlike* excitement in his face" (emphasis mine) as he develops a machinelike consciousness during the long hours he spends

> tapping away at the keyboard of his home computer terminal. Next to desk are racks of sophisticated gear. On a Sunday morning, when most men are relaxing, spending time with their families, Dyson is hard at work.
> IN A PROFILE CLOSEUP we see him in deep concentration, his mind prowling the labyrinth of his new microprocessor.

In the iconic text of the production still, we read the fruits of Dyson's innocent devotion to his computer work. Though partially obscured, the words on the shirt of John Connor, future leader of the human resistance, read "Public Enemy." According to the message sent from the future, Miles Dyson's research makes him public enemy number one. Public Enemy's breakthrough rap album, *Fear of a Black Planet,* touched upon a deep white phobia that the Terminator future horrifically realizes; for fear of a black planet, Dyson must be stopped. Linguistically and visually, the script and film make a direct connection between blackness and Dyson's technological advances. Sarah Connor's fear of what she calls "the dark future" commits her to "war against those who build the wrong machines." In a bit of description from the screenplay, when Dyson manages to tear himself away from the computer screen for a rare break, the exposition comments that, as no further progress will be made that day, "The forces of darkness have lost this round." In an earlier, ominous scene at Cyberdyne, Dyson turns for inspiration to a Terminator relic from the future; his sublime techno-logical object before him, "Dyson stares at it, lost in thought. Then he closes the cabinet, BLACKING OUT [THE] FRAME."[41] His contemplative actions black out the frame as they will later black out the sun: the film's scenes of the post–nuclear holocaust future portray an endless night. By the time John Connor and the good Terminator bring him back to Cyberdyne to destroy his research, the film has repeatedly insisted that Dyson poses the greatest "DANGER" to society; the plainly marked volatile chemicals arranged beside him will soon be put to deadly use in his noble immolation scene.

These groupings may be read as sacrificial diagrams, with the victim at the center, presided over by the community that seeks to preserve its social order through ritual offering. Discussing the spectacles of white-generated mass culture, "invariably," claims Guerrero in what is hardly an overstate-ment, "it is the Black man who makes a sacrifice to solve the White man's problems."[42] Nor are we merely discussing imaginary diagrams that desig-nate symbolic victims; we should not neglect to enumerate some of the de-pictions of violence and disembodiment to which these diagrams fre-quently correspond. In some instances, the disembodiment does remain on the level of a limiting instrumentalization: Seaman Jones's reduction to a pair of ears and a calculator; Major Salt's incorporation into the computer-imaging equipment. But in many of these movies, the black body bears literalized markings of technological disembodiment. Jingo in *Rising Sun* is crippled, her stump of an arm merging with the computer mouse, her digits digitally replaced. Arnold in *Jurassic Park* undergoes dis-memberment: the last we see of him is his severed arm, which one charac-ter, in a horrible misapprehension, addresses by name. Dyson in *T2* is pro-gressively incapacitated by bullet wounds, finally diminished to being no more than the triggering mechanism for the explosive device that will fin-ish him off; he nobly devotes his final desperate gasps to holding up the detonating plunger just long enough for the white police officers who have been shooting at him to get clear of the blast zone. Part of the director's original vision was a scene cut from the final film, one hardly necessary to make clear Dyson's role but useful for its explicitness in showing Dyson "making peace with himself and his family at his sacrifice for the good of mankind."[43] Both the radar commander and the radiation-detector die in *Broken Arrow*'s line of duty; the first goes down in flames while protecting the white hero and his love interest, the latter takes a bullet as soon as his usefulness to the white traitor expires—that is, as soon as he locates the missing nuclear warhead by means of the high-tech sensory equipment strapped to his body.

In *Executive Decision,* the involuntarily immobile Cappy (lashed to the sacrificial altar, as it were) uses a snaking fiber optic eye to inspect the interior of the electronic explosives device.[44] Among the computer components he confidently identifies is what he calls the system's "dedicated hard drive." He, too, is a dedicated hard drive: a disembodied supplier of information dedicated to a single task. Nor would anyone question that he is a dedicated soldier, in the two interchangeable senses of that label: not only is he a "dedicated" patriot, he is also "dedicated" in the original sacrificial sense ("dedicated to the gods")—only in this case he is dedicated to the gods of American escapism.

I will conclude this introductory chapter by looking at one more figure dedicated to these same gods, "computer genius" Luther Stickell (Ving Rhames) of *Mission: Impossible* (1996).[45] Though he sheds no blood, his instrumentalization, containment, disembodiment, and ideological sacrifice in many ways sum up the trajectory we have been tracing. Unlike Barney Collier from the original series, a black handyman with a variety of gadgets and technical illusions, Luther's specialization is total: he is a world-class computer hacker. Hero Ethan Hunt (Tom Cruise) indulges in a fanfare introduction of Luther, painting him as a living legend, the only man ever to hack into NATO's top secret computer system. This latter feat points to another difference in Luther's character; he's a renegade, not a member of the Impossible Missions Force at the movie's outset. When treachery runs Ethan Hunt afoul of the CIA, he recruits Luther from the CIA's "disavowed" list to help set things straight with some dazzling computer hacking. We later discover that Luther has no idea what the information that Ethan has asked him to steal even is; Ethan unapologetically asserts that if Luther had known how sensitive the data was, Luther never would have accepted the job. But Luther is a well-tempered instrument; he not only smoothly enables the data retrieval, he also makes not a single recriminatory statement about the way Ethan has used him. The film makes clear that technology entirely controls Luther's desire; his only contractual condition is to be allowed to keep the laptop computer—an "artificial intelligence" dream machine whose list of state-of-the-art specifications he lov-ingly recites—he will require to pull off the job.

Luther's creed as a wired professional focuses on the imperative of dis-embodiment. When Ethan recounts the NATO hacking escapade, Luther replies with great pride, and emphasis, that "there was never any *physical* evidence that I had anything to do with that . . . with that [Luther pauses, grins] . . . *exceptional* piece of work." When Ethan outlines a plan that in-volves Luther's hacking into CIA headquarters in Langley, Virginia, Luther patiently explains that the computers at Langley run on a self-contained system inaccessible by modem, and thus(as his face clouds over) in order to crack the database, "I'll have to be physically at the terminal." Ethan tells Luther not to worry; the white action hero will perform the actual breaking and entering while Luther operates in remote virtuality. Ethan dubs Luther with the codename "Cyber-Op," and cyberspace remains his effective arena. In the climactic train sequence, the fact that he must operate in a space where his physical body is visible very nearly compromises the mis-sion. The movie strikingly excludes Luther almost entirely from physical motion, and he never makes a single move that even hints at violence. In a tension-filled exchange between Ethan and Franz Krieger (Jean Reno), an-other, less tractable, recruit from the "disavowed" list, Luther remains to-tally stationary, blocked from the action by his computer desk, with what appears to be some sort of cyber-goggles contraption encircling his brow. Of all the actors who have portrayed techno-wizards, Rhames brings the most physically imposing presence to the role. Neither pencil-necked micro-geek (Theo) nor comfortable family man (Dyson) is Luther. When the man who once played "the dreaded Marsellus Wallace" in *Pulp Fiction* (1994) and the menacing Garvey in the Afro-centrist *Drop Squad* (1994) re-mains passively seated behind his computer screen, the sense of technolog-ical bodily containment is all the more palpable.[46]

All Luther wanted from his bargain with Ethan was to keep the neat computer, but he gets something more. For an international espionage job well done, Luther gets cleared from the CIA "disavowed" list and wins a do-mesticated career in preserving the American way. In the denouement, Ethan, relaxing over drinks, asks Luther, "How does it feel to be a solid cit-izen?" Expressing some uncertainty, Luther says he's going to "miss being disreputable." "If it makes you feel any better," replies Ethan, "I'll always think of you that way." Luther's sense of loss at no longer "being disrep-utable" bespeaks the pathos of having sacrificed his potentially dangerous, subversive identity to become just another company man. Ethan's promise, however jocular, to retain his previous perception of Luther testifies to the lingering of the ambivalence we hear in Baldwin's Freud. To the mind that has first learned to say "savage," the "civilized savage" is always just what the phrase says, and never merely "civilized." Which is not to say that same mind won't eagerly bestow upon the savage all the trappings that civilization can muster, whatever the latest technology happens to be. Ethan congratulates Luther for having earned a job doing CIA computer work. "Hey," Luther shrugs, "I'm the flavor of the month." No, Luther. You're the flavor of the age.

chapter TWO

LOST WORLDS

Technologies for Dark Places

A small black child advances through the tall grass of the African veldt. Wearing a floppy safari hat, the boy faces the camera with a determined expression. Following slightly behind him, a zebra matches the boy's forward stride. The boy's arms are raised, hands gripping the keyboard of a notebook computer that he balances atop his head. The computer screen faces the viewer, displaying an oblong, gridded projection of the world. The African continent occupies the center of the map's crosshairs. A large slogan runs across the bodies of zebra and boy and onto a white space that takes up the rightmost portion of the poster: "Technology Is Changing the Face of the Earth."

The advertisement celebrates the power of technology and all its civilizing blessings. The face of the earth as displayed on the computer demonstrates technology's capacity to span the globe and to present even its darkest continent as an object for rational scrutiny. Indeed, every element of the poster contributes to the theme of technology's complete triumph *even* in the most extreme circumstances. Africa—its geography, its people, its nature—yields to the advance of technology. In the advertisement, the boy's fully clothed body contrasts with more commonly presented African ob-

jects of anthropological curiosity and charitable pity. Naked African children have served again and again in appeals for civilizing intervention. This
black child stands as a demonstration of that intervention's success. Not
merely civilized, he has himself become a civilizer. Equipped with an outfit
for adventure, he is a colonial subject who has signed on as a colonizing
agent. On his head, he wears a hat that salutes empire; on that supple
crown, he bears the forces of technology. He marches confidently across the
savanna, bringing even the wild zebra to heel.

"Can a zebra change its stripes?" In that question's traditional rhetorical
form, the implicit answer is no. In this cultural touchstone, the zebra represents the recalcitrance of nature. As with its rhetorical cousin the leopard
and its spots, the beast's markings signify the indelibility of natural color,
the intransigence of nature as indexed by color. So, whether stripes or
spots, Africa stands for the source of nature's most resistant specimens. But
this advertisement implies a different answer to the canonical question:
sufficient technology *can* transform the unalterable essence. The stripes
themselves may not change, but nature itself falls into line with the program of progress. The child's face, leading the charge, presents blackness on
a technological mission. What technology promises is the power to change
a face without having to change its color. In this account, one need not fear
a black planet—as long as its black bodies serve as bearers of civilizing
technology.

Empire, as conceived for the globalized millennium by Michael Hardt
and Antonio Negri in the book with that title, no longer possesses an "outside."[1] This "Marx and Engels of the internet age" argue that with the passage to Empire, "no identity is designated as Other, no one is excluded
from the domain, there is no outside."[2] Empire's racism "integrates others
with its order and then orchestrates those differences in a system of control."[3] Color monitoring undertakes just such "management" of difference
(195); nevertheless, as this chapter will demonstrate, that integration takes
place through representations that manifest a nostalgia for the older political topologies. Africa, for example, still functions imaginatively as an "outside" to the project of technological incorporation, a space for the managed
black body to claim for American control.

That technologizing role for ideal blackness is revealed anew in the selection of "Survivors" recently sent to populate the remote island of Koh
Tarutao, another "outside" fantasized for American audiences. In late 2002,
the reality-TV hit *Survivor* introduced us to "Ted Rogers, Jr., Software Developer, Durham, NC"—the cast's sole black man and the cast's sole techie.

Through such selections, the careful molding of "reality" TV does indeed reflect something real: America's ideals of representative identities for colonial adventure.[4] Preeminent in this regard are characters like the white elder statesman of the group, a rugged "Land Broker" from Texas, a man of indomitable resourcefulness and folksy leadership. But the youthful Ted fills in as an important supplement to such heroic identities. An introductory interview with this Mr. Rogers focused on the issue of his "adaptability," the special quality that he brought to the "Survivor" challenge.[5] "Working in corporate America, you do have to adapt," he explains. The software developer is said to have "developed" his adaptability though "years and years" of practice—that is, his capacity to acquire new traits is itself an acquired trait. One could say that he is presented as having developed his own software—his internal, personal software—for maximum accommodation of compatibility demands. *Survivor* presents Ted Jr. as an American success story, an achiever who has learned how to change his nature; he is thus an emblematic asset for the U.S. expedition to colonize the exotic island.

The aforementioned poster for a technology that is "Changing the Face of the Earth" shows how the figure of the technologized black adventurer, similarly projected onto a distant colonial horizon, can be brought home to a tightly focused demographic. The company, Star Power, despite trumpeting a slogan about changing the world, is not selling the globalization of technology. Rather, Star Power uses the image of a technologized globe, specifically a technologized Africa, to sell networking technology in a highly localized American context. Star Power promises that Washington, D.C., "Is Next in Line for a Makeover"; the image of African conquest supplies the guarantee: what technology can accomplish in the Dark Continent, Star Power networking will accomplish in the District of Columbia. The Star Power campaign specifically targets "the affluent suburban rail audience" to reach desirable viewers "during the journey between their suburban home" and their urban workplace.[6]

The advertisers' awareness of class distinction maps readily onto a racializing dynamic of their message. "The Chocolate City," a moniker popularized by Parliament's 1975 album and used affectionately among African Americans to refer to the District, reflects a demographic fact not perceived with equal sweetness in all quarters. The Star Power ads greet commuters from the "Vanilla Suburbs" as they travel into the heart of the city. Star Power promises that the urban passage these commuters traverse en route to the interior is next in line for a change of face. With Star Power's fiber optics on their side, whatever darkness these travelers may encounter will be made over in the light of technological progress. Thus the ad's image of an "outward" thrust of technological civilization, toward the domestication of African nature, serves as a model for an "inward"-focused program of urban enlightenment.

A well-established and still-available vocabulary of urban metaphors facilitates that translation. As late as 2001, one could still overhear a police officer from the region refer to the urban sphere as a "jungle" and to the proper role of cops as "animal tamers."[7] Star Power's ad offers a preemptive solution to such urban nightmares. The black child pictured is probably not yet old enough to be considered as belonging to those fearsome categories, the Young Black Man or the Black Male Youth.[8] Rather than threatening to grow into a primary target for police surveillance, this exemplary young man is already enlisted in the work of policing. With a face enhanced by its technological framing, he has himself become an animal tamer.

The overall logic of the ad equates technology with civility, with the cosmetic beauty of urbs and orbs, with attractive makeovers for Washington and the world. Such an equation may seem rather mundane. That an American advertisement would base its appeal upon a narrative of "progress" scarcely seems noteworthy. But of greater interest to the *Color Monitors* project is the tenuous status of technology as a term within the formula for progress. Other cultural examples to be examined in this study of "Lost Worlds" will show just how unstable a value technology exhibits with respect to civilization.

This chapter pursues the premise that Americans maintain an uneasy fascination with the power of computers. In particular, we will consider how that cultural unease responds to perceptions that information technology may not only disrupt individual lives but may also unsettle America's status as a nation. The quintessentially American narratives crafted in response to this unease are paranoid and sentimental and concerned with race; specifically, these technophobic narratives often exploit sentimental treatments of race to assuage paranoia. To explicate this dynamic, the chapter will draw many of its later examples from the career of Michael Crichton: as measured by box office returns and book sales, Crichton may well be counted as the most successful cultural producer of the era; his genre, the "techno-thriller," consistently engages the anxieties of the computer age. This chapter examines the characteristic cultural transformation performed in the techno-thriller: a retooling of nineteenth-century colonial adventure paradigms, via the instrumentalization of race, to serve the twenty-first–century needs of American national identity.

plugs for the Digital Gap

If the power of the stars derives from fusion, Star Power's networking appeal runs on the fusion of the young black body with new computer technology. The much-discussed issue of the "digital divide" illuminates the desire for that fusion. Some who study the issue try to insist that the gap not be viewed as a primarily racial matter. In popular usage, the phrase "digital divide" tends to serve as a polite shorthand from which explicit reference to race has been omitted in describing the gap between technological haves and have-nots. Of course, the degree of technological access does correlate to a range of categories, including geography, income, and ethnicity. But attempts to depict the access situation in its true complexity run up against the strength of established perception: when people hear "digital divide," they tend to think in terms of black and white.

People think that way about the gap because that is, quite literally, how they see it. In image after published image, the face of that gap is black. A front-page news story on a "program [that] bridges technology gap" typifies the phenomenon. The Computers for Learning project, backed by Dell, Southwestern Bell, Time Warner, AMD, Intel, Samsung, and others, aims to benefit tens of thousands of "needy schoolchildren." The color photo shows just one: a nine-year-old black boy, hands on the keyboard, eyes earnestly glued to the screen.[9] Fostering such initiatives has become the feel-good charity of the cash-flush tech set. *Forbes*'s 2001 issue on the four hundred richest people in America included a feature on 800-million-dollar man Todd Wagner, who in 1999 had sold his tech start-up to Yahoo.[10] Within the next two years, he had spent ten million dollars on his Miracles program, through which he sought "to try out different educational software on poor kids, then track their progress through a battery of tests." (This gesture calls to mind the skeptical voice of George Schuyler and his scathing 1931 satire of "retired white capitalists, whose guilty consciences persuaded them to indulge in philanthropy" and who customarily direct their generosity to "The Negro Data League."[11]) The accompanying photo cues the reader on how to interpret "poor": the white experimenter/philanthropist shares the frame with a roomful of computers and a cluster of his would-be test subjects, seven beaming black children. The caption's tagline, "Boxed in," refers to the way the kids affectionately surround the man, but it could just as well refer to the way the computers surround the children. A 2001 United Way newspaper ad strikes a similar chord, in which the image completes the content of the charitable thought. "Technology is an important tool in our children's education," so "Tech Tots is taking steps to bridge the digital divide by providing technological solutions to low-income families with preschool-age children."[12] The tiny Tech Tot shown receiving this tool, thanks to Dell and IBM, is a black boy in profile, fingers on the keys, face sober with concentration.

Reading such scenes of "boxed in" youth with his characteristic biting skepticism, David Mamet probes the unconscious of digital largess:

> Consider Newt Gingrich's suggestion that the plight of the underprivileged would be ameliorated by putting a computer onto every schoolroom desk.
> This was the occasion of mirth on the part of his detractors.
> They saw it as an inept, untutored, and disingenuous attempt to suggest social improvement.
> But perhaps his suggestion reveals a deeper, an unconscious, understanding of the role of the machine.
> What did he want from the poor, and what possible good could their use of the computer do for him? It could get the poor to shut up.[13]

It could also make them disappear, as virtual benevolence may convey both a patronizing concern and a reinforcement of geographic segregation. IBM, in their 1999 Annual Report to Investors, entitled ".COM," highlights the company's involvement with the "Acorn Smart Housing Project" in Oakland, California: "Learning to read just got a little bit easier for 9–year-old Frank Martin, thanks to IBM's participation. . . . Acorn's 293 families each get an IBM Network Station 'thin client' computer and high-speed links to the Internet" (24). The nine–year-old boy in the full-page profile tapping the keyboard is, again, black. EDS (Electronic Data Systems) boasts a larger-scale operation with a similar focus. In "trust," their 2001 Annual Report, EDS points to the worthiness of their thirteen–year technology sponsorship of the JASON project, "the world's premier distance-learning program, teaching more than 11 million students to date" (11). The photo picks just one: a black boy, in profile, typing at the computer. If the Miracles project boxes such children in, the JASON project makes sure they keep their distance—this "distance-learning" image implies the ability to teach black children without having to bus them to other, possibly whiter, neighborhoods.[14]

The strong appeal of such computer philanthropy as an image-building program has made even nontech firms eager to get in the game. Coca-Cola Enterprises, as their 2000 Annual Report announces, is "Striving to be more than the World's largest bottler." In one demonstration of that ambition, employees "work to help local youth understand how to use computers at a local community center in Dorchester [Mass.]" (14). The photo shows two company representatives supervising six preadolescent black children arrayed behind a bank of computers. This kind of "Close to Home" focus, the company explains, helps Coca-Cola Enterprises secure goodwill "across all of our territories."

The imperial echoes of that last word find more overt formulation in Microsoft's designs for "Strengthening Communities Around the World." W. E. B. DuBois's analysis, linking narrow vocational training for blacks to the global economic scene of 1903, still resonates: "The tendency is here, born of slavery and quickened by the crazy imperialism of the day, to regard human beings as among the material resources of the land to be trained with an eye single to future dividends."[15] In the 2001 Annual Report to investors, Microsoft expresses its commitment to providing "technology training programs to diverse and underserved populations" (5). These words appear superimposed on a full two-page photo of an elementary school–aged black girl holding a notebook computer. Smaller inset photos dot the page, including pictures of the mentally challenged, the physically disabled, and black people working on desktop computers. Like IBM's assertion that its digital behest will make learning to read "a little bit easier" for a black child, Microsoft's diversity grouping suggests a liberal condescension. Here, blackness gets lumped with other diagnosable disadvantages that mark bodies as requiring special technological attention. In the layout's climactic display, Microsoft seeks to impress with the lengths to which the company will go to put that apparatus in place. The layout as a whole underlines diversity, but the photo of the black computer users corresponds specifically to Microsoft's global focus, as made clear in the spread's final paragraph: "Microsoft has opened eight centers with trained staff and multimedia, Internet-connected PCs. More than 2,000 people have benefitted from the Digital Villages in South Africa alone" (5).[16] Whereas Star Power, a company located in the Potomac region, uses the trope of African colonization to sell its program for urban technology, Microsoft's global reach gives it the power to literalize that trope. For Microsoft, success at establishing digital settlements in Africa and competence at containing diverse domestic bodies serve as mutually credentialing projects. Microsoft can boast of delivering technology to forms of blackness interchangeably African and American.

One need not believe that such programs are devoid of good intentions or effects. As for the good intentions, the individuals who spearhead these programs tend to be true technophiles, people most likely to cherish genuine beliefs about the virtues of technology, a mastery of which has, indeed, made them rich. As for the effects, a cynic might point out that the children targeted for digital training are in effect being fast-tracked for future drudgery at data-entry farms and call center operations: tracking the "Low-Wage Factor of High-Tech," the Bureau of Labor Statistics expects that "six of the 10 occupations expected to add the most jobs by 2006 pay poverty-level wages."[17] But one would be hard-pressed to deny outright that early exposure to computers could increase the chances that some of these children will make the leap to the creative class—and, moreover, do so in an era when the service-class path is becoming ever more difficult to escape.[18] Nevertheless, one may remain skeptical of the representational patterns that surround digital gap-stopping, starting with the phenomenon's representedness. The pictures show people of good will, people who believe in technology, giving aid to children who may otherwise have difficulty gaining digital access. Over and over, the pictures *show* this good deed; one cannot quite shake the impression that the deed exists primarily to *be* shown. The display of the charitable transaction implies a third party for whose benefit the benevolent scene has been scripted. And this audience—consumers, investors, mere jurors in the court of public opinion—does not necessarily share the techno-philanthropists' preconceptions about the joys and benefits of computing. The companies selling the machines know this fear, they have taken its measure. One oft-cited industry study from the mid-1990s reported that over half of Americans are cyberphobic, afraid of computers to a significant degree.[19] Such a wary public must be persuaded of the computer technology's salutary effects. Tech firms can mine the digital divide to make that case, one reason digital gap-stopping has become the charity of choice for the information age.

In the mid-1980s, Mark Crispin Miller identified the way television assuages viewers' fears about "poor blacks": "in suburbs reassuringly remote from the cities' 'bad neighborhoods,' whites may, unconsciously, be reassured by watching . . . a whole set of TV shows that negate the possibility of black violence with lunatic fantasies of containment: *Diff'rent Strokes,* and *Webster,* starring Gary Coleman and Emmanuel Lewis, respectively, each an overcute, miniaturized black person, each playing the adopted son of good white parents."[20] Miller refers to these programs as "corporate showcases" that present "consumption as a way of life" amidst minivans and refrigerators, microwaves and juicers (646, 648). Though Miller does not attribute any inherently "containing" function to these devices, he emphasizes their presence as props for American success stories, for the materialist placation of historical resentment (651). Surrounded by these appliances, the smiling black faces that define these programs present "a strained denial of all animosity" (651). The broad smiles that span the digital divide update Miller's scenarios—and do so in a way that connects the specific hardware more closely to the logic of containment. In the interval between *Diff'rent Strokes* (1978–86) and, say, *Family Matters*'s Urkel-bot (1989–98) or *Malcolm in the Middle*'s Stevie Kenarban (2000–present), the personal computer became the appliance of containment par excellence.[21] More directly than the situation comedies, the digital-gap charity stories play up the way instructional technology meets an implied deficit in black culture. Often bequeathed by good white adults, the microcomputers electronically extend a kind of surrogate parenting to small black children. But it is not simply anxieties about poor blacks that drive these depictions. The digital-gap media campaigns suggest that the computer has been deployed in this fashion in part so as to cast the *computer* in a positive role. In these instances of tech-sector public relations, the affirmative action is technological: the placement of small colored people next to the machines forms an association for the advancement of computers.

Machines Gone Savage

Inviting Disaster: Lessons from the Edge of Technology shows just how sharply the technological blade may cut in another direction. This 2001 study by James Chiles warns us of the precarious position we humans occupy in "our new world surrounded by machines occasionally gone savage."[22] These "savage" machines, far from advancing the interests of civilization, threaten to turn against and destroy it. The figuration that these entities have *gone* savage indicates a loss of prior colonial control; indeed, it names the most dreadful scenario for such a loss. Going savage, or going native, refers to the corruption of a colonizer gone bad.[23] The notion that a machine could *go* savage still presumes that technology, by birthright, *ought* to function on behalf of social decorum. But some machines (Chiles points, for example, to computers entrusted with automating crucial safety systems) manifest a disturbing capacity to abandon the glorious cause of civilization and defect to the side of savagery. Quite simply, the author of these "lessons from the edge" suggests that such dereliction becomes dangerously likely once it becomes possible. We "invite disaster" to the extent that we abdicate the human duty to exercise control and instead grant regulatory autonomy to machines. If Star Power sells the dream of the colonized subject's joining the forces of colonization, *Lessons from the Edge of Technology* details the nightmare of the colonial agents' switching to the side of the uncolonized.

The more complex and autonomous the technology, the more likely it is to lose its status as a civilizing tool and appear instead as a candidate for colonization. The vision of Peter Menzel and Faith D'Aluisio's *Robo Sapiens: Evolution of a New Species* (2001) vividly illustrates this paradoxical value shift. An astute reviewer of that volume captures the attitude conveyed by the book's pictorial manner: "True to the *National Geographic* style, robots of all shapes and sizes are photographed as if they were aboriginal tribesmen from Pago Pago staring at us from the glossy colored pages with unblinking camera-eyes."[24] In the uncanny moment of a face-to-face encounter, the technological origins of the seemingly sapient robots are almost forgotten, and the presumption of the machines' civilizing influence is lost. In their near-perfect mimicry of a species—a sapient, thinking species—the machines qualify as new objects for the imperial gaze. In this regard, we may note that the technological trappings are not entirely forgotten. Exhibiting what may count as menacing behavior, this new breed of natives threatens to return the gaze. Worse yet, they do so with that favored apparatus of traditional imperialism, the camera eye. In a study of film and the imperial gaze, E. Ann Kaplan points out that "cinema was invented at the height of colonialism at the end of the nineteenth century. The camera was crucial as a machine used by western travellers . . . —and the entire array of colonial agents—to document and control the 'primitive' cultures they had seen and found."[25] The sapient robots, though photographed *as if* they were aboriginal peoples, return the gaze with a critical difference: they possess the power to photograph us in like manner. These unsettling images call out for a new wave of colonial control, although the encounter may shape up to be less one-sided than a meeting with other

"primitive" or "pre-technological" races. The interface zone with these incipient robo-races may well present new dangers, albeit ones indexed to
fears with readily available historical analogs.

The foremost source for such analogies is the matter of slavery and the
fearsome specter of slave revolt. In *Robots and Empire,* sci-fi master Isaac
Asimov develops at length the conceit of robots as slaves, exploring in particular their unstable role in colonizing a galactic empire.[26] Robots are referred to as "chattels," to be passed from human "overlord" to descendant
as inheritance or "put up for sale" if ever found to "hesitate in fulfilling an
order" (14, 76). The plot of the novel involves the return of a human
named Gladia, a galactic VIP, to Solaria, her birth planet and "the last of the
Spacer worlds to be settled and made into a home for humanity" (12). Over
the years of Gladia's absence, some mysterious malaise has descended upon
the Solarian outpost: it has become the "Abandoned World" (93). Most recently, two trader ships that had landed on Solaria have been destroyed—
and robot violence is suspected. The human settlers send an armed ship to
investigate; they bring along Gladia in the particular hope that she may
hold a commanding sway over some of the robots.[27] The ship aims to land
at the site of Gladia's old "estate," where she owned some ten thousand robots, mostly "agricultural robots" along with a few "household robots"
(107). One crew member "dryly" sketches the effect that the police force
hopes Gladia's presence will have upon her property: "They'll remember
Ol' Missy and fall to their knees" (109); the pastiche of plantation slave
speech here is unmistakable. Returning to Solaria, Gladia herself fondly re-
members the happy days of her youth, a time experienced as "freedom," a
freedom supported by the dozen robots that personally attended her (111).
In those days, the human/robot hierarchy was clear. Gladia recalls that fact
of status as reflected in the conventions of looking: "The robots said 'seeing' as though it were a word they must not say, so that they had to whisper
it. She could see *them,* but they were not human" (111).[28] Of course the robots had "watched" her carefully, anticipating her every need, reading her
every gesture (111, 76). Yet they dared not arrogate the privilege of "seeing"
her; the customs of the Spacer worlds had forbidden them to enter into
what E. Ann Kaplan calls a "looking relationship" with the human mistress. Governed by such protocols, the settler outpost appeared to flourish,
for a time.

But in the latter days of colonial adventure, the "and" in Asimov's title
Robots and Empire, becomes ambiguous: the first term poses an insurgent

threat to the latter. Asimov's "Abandoned World" scenario suggests that when governance has declined to the point of permitting robots to look back, an immediate corollary danger arises: the looking robots become free to attack humans and thus to violate the precious First Law of Robotics itself (117). Much of the novel turns out to be a testing of the limits of this First Law—that no robot may harm a human or, through inaction, allow a human to come to harm (142, 151). One could note that Asimov's Three Laws of Robotics, the foundation of his many robot stories and arguably his most famous fictional invention, are predicated on the fear of robot violence. When Gladia and the settlers land on Solaria, the first confirmation that all is not well arrives in the form of robots, gathered quietly, *looking* at the intruders. This looking indeed proves to be a prelude to a robot attack (117). Robots and empire go hand in hand only so long as the robots do not return the objectifying gaze.

Postmodern culture has become increasingly attuned to the ways in which such a gaze produces death. In *Technology as Symptom and Dream,* a fascinating work of academic cultural criticism, Robert D. Romanyshyn analyzes the history of western fantasies of technological vision.[29] Along the way, he produces a revealing fantasy about a colonial role for technology today. Romanyshyn's major argument illuminates the way technologies of linear perspective, from the window to the camera, have positioned the self as a detached spectator. A special case arises when this detached human subject considers the human form as object: at the focal point of the technological gaze, the body appears as a mere specimen. Romanyshyn laments that this mechanistic view obscures "the living body" and finds in its place what he calls "the corpse" (132). The centerpiece of his book is an elegy for "the abandoned body and its shadows," through which he hopes to recover, from beneath the corpse, shadowy traces that will lead us back to a nonreductive appreciation of the living body (133–75). Overall, technology emerges as a menace to humanity. But, in a fleeting reverie, the tech-wary author imagines a significant exception to his strictures:

On a dry African plain, in the silence of the early morning, one can still imagine technology as *vocation,* as the earth's call to become its agent and instrument of awakening. But in the shadows [earlier the author had referenced "the shadows of Chernobyl and the space shuttle disaster"], the imagination falters and technology seems less the

earth's way of coming to know itself and more the earth's way of coming to cleanse itself of us (3).

The analyst snaps back quickly from the reverie, reminded of the threat that
technology poses as a means of cleansing "us" from the face of the planet;
yet that threat can "still" be deferred as long as we can imagine a space
where a *not-us*, an unknown, resides ("On a dry African plain," in the "silence" awaiting human civilization, "one can still imagine technology" as a
higher calling). Though the danger from machines assumes the form of
shadows, though technology threatens to cast us into the darkness, it can
still be counted upon to bring light to a dark continent.

What remains unstated in Romanyshyn's revealing reverie is the explicit
figuration of the black body. Somewhere between the Maryland suburbs
and the urban interior, Star Power crosses that line. The black child with
computer puts on display the fulfillment of that defining American impulse
identified by James Baldwin as the imperative to "civilize these savages."
While presenting a black body under control, the image simultaneously reassures that the *technology* functions properly as part of that civilizing program and not as a source of savagery. In light of this ad, one could conclude
that the problem with those machines at the edge that have "gone savage"
was that they were not attended by black bodies. For the control-loving
technophobe, the black child and computer form a perfect couple: the
black body draws the hazardous duty of keeping the machines from running amok, while the activity of tending technology occupies and develops
the growing black body in a civil fashion.

But even cultural producers with relatively little vested interest in such
hardware merchandising have evidently found compelling reasons to love
the juxtaposition of black person and personal computer. This pattern of
color monitoring appears with comparable frequency within narratives
that have no deep commitment to extolling the virtues of technology, narratives indeed driven by the premise of technology-as-menace. The previous chapter examined a number of Hollywood narratives that assign black
bodies to the computer seat as a way of absorbing that menace. From the
perspective of these narratives, a reciprocal benefit of that seating arrangement is the safe occupation of the black body with technological tasks; if
this benefit does not exactly redeem technology itself, it certainly affirms
the desirability of a proper deployment of technologized blackness. We will
soon see how a larger American cultural ideal finds itself served through

the mutual containment of technology by blackness and of blackness by technology.

Maps of the American Techno-Thriller

To restate our initial question: What do the consistent portrayals of black faces before the computer screen achieve beyond satisfying a need for what narrowly could be termed "positive black images"? What do such portrayals reveal about the creative transactions between storytellers and the audiences whose fears and desires those tellers both serve and shape? I argue that the designation of the techno-whiz as African American contributes a crucial gesture toward reconstituting a national identity. In a global economy wired on information technology, the *multi*national corporation asserts itself as the distributed body with the most power, threatening to displace the sovereignty of nationhood. As noted, Sobchack and Jameson have argued that postmodernism is characterized by multinationalism as the dominant economic form and by electronic mediation as the dominant mode of representation; these correlated elements of cultural logic constitute a worldview "distinct from the older imperialism, which was little more than a rivalry between the various colonial powers." The deployment of the black computer expert, specified as a uniquely American subject, serves to mark an online national vitality that hearkens back to that earlier colonial contest. The African American man at the keyboard affirms America's enduring ability to reinvent implements for a colonial game, whatever the techno-economic stage.

The case of Michael Crichton is replete with instructive examples of such tools for national recovery. Crichton participates in a larger cultural phenomenon, leading the way as a spectacular and highly influential instance of it. Crichton's métier is the techno-thriller, a genre he is sometimes credited with inventing. In the often-imitated Crichton formula, much of the thrill derives from the threat of the techno. Crichton's broad success depends in part on his ability to concoct entertaining strategies for managing that threat.[30]

The nature of the threat itself is well-established to the point of predictability. Ian Frazier has offered up a parody of the genre in a brief piece for *The Atlantic*: "Techno-Thriller: *Now showing continuously at a theater near you.*"[31] This disdainful, highbrow dismissal manages to highlight some key features in a few rapidly sketched scenes:

Opening shot of the Mall in Washington, D.C., seen from above through an office window. Then the focus becomes blurry.
Sound of clicking keys on a computer keyboard.
KEYS: *Click-click-click-click-click. Click-click-click. Click-click-click-click-click-click-click-click-click-click-click-click.* . . .
Shot of microchip magnified 10,000 times. Sudden close-up of its circuitry. Burst of scary *whang-ang-ang-ang-ang* sound.

Frazier's successive shots register both the tedium and the threat of the computer. To some degree, most notably from the parodist's ostensibly bored perspective, the tedium *is* the threat. But the mocker remains faithful to the genre's conventions, which insist that visions of the electronic realm strike the audience as genuinely frightening; the jump cut to extreme close-up communicates the fear of being dwarfed by the digital, engulfed by such tiny technology. And, as the establishing shot makes clear, the plot will involve nothing less than a threat to national security. The "seen from above" viewpoint already subtly implies the way cyber-operations can subordinate and destabilize the foundations of the American state: the computer operates on a plane above—a stage beyond—the icons of national identity. In a global information economy, the defining edges of the monuments can dissolve at the stroke of a key.

This slight pastiche omits at least one leavening ingredient: race. In the techno-thriller's bag of tricks, racial tools occupy a crucial but usually unmentioned compartment. Frazier does identify the panic buttons that the genre repeatedly pushes: the looming microprocessor and the vanishing nation. Here I spotlight the techno-thriller's use of the black body to negotiate that set of threats. Crichton's oeuvre, as it unfolds, provides increasing insights into this dynamic. From the beginnings of his career, fear supplies the thumping bass line: concern with the perils of computer technology pervades Crichton's publications, from *The Andromeda Strain* (1969) to *Prey* (2002). As an imagined corollary to the encroachment of electronics, an unease about the erosion of political borders consistently shadows these works. The novels, best-sellers all, appear to speak to an anxious American audience for whom the national pastime becomes a punctuated suspense, for one breathless book after another, about whether the information age has led the United States past its national time. Can the exceptional American empire still lead in a networked world increasingly controlled by the computer command line? In Crichton's cautionary tales, the modes and degrees of patriotic reassurance vary; in some cases, as in *The Andromeda Strain,* the reader receives little comfort beyond the implication that America at least still nurtures a writer alert enough to sound the alarm. But in a sequence that extends from *Congo* (1980) to *The Lost World* (1995), Crichton has developed a formula that exploits exotic locales as sites for affirming American identity. In this neocolonial sequence, to be discussed below, black computer expertise emerges as the backup for heroic Yankee crisis management. Piotr Siemion, in his groundbreaking study of technothrillers, speaks of these narratives as "routinized epics."[32] In these postmodern rebirths of the nation, race plays a key role in the routine.

One set of terms for framing Crichton's American literary project comes by way of the author's engagement with the work of Jasper Johns. As it happens, Crichton has published an appreciation of the artist, *Jasper Johns,* in two editions, 1977 and 1994, issued in cooperation with the Whitney Museum of American Art. The author's studious fascination with Johns's American artistry thus predates *Congo* and extends up to the threshold of *The Lost World.*[33] Most pertinent to Crichton's own poetics is his consideration of the artist's methodology in "A Brief History of *The Work.*" Crichton locates the genesis of Johns's career in the moment when, soon after destroying all his previous work in 1954, "Johns had a dream of painting a large American flag" (30). In realizing that dream, "the young artist found his self-identity" (30). Crichton lingers over Johns's explanation of how this choice freed him: "Using the design of the American flag took care of a great deal for me because I didn't have to design it" (30). This remark suggests to Crichton a paradox, one that raises the "crucial" question of Johns's "method of operation": "If he does not create an image, but uses ready-made designs, images, and lettering, what does his work consist of?" The way Crichton sets about answering that question unfurls both formal and thematic implications for Crichton's own literary methods and authorial success.

In glossing Johns's comments on the composition of "Flag on Orange Field" (1957), Crichton focuses on the *additive* approach that he finds typical of Johns's procedure: " 'I wanted to add something.' He doesn't say that he wants to make a break, or that he wants to do something else. Rather he wishes to build—to add to what is already there. In this sense, his approach is fundamentally conservative" (35). Not lost on Crichton is the position that a certain formal conservatism may have contributed to Johns's success. Johns's "assured and finely worked paintings of flags and targets offered an alternative to Abstract Expressionism, and reintroduced representation—

the recognizable image—into painting" (37). Thus Johns pleases art crowds with work that resounds as "something fresh and new" by *rein*troducing earlier, familiar, comforting representational schemes—with something added (37). The choice of subject matter does nothing to dampen the energizing sense of tradition renewed. Crichton notes that, in alignment with the identity-making flags, an important expansion of Johns's repertoire involves "the schematic American map of the sort used in a school notebook" (44). These recognizable images blazed the trail for Johns's public recognition; Crichton cites Barbara Rose's assessment that Johns's rapid attainment of early success had much to do "with the ease of mass-media dissemination of his simple American images" (38).

Crichton's rise to cultural prominence owes much to analogous choices of form, content, and method. In forging a new genre, the techno-thriller, Crichton self-consciously built upon what was already there, frequently adopting his plot designs whole cloth from earlier, beloved tales of adventure; as Siemion observes, the techno-thriller uses "familiar categories and figures to explain *everything*" (197).[34] Rather than looking to writerly modernist predecessors, Crichton reintroduces the readerly stories of late imperial romance. He achieves international acclaim for these retellings while bundling them with iconic American imagery, heroes, and ideals. And he always writes with an eye for mass media dissemination. A frequent criticism of Crichton's novels identifies one of their obvious strengths: they read like screenplays.

Starting with *The Andromeda Strain,* a hit movie shot the year after the novel's publication and released in 1971, he has succeeded on a grand scale with a series of fictions that transmits the shock of the new in the outline of the familiar. Tracing a pattern that evokes his own production line, Crichton points to " 'Flag' I, II, and III, a series of transformed images [that] exemplify the Johns dictum, 'Take an object/Do something to it/Do something else to it' " (43). Crichton's own versions of "Flag" I, II, and III can be found in his postcolonial/neo-imperial triad, *Congo, Sphere,* and *The Lost World.* The Johns dictum returns within a Crichton formula: *Take a late imperial adventure/Coat with a coruscating layer of techno-menace/Mask selectively with assorted American characters.* Further specification of this secondary process to Americanize the genre—such as the addition of a representative American black techno-whiz, dispatched to a troubled colonial outpost as the mop-up team's designated information absorber—does not develop immediately. Crichton first puts himself on the map by establishing techno-menace as domestic crisis.

The Andromeda Strain, as Crichton's trademark factitious "acknowledgments" solemnly report, "recounts the five-day history of a major American scientific crisis" (3).[35] The nature of the crisis derives only partially from the virulent strain of the title. Crichton's analysis of the disaster response reveals the real villain of the piece: the ceding of power to computer automation. The final words of the epilogue, in the form of a postcrisis debriefing interview, hammer home Crichton's diagnostic outrage: a hapless NASA representative concludes that the failure that precipitated the crisis ought to be regarded as "a breakdown in systems technology, not as a specifically human error. . . . The decision is really out of our hands." These culminating words resonate with a series of human derelictions exposed throughout the novel. Anticipating the argument of Chiles's *Lessons from the Edge of Technology,* the narrative continually emphasizes the ways that an ill-considered dependence on computerization amounts to *Inviting Disaster.* Even before the alien contaminant reaches the earth's atmosphere, a deadly contagion has already struck: the unchecked spread of autonomous technology.

The cover image for the mass market paperback encapsulates the novel's fundamental conflict and its elemental solution. A small blue and green image of the earth forms the bulls-eye of a target pattern. The pattern consists of a computer printout that fills the page with a circular arrangement of black dots and digits superimposed across the globe and a white background. Over this computer display font, a third picture element occupies the top layer of the illustration: a naked man, stern and upright, the top of his head just cresting the sea of numbers. Picturing the hero as vulnerable, brave, and alone, the cover illustration intimates that this man, in his brain and in the raw physicality of his body, still retains something that sets him apart from and above the electronic realm. If the computer output threatens to overwhelm the world with digitization, the masculine hero stands by, ready to perform the rescue mission.

From this graphical perspective, the problem the hero must rectify is one of mapping. The globe has been reconfigured, subjected to a numerical regime without respect to geographical boundaries. The numerical screen that covers the earth reappears as a figure within the novel, where it is identified as a "scanner printout," with the numbers indicating the density of Andromeda "colonies" in growth media, as measured by a "photoelectric eye" (245). The numbers thus *represent* the spreading colonies of the alien agent, but within the overall argument of Crichton's narrative, the numerical clusters *are themselves* colonies, placeholders for a new world order determined by the internal logic of computer systems. These circuits render decisions subject to no higher court of appeals, and owe allegiance to no nation under God.

The title of the first chapter sings the lament for what the machines have unwrought: "The Country of Lost Borders." A lonely U.S. soldier gazes across "the flat expanse of the Mojave Desert, trackless and vast. The Indians called it the Country of Lost Borders" (10). The U.S. Army would prefer to call it "Arizona" (9), but the soldier, riding in a search van that electronically performs "its own triangulation" (11), traverses an unbounded infoscape. Almost immediately after establishing the setting as the Country of Lost Borders, Crichton drops in a descriptive detail that hints at how we have arrived at such a place: "the banks of instruments and electronic equipment glowed greenly" (10). One may be tempted to read the quick transition from Indian tradition to electronic glow as a deliberately jarring time shift, a conventional contrastive juxtaposition to illustrate how much things have changed since the old times. But the labeling claim of the title, the first words of the novel proper, insists that the Country of Lost Borders names the terrain we inhabit *now*. Under a screen of data points continuously, dynamically, electronically remapped, the land is imagined to revert from national to precolonial status, with which the Indian nomenclature acquires renewed currency.

Crichton's choice of epigraph for his next novel cues a further exploration of this same troubled territory. He invokes Frederick Jackson Turner, author of the Frontier Thesis, here captured in one of his less sanguine moments: "The wilderness masters the colonist" (xiii).[36] Superficially, the novel to which Crichton affixes this sobering thought has nothing to do with the wilderness or colonist, at least in Turner's sense of those terms. *The Terminal Man* (1972) has everything to do with cybernetics: specifically with—to adapt the Norbert Wiener title featured in Crichton's bibliography—information control and the use of human beings. Crichton's chosen epigraph, precisely because of its non-obvious relationship to this immediate subject matter, with a single stroke makes plain everything that the previous novel had merely hinted: Crichton draws a direct connection between information technology and the decline and fall of the American empire. "Perhaps computers really were taking over," the hero worries (195). In this account, wilderness masters the colonist at the cutting edge of the electronic frontier.

As Crichton's invocation of Turner suggests, such discomfort has deep historical roots. In wrapping up a survey of America's "literature of colonization" from 1590 to 1820, Myra Jehlen describes the Indian-hunting, Indian-haunted landscapes of Charles Brockden Brown as the source of his protagonists' unease. Their psyches "a battlefield where savagery and civilization clash," Brown's troubled characters find themselves doomed to reenact unconsciously the savagery of civilization (165). From the nightmare motions of Wieland as he slays his family to the violent sleepwalking of Edgar Huntly (1798, 1799), Brown's central figures act out of an irrational yet causally explicable compulsion: "His characters are mad, but it is history that has made them so."[37] I would add that Brown describes both Wieland and Huntly as acting "mechanically"; mastered by the wilderness, these colonists find their will usurped by an inhuman determinism. The "Terminal Man" updates this history-induced madness of the colonists.

Crichton's nightmares find similar resonance with Renée Bergland's analytical contribution to Dartmouth College's "Reencounters with Colonialism" series: in Bergland's argument, "Indian Ghosts" constitute the "national uncanny" for "American subjects."[38] In *The Andromeda Strain* and *The Terminal Man*, Crichton fuses the legacy of America's Indian displacement with the specter of an electronic life that threatens to displace America itself. When the alien plague strikes in *The Andromeda Strain*, one of the first to fall is Old Doc Benedict, who used to take "care of everybody around, even the Indians" (233); his passing signals the collapse of the old colonial order, leaving the new docs to contend with the spooky machines. *The Terminal Man* displays that red afterimage in "hi-res." In observing such continuity, we may note Bergland's use of the term "uncanny." Bergland explicates Freud's famous 1919 exploration of the concept in his essay "The Uncanny":

> In German, the word that Freud uses is *unheimlich*, which can also be translated as un-home-y, or, more gracefully, as unsettling. The sense of unsettledness in the word *unheimlich* is important, because it evokes the colonialist paradigm that opposes civilization to the dark and mysterious world of the irrational and savage. Quite literally, the uncanny is the unsettled, the not-yet-colonized, the unsuccessfully colonized, or the decolonized (11).

Our cyber-analytic perspective will dwell upon the latter unsettling possibilities in their most extreme forms: colonial subjects and spaces turned decolonized, colonial agents and forces suddenly decolonizing.

The literary origin of Freud's "*unheimlich*," E. T. A. Hoffmann's "The Sandman," casts a lurid light on the explicitly technological direction of Crichton's decolonized terminus. As Terry Castle reminds us, Hoffmann's notion of the "uncanny" was bound to "technological innovation."[39] More to the point, "As Freud himself observes, one of the most uncanny (yet typical) of Hoffmann's themes is that of the 'dancing doll' or automaton," with "The Sandman" featuring just such a terrifying mechanical exemplar (10). The distinct emphases of Bergland and Castle—the uncanny as the decolonized and the uncanny as the mechanical—merge in the figure of a terrifyingly uncontrollable being, the man controlled by technology. "The Terminal Man" lurches into the frame as Crichton's bid for the uncanniest of that race.

For Benson, the title character, the issue of computers has become intensely personal. He has undergone an experimental surgical procedure to help him control seizures—with easily anticipated results to the contrary. A post-op X-ray sets up the tale: Benson's head, in profile, with "electrodes in temporal lobe and computer in neck" (71). In Crichton's horror scenario, the computer takes over Benson's mind, ultimately turning him into parallel-port peripheral that functions as a serial killer. Before the homicidal pattern develops, a blithe neuroscientist dictates the operation's results in terms that already indicate an unhappy outcome:

> the patient's biological brain, and indeed his whole body, has become a terminal for the new computer. We have created a man who is one single, large, complex computer terminal. The patient is a read-out device for the new computer, and he is as helpless to control the readout as a TV screen is helpless to control the information presented on it.
>
> Perhaps that was a bit strong, he thought. He pressed the button and said, "Harriet, type that last paragraph but I want to look at it, okay?" (78)

The scientist thinks he can consider the case with cold detachment. After all, he occupies the comfortably masculine position of a professional dictating to his female secretary.[40] He still inhabits the "discourse network of 1900," which, as recorded in Friedrich Kittler's study of inscription systems, brought typewriters into the office and women to operate them, women "with the admirable ability 'to sink to the level of mere writing machines.' "[41] Among *Terminal Man*'s men, only the pathetic Benson must

take dictation as a mere writing machine—or so the smug technocrat believes. But Crichton elsewhere suggests that the threat of machinic emascu-
lation unfloats all boats within the discourse network of the computer. The
terminal man, however freakish, is the harbinger of a more general fate: the
terminus of Man.

Men on the Verge of a National Breakdown

"Perhaps you think that a few people have power. . . . [but] Everyone is
locked into a system. . . . We are all trapped, my friends. That is the meaning of the twentieth century. It is the century of impotence."[42] Thus spake
John Wright, another of Crichton's dangerous gentleman-madmen from
1972. And, like Benson in *The Terminal Man*, Wright appears in a novel, *Binary*, set up to prove that just because the alarmist is paranoid, it doesn't
mean that the system isn't out to get American manhood. "Wright's voice
dropped lower, became more ominous. His face was grim. 'Impotence,' he
repeated" (21). That ominous emphasis strikes a chord with hero-
investigator Graves, as he studies a statistical analysis of the words Wright
uses most frequently. Two stand out together: "Two-Component" and
"Impotence"; "Graves frowned, staring at the last word" (32). The action of
the novel requires the hero to overcome impotence by escaping the two-
component dictates of binary coding, a coding that the novel identifies
with the emasculating determinism of the computer. He must slip the chain
of ones and zeros to dwell in the world as a man.

An even more insidious form of binary enslavement beckons the
techno-thriller hero with simulated fantasies of potency; Crichton's next
production explores how dangerous these illusions can become. *Westworld*
(1973), a feature film Crichton wrote and directed, hit theaters under the
banner of two marketing taglines: "Westworld . . . where robot men and
women are programmed to serve you" and "Boy, have we got a vacation for
you."[43] *Westworld* lures its unsuspecting victims onto the electronic grid by
offering adult males a chance to play cowboy. After arriving at the resort,
the guests settle in for an orientation film: "Western World is a complete
recreation of the American frontier of the 1880s."

Westworld captures the protagonist's imagination by staging a series of
scenes calculated to buttress his sense of manhood. Peter (a nervous Richard Benjamin) is newly single, still stuck on the wife who has abandoned
him. His friends have proposed a trip to Westworld as therapy for his bat-

tered male ego. And the resort appears to deliver just what the doctor ordered. He knows he's not in the American West of the 1880s, but he fully approves of this diverting choice of backdrop for the programmed reality he learns to enjoy. What he grows to accept is the desirability of a completely computerized environment in which robots serve up a life of entertainment. The buddies share a chortle after a night at a brothel: "Boy, machines are the servants of man!" Having sampled the animatronic pleasures, the men do not find that the acknowledgment of their hostesses' robotic nature in any way interferes with their enjoyment. In a way, that knowledge appears necessary to the fantasy's realization: the men get to do it to the machines. From this perspective, the real trick of Westworld is to permit its guests to feel utterly superior to the machines, to treat the robots as servants. That's the real fantasy that Westworld delivers: that autonomous machines are under control. But as Crichton's narrative insists, that presumption is the most dangerous of westworldly delusions.

The star attraction in this fantasy of masculine mastery is the Robot Gunslinger, a real glutton for punishment. The guests never tire of his shtick: he provokes a gunfight, eats lead, and gets dragged off, bleeding, to the repair shop. The Robot Gunslinger (portrayed by Yul Brynner with fierce, simmering anger) plies his trade with the protagonist, pushing all the right buttons. The black-hatted stranger strolls into the saloon, jostles Peter's drink, and then insults him for spilling: "Give this boy a bib. [the robot pauses, tilts back his whiskey] He needs his mamma." After some prompting from his buddy, Peter delivers the proper retorts, finally punctuated with a bullet to the gut:

> PETER: [*quietly*] You talk too much.
> ROBOT: You say something, boy?
> PETER: [*louder*] I said you talk too much.
> ROBOT: Why don't you make me shut up?

So Peter does just that. The fantasy is complete, intensified by the nature of the verbal output that the protagonist has silenced. Westworld has vouchsafed to Peter the opportunity to defeat in combat not just any machine but a machine that in no uncertain terms has slighted him. The robot's slurs, calling Peter a "boy" and referencing his "mamma," establish a face-off with the protagonist's masculine honor explicitly at stake. The staged scenario of provoked hostility licenses the vacationer to reassert his manhood through violence against the machine.

But a subsequent encounter with the gunslinger ends with an abrupt rupture of the subservient-machine hypothesis. The electronic desperado coolly pulls out his revolver and shoots Peter's buddy dead. This sudden reversal stuns Peter, but Crichton has cued the audience to a rapidly unraveling Western World by periodically intercutting scenes from backstage at the resort. When all is humming smoothly, a robot must clear a series of checks before the team of humans in the control room releases the droid to perform a delimited, albeit autonomous, action. The typical chain of command gives an early glimpse of racialized tech work. For example, in staging a successful showdown with the gunslinger, a white "Supervisor" asks, "Are you ready on phase 443?" A black "Technician" confirms: "443." The technician says nothing else in the scene; the black man speaks in numbers, forming a link between white command and robot execution. Again, setting up the action at nearby Medieval World, a white supervisor delivers a guest order for a duel with the robotic "Black Knight"; the black technician confirms a locked schedule for that programming.[44]

But somehow, this white supervisor > black technician > (black) machine hierarchy has broken down. A "central malfunction" evidently began at Roman World, and "now we're seeing more Western World breakdowns. There's a clear pattern here which suggests an analogy to an infectious disease process." As a contagious insurrection spreads from the dark interior of one incomprehensible machine to the next, so does the West decline.

Crichton's film dramatizes this systemic debacle by focusing on a single insurgent figure, the Robot Gunslinger. Its inexorable pursuit drives the protagonist out across the trackless desert, past a historical terminus, marked by a sign that reads, "Leaving Westworld." Just beyond this boundary, Crichton shows us the end of the American imperial course projected backwards onto its classical model: fallen busts of Caesar and "Cyber-Mayhem" at Roman World.[45] Chased by the implacable gaze of the gunslinger gone haywire, the dream of an endlessly renewed American frontier, programmed to replay the prospects of the 1880s, gives way to a techno-nightmare of imperial decadence.

In dispelling the mirage of man-over-machine dominance, the face of Yul Brynner bears a special weight in Crichton's history lesson. Casting plays an important role in any movie, but the casting of Brynner as the resistant robot affects the viewing experience to an unusual degree, brilliantly amplifying the film's eerie score and animating its unsettling cinematography.[46] As film critic Leonard Maltin asserts, in an all-but-indisputable career summary, "Rarely has an actor been so identified with one role as

Brynner with the King of Siam."[47] Through his years doing the stage role in the 1951 musical and his 1956 Oscar-winning screen performance, Brynner became "The King," the objectified counterpart to the subjective audience proxy, "I." Brynner's presence forever evokes the exotic monarch who succumbs to the manifest domesticity of U.S. literary culture; swayed by the "Poor Eliza" sentiment bestowed upon him courtesy of an English teacher, he becomes the splendid puppet of colonial pedagogy.[48] When, in *Westworld,* Brynner's roboticized body raises its hand against the puppet masters, his violent uprising signals the decisive breakdown of the colonial apparatus across a whole range of global operations. *Westworld* shows us the robot at the end of the empire: a decolonized machine, an uncanny *robo sapiens* that looks back at us—and aims to kill.

The Technological Mind of the Mindless Primitive

Crichton's prophecy of imperial doom taps into a classic sci-fi menace, one memorably presented in the celebrated 1956 film *Forbidden Planet.* "Some dark incomprehensible force" prowls that planet, and its source proves to be a forbidden conjunction of Western mind with machine. The fatal interface takes place on an "Earth-type" planet referred to by one colonizer early in the film as "another one of them new worlds." Here the ambitious Dr. Morbius—consistently identified by commentators as a Prospero figure in this loose adaptation of *The Tempest*—has happened upon the ruins of a departed race, their advanced, annihilating, technology still intact. This "alien" technology, a sort of high-impact virtual reality device that connects conveniently to the human skull, enables the dream of "true creation," creation through dreams, thought into action. Dr. Morbius dives headfirst into this engine of creation, hoping to harness a superior mode of production, but he, like the mysteriously vanished inventors, forgets one thing: the "monsters from the id." Morbius's own repressed desires fuel the dark destructive force that hunts them all. At the film's climax, the United Planets military commander confronts the doomed man of learning with the unhappy truth, the nature of "the beast" that his contact with the advanced technology has revealed: "In you there still exists the mindless primitive."

This same premise drives the plot of Crichton's *Sphere* and its deadly monsters from the id (novel, 1987; movie, 1998): a human encounter with a more advanced alien technology, one that manifests and enacts the user's unconscious, eventuates in the revelation of humanity's own destructive tendencies toward savage technicity. Once again, there's a bit of *The Tempest* surrounding *Sphere,* but whereas *Forbidden Planet* tipped its literary hand with the allusion to "new worlds"—brave or otherwise—*Sphere* charts its trajectory with reference to a much later work about imperialism. An American team is exploring a mysterious wreck near Guam: in the movie, they descend in a submarine, as the white military commander puts it, "into the heart of darkness." Conrad's tale unveils the horror of the white man gone native, his savagery unleashed through contact with the primitive, the dark interior furnishing a mirror to his soul; *Sphere* revisits this horror as reflected in the gleaming surfaces of advanced technology. Crichton's literally wishful conclusion renounces all contact with the shimmering high-tech sphere—in one of the weakest moments in all of Crichton's fiction, the team joins hands and closes eyes and wishes the horrid alien Tinkerbell out of existence. But along the way, a more pragmatic strategy takes shape; for those pesky terrestrial technologies less prone to vanishing, the most effective intermediate buffers are screened according to racial difference.

In *Sphere,* on the mission to an American colonial destination, the team's computational expert is black. Samuel L. Jackson is cast as math "wunderkind" Harry Adams; though obviously an adult at the time of the story's action, he retains from an earlier labeling the identity of a numerically precocious child. Norman, the familiar Crichton hero-doctor-investigator, refers in his notebook to "the subject" as a "black mathematician" (134).[49] Numbers define Adams; he speaks and thinks numbers. Here is his first line from the movie in its entirety: "1709." His second line, similarly unabridged: "288." To be sure, the screenplay does explore a somewhat wider range of alphanumeric possibilities for his character. A third line: "K-447."[50] But what most sets the black man apart is his ability to think in those number systems most dear to the heart of the computer. Early in the investigation, the sub's computer screen fills with a stream of numbers that a white scientist dismisses as "random," the result of a hardware problem that will require them to replace the chips. But Harry Adams squints for a moment and says, "Try binary": he sees the "pattern," understands the "code," and sits at the keyboard to communicate with the machine.

Crichton's nonfiction cautions a privileged readership against this level of machine intimacy. In *Electronic Life: How to Think about Computers* (1983), Crichton has written a handbook to address the fear brought on by the prospect of, as one of his chapter headings poses the question, "The

Final Days of Man Before the Machines Take Over?" (135). He wants in part to assuage that fear, but he takes it as a very real given: "Today we are threatened by computers" (136). Crichton advises that one way to be more comfortable with computers is to limit one's interaction with the machines to "high-level languages. They are closer to English than binary numbers" (84). He establishes a first-person-plural bond with those of "us" who need not trouble ourselves with binary code, while setting aside a minority to handle such headaches: "Computers carry out their work through . . . binary notation. . . . (A few people can program in direct binary notation but that's beyond most of us.)" (83).[51] The preposition of the handbook's prescriptive subtitle suggests at least an arm's-length quarantine; one thinks *about* computers, rather than prying open the black box and studying their basic functioning. Similarly, an intermediate form below "high-level" is also to be avoided: "There is something more primitive, called assembly language . . . close to direct binary machine code" (84–85). In *Sphere,* only Harry Adams can speak the "primitive" language of the machine; as the black technologist, he must deal with that realm "beyond" everyday comfort, the binary code.

In *Congo* (1980), the great white hunter and leader of the expedition, Munro Kelly, muses nostalgically about an adventurous past, before he was "forced" to learn computer language: "It wasn't like the old days, Munro thought. . . . Now every major expedition employed real-time computer planning. Munro had long since been forced to learn . . . [the] major interactive languages. . . . The business had changed" (121). "They were seduced by the technology"; the narrator shakes his head at this sad state of affairs and stands by his man in stalwart resistance to the virus that is computerization: "Only Munro remained immune" (247). At a critical juncture, Munro decides to ignore the prognostications of the computer, presses the "override button" and hatches his own heroic course of action (122). But in the 1995 movie version, the great white hunter is cast as black, and we hear no grumbling about his dislike of computers.

Like the white Munro of the novel, *Congo*'s white hero-scientist Peter Elliot doesn't like computers, and he especially resents the use of computers in the decision-making process: "Elliot was appalled by this prospect of turning control over to the creations of men. . . . 'No,' Elliot said, 'We can make our own decisions'" (293). The only character in *Congo* to demonstrate a love for computers is Amy, the protagonist's trained gorilla, as Elliot explains: "'She likes computers. She's worked around them ever since she was very young.' . . . Amy signed, *Amy good gorilla,* and pushed the keys on the computer again. She appeared relaxed, and Elliot was grateful for the distraction the computer provided. He was always amused by the sight of Amy's heavy dark form before the computer console. She would touch her lower lip thoughtfully before pushing the keys, in what seemed a parody of human behavior" (63–64). This description of the amusement supplied by a large "dark form" at the keyboard, pacified by the distraction of the computer, scarcely requires further comment; at the very least, the good primate's instinctive affinity for computers reinforces the view that the digital realm is something "primitive," highly compatible with subhuman linguistic performance.[52]

Digital Distractions

The Lost World (1995) also makes clear distinctions about the value and desirability of computer work, assigning digital tasks according to a racial binary system. The division exists most clearly between the two stowaway children at the center of the novel's adventure:

> Arby drifted over to Kelly. He looked up at her mournfully. Arby was a head shorter than Kelly; he was the shortest person in the class. . . .
> He had already been skipped two grades, because he was so smart. . . .
> Arby was a genius, particularly with computers.
> Arby put his pen in the pocket of his white button-down shirt, and pushed his horn-rim glasses up on his nose. R. B. Benton was black. . . . (46)

Unlike Arby, the white girl Kelly is not especially interested in computers. She wants to be a real scientist; the novel repeatedly and approvingly emphasizes how Kelly emulates the heroic scientists she meets. Thus, in turn, the novel presents Kelly as a role model for younger readers. Arby emulates nobody, and is nobody's role model. A simple narrative device makes the preferred readerly identification clear: Kelly and Arby are virtually inseparable, but throughout all of their scenes together, the third person narration adopts only Kelly's point of view.

The novel sees things through Kelly's eyes but looks down on Arby with nothing but condescension for his special abilities. At one point, the team wants to recover and decode some secret computer files:

[Doctor] Thorne said, "How are you going to—"

"Give me a minute here," Arby said. . . . Then he began to type rapidly.

"Okay, Arb," Thorne said. He was amused by the imperious way Arby behaved whenever he was working with a computer. . . . The electronic world was really his element. (72)

While indulging in a chuckle at the boy's play imperialism in the virtual world, the white engineer Thorne patronizes Arby's whiz-kid status; despite moments of urgency, the kid's work turns out to be largely superfluous:

"Arb," Kelly said, "don't just sit there. Come on! Recover the map! That's what we need!"

"I don't know if I can," Arby said. "It's a proprietary thirty-two-bit format. . . . I mean, it's a big job."

"Stop whining, Arb. Just do it."

"Never mind," Malcolm said. . . . "It's not important."

"It's not?" Arby said, a little wounded.

"No, Arby." (80)

The wise white scientist (Malcolm, a kind of Yankee Sherlock Holmes in this scene) informs Arby that they already have sufficient clues to deduce the answer they need: American mother wit trumps mere number-crunching.

Again: at the climactic moment, the team encounters an electronic impasse. Huddled in front of a computer terminal, the characters attempt to formulate a plan. This time, Kelly ends up at the keyboard, confronted with a bewildering graphical display:

Everyone in the room was shouting. Kelly stared at the cube on the screen, feeling hopeless and lost. . . .

Standing beside her, Arby said, "Come on. Do the icons one at a time, Kel. . . . Stay with it. Focus."

But she couldn't focus. She couldn't click on the icons, they were rotating too fast on the screen. . . .

"It's important, Kel," Arby said. He was trembling as he stood beside her. She knew he concentrated on computers as a way to block things out. As a way to—

> The wall splintered wide, an eight-inch plank cracking inward,
> and a raptor stuck his head through, snarling, snapping his jaws. . . .
>   Arby said, "It's important."
>   And then it hit her.
>   "No," she said to him. "It's not important." (383–84)

Though Arby fixates on the computer, Kelly has learned her lesson. What
turns out to be important is that Kelly discovers a crawl space beneath the
terminal, a tunnel to hold the cabling. Their escape thus hinges upon turning away from the virtual distractions of Arby's realm, back toward Kelly's
reality. In each of these instances black, peripheral characters serve to outline a central whiteness unhampered by technological constraints.[53] Alongside a colonial instrumentalization of blackness, Crichton's plots drive
home an imperative for a firm white grip on reality.

   This insistence on a physical rather than a computational solution finds
an even more explicit formulation in Crichton's recent novel, *Prey* (2002).
Those who lose their grip on reality shall suffer the deadly embrace of digitality: with punitive logic, the narrative links information technology to an
unhealthy blackness that overtakes the white body. In this thriller of nano-
technology, the hero must do battle with swarms of tiny robots, which have
evolved an intelligence of their own. An attack of the nanomachines threatens him with the prospect of a black death: "I looked down at my body but
could barely see it. My skin appeared black" (168). The hero, Jack Forman,
manages to cleanse himself of this computer coating and overcome the
bodily alienation it produces. But surviving this brush with blackness gives
him nothing more than a temporary reprieve from a structural crisis he
must resolve. The colonies of nanomachines behave in a manner that poses
not only an immediate threat to Jack's life but also a functional challenge to
the way of life that gives him his identity: the swarming bots exhibit the
kind of self-organization characteristic of "African termites," creatures capable of complex accomplishments "with no architect, no foreman, no
central authority" (274). If left unchecked, the swarms would overwhelm
and suffocate Jack; more fundamentally, their mode of production would
make obsolete the Forman/foreman. The hero insists on the ultimate un-
manageability of such self-managing mechanisms, particularly when they
move to recolor his own skin.

   But the villains of the piece, the human collaborationists with *Prey*'s
predators, appear to embrace this technologized blackness willingly. Signaling their unnatural natures, a white man and woman immerse them-

selves in "the black cloud" and wrap themselves in "the black cloak" that
will bring about the "new world" and "the birth of the new world order"
(88–89). Pursuing an adulterous affair, the couple commits infidelities that
break both marital and human covenants and that make them race traitors
into the bargain. The blackness that engulfs their white bodies, outwardly
pure artifice, partakes of an Africanist origin. The electronic code that mo-
bilizes the nanobots models itself on the movements of "African hunting
dogs, stalking lionesses, and attacking columns of army ants"; from these
patterns emerges "a program module called PREDPREY, which could be
used to control any system of agents" (127). In theory. But when the white
folks develop too much intimacy with the machines, these digital beasts of
the wilderness master the colonists. Technology goes savage, the technologists go native: together, they are black, violent, deadly. The fools choose a
life formed by information, a choice made at the expense of their fleshly
bodies. When a magnetic field momentarily disperses the nanoparticles
from an initially willing host, only a "cadaverous form" remains. Too late,
the unfaithful wife confesses the horror of the cybernetic embrace: " 'Jack,'
she whispered. 'It's eating me' " (338).

When the swarm reintegrates with its host, we see that something else is
eating Jack: "Suddenly, in a *whoosh,* all the particles returned, and Julia was
full and beautiful and strong as before, and she pushed me away from her
with a contemptuous look" (339–40). In the face of this apparition, the
hero's anxiety has much to do with gender power. From the opening pages
of the novel, the narration dwells repeatedly on the (unemployed) protagonist's growing perception that his (tech professional) wife is metamorphos-
ing; he registers his unease about her acquisition of strength and hardness:
"I had the feeling that her appearance had changed, somehow. Of course
she had lost weight recently, part of the strain of the job. A certain softness
in her face was gone; her cheekbones protruded more; her chin seemed
sharper" (17). This chiseled glamour awakens his insecurities: "I had read
somewhere that this was a syndrome. The husband's out of work, his masculine appeal declines, his wife no longer respects him, and she wanders"
(18). The figure of Julia as potent libertine recalls another strong and evil
woman from the Crichton catalog, *Disclosure*'s Meredith Johnson (played
by Demi Moore in the 1994 movie of the 1993 novel), who gets promoted
over the male protagonist for an upper management slot at DigiCom. As
even these brief summaries suggest, the obvious gender politics of these
threatening female characters comes bundled in a digital package. In both
cases, the woman's power is closely associated with her professional and

personal commitment to antinatural technology—information technology that consumes the softness of feminine flesh and demeanor, that eats up all manner of comforting cultural markers along the way.

At DigiCom, Ms. Johnson (Moore) pilots a project that will serve up a virtual world, "When Reality is Not Enough." Pitching the digital vision, she preaches a hard-core techno-idealist philosophy: "Freedom from the physical body" and "Freedom from nationality and personality." With carefully placed disharmonies, the writer tips his hand: we are not to trust this woman with our future. She disavows the life of the body—and thus categorically disqualifies herself from heroic identity.[54] And in no example of even the most starry-eyed techno-utopianism have I ever seen an appeal for the abolition of *personality*. Some dissident dreamers may foretell a farewell to nationality, perhaps; but not with the blessings of Crichton's narrative—and not along with the baby of personality. *Disclosure* insists that the two items go together: the digital agenda has its eyes on both our personality and our nationality. Right-thinking viewers must rush to defend both from the clutches of wicked and emasculating technologists. The American nation must thrive upon American individualism.[55] We are, and of right ought to be, free. But not from nationality.

The American techno-thriller boasts plenty of stern visages bidding to uphold national personality. Entering the fray in the same spirit as Crichton's Representative Men, Arnold Schwarzenegger rages for American reality. Confronted with digital displays, as at the climax of *The Lost World*, Crichton's white protagonists crawl, climb, and leap toward daylight and fresh air; a solid portion of the recent career of Arnold Schwarzenegger seeks to squeeze through this same opening. Arnold, antithesis of the diminutive black Arby, follows Crichton's Kelly in her turn away from the computer to the path of physical escape. *The 6th Day* (2000), a warning against the imminent perils of biocybernetic reproduction, finds Adam Gibson (Schwarzenegger) being interrogated by a "Virtual Psychiatrist."[56] When Adam fails to cooperate with the program, a cyber-agent issues an order to "detain the subject." But no action hero portrayed by Arnold Schwarzenegger will long submit to having his subjectivity policed and detained by cybernetic control. His detention cell prominently features the electronic mediation he will fight to overcome, a wall-sized screen wired to the Internet. Ignoring the streaming media, Adam approaches the screen with suspicion and hostility; closer inspection reveals that the monitor doubles as a surveillance device, a one-way window. Having detected the screen's insubstantiality—an object lesson to other detained subjects who may have unquestioningly allowed the World Wide Web to trap them within narrow confines—Adam rips through the electronic display with his bare hands. In the process of escaping the control facilities, he uses a blaster to destroy yet another computer screen. Getaway scenes throughout the movie underscore Adam's scorn for the digital domain and his commitment to traditional, masculine relations to technology. Unlike his doomed partner, the invention-happy Hank Morgan—a take on Twain's Connecticut Yankee, amused to death by technologies of simulation such as a virtual girlfriend—Adam is proudly "old school." Driving his trusty 1957 Cadillac, Adam plows through a living room, driving a man away from a computer while smashing the screen. In such scenes, the kinetic force of Schwarzenegger's persona acts as a calculated intervention; Arnold defends men against the immobilizing effects of digital temptation.

In *End of Days* (1999), the Devil himself tempts Schwarzenegger's Jericho Cane with a virtual vista. But Cane resists the lure of the vividly conjured images. Why? "Because they are not real." His refusal marks Satan as an evil purveyor of virtuality; within the story, if Arnold's character were to give in to the image-enhanced blandishments of the Devil, the "end of days" would be upon us. But Jericho remains resolute against the Beast and his Numbers game: "I prefer reality." In the movie-making imagination, Schwarzenegger has himself come to embody that preference. In "Imagining *Total Recall*" (2001), a featurette created for the DVD of the 1990 movie, the director of that "is it virtual?" adventure explains that "by choosing Arnold, there was a preference for reality."

Fighting his way out of the "Dark Territory" of *Under Siege 2: Dark Territory* (1995), Steven Seagal wants a piece of this same action. Seagal (here playing Casey Ryback) finds himself up against a mad cyberterrorist who holds the Pentagon hostage, issuing orders from an unmappable locale.[57] The multiracial U.S. team responds the way it knows best: "Give me a report, Captain Williams!" orders the white general, standing. Seated at the computer, a black man types furiously: "I'm still searching." And he keeps on searching. As the zero hour approaches, some sixty screen minutes later, poor Captain Williams is still sitting in the same spot, trying to find the electronic key by exhaustively processing the possible permutations. Like Arby in *The Lost World,* he will never find it. But thanks to Casey's steady hand, the black man's computer efforts turn out to be superfluous. At *Dark Territory*'s climax, Seagal meets the cybervillain face to face. Eric Bogosian, playing wild-eyed and woolly madman Travis Dane, cradles his laptop, the computer controlling the countdown to national destruction. Dane smugly informs the action hero that he will never break "my encrypted code."

> CASEY: You mean to say there's no way I can shut that off?
> TRAVIS: That's right.

Casey levels his gun and puts a bullet through the Toshiba and its operator. The dying Travis's last words: "I never thought of that."

One didactic point of the techno-thriller is to remind us always to think of exactly *that*: never to mistake electronic control for physical mastery, forever to privilege the decisive action over the digital distraction. Holding the line against an ungovernable cyber-chaos that threatens to derail America into the "dark territory" of the digital, the techno-thriller stands firm for the state of reality. No one pounds this lesson more relentlessly than Crichton.

Seeking to dispel the "black cloud" of nanobots, the hero of *Prey* momentarily considers actually looking at how these machines have been programmed. He goes so far as to have the code printed out for him. But a quick glance suffices to snap him back to reality: "The hell with it, I thought. I crumpled up the sheet of paper, and tossed it in the wastebasket. However this problem got solved, it wasn't going to be with computer code. That much was clear" (249).

Lost Worlds Regained

Computers get us into the dark territory, get us lost in the lost worlds; they don't help us find our way out. Computers are not important, the techno-thriller tells us. But Arby and his brothers somehow are important, the techno-thriller implicitly shows us by presenting them repeatedly. Though the black male at the keyboard is not pragmatically instrumental to the successful resolution of the plot, he is symbolically instrumental to a narrative of America's cultural efficacy. "It's not important," as Malcolm and Kelly have both learned to say, referring to Arby's futile efforts to forge a digital evasion of a grave physical threat. No, it's not important. But *he* is. In a narrow sense, his computer work accomplishes nothing substantial. But his intense engagement and preoccupation with the computer is an end unto itself. R. B. Benton serves as a proof of American colonial competence. In her recent genealogical recovery of overlooked black film criticism, Anna Everett notes that Lawrence Reddick identified this strategy as early as 1944: *The Lost World*'s R. B. Benton lines up with a tradition of positive black characters who "were crafted as alibis, 'justifications and apologies for colonial imperialism.'"[58]

We have noted in chapter 1 that *Jurassic Park* recapitulates a colonial division of labor. But, more specifically, Crichton sets the scene for an American disciplinary rehabilitation of botched British rule. The narrative initially places the Brit, John Hammond, in command of the island venture, but only in order to emphasize his incompetent rule, his inability to control the course of events, human and otherwise. When things get messy, it becomes necessary for the American experts to come in, mop up, and whip things back into shape.

This recuperative scheme becomes even clearer in the sequel, *The Lost World*, beginning with the historical framing of the novel. The first words of the introduction announce the subject of the book, "Extinction": "The late twentieth century has witnessed a remarkable growth in scientific interest in the subject of extinction. It is hardly a new subject—Baron Georges Cuvier had first demonstrated that species become extinct back in 1786, not long after the American Revolution" (ix). The reference to the American Revolution may at first seem gratuitous—do we really need this historical marker to have a sense of when 1786 was?—but as the narrative unfolds, this allusion takes on added significance: what the book bears witness to is the extinction of the British Empire from an American perspective, a process presumably first demonstrated when the "world turned upside down" with the spirit of '76. The very last page of the novel completes the frame, again invoking the time "when America was a new country" (393), as the surviving heroic Americans optimistically set sail for home. British imperial dissolution is evident in the overall plot trajectory, as well as a few key details: for example, the cause of the island crisis is at one point traced to the fact that the animals have been fed tainted British meat, with "mad cow" disease held up as an emblem of degeneracy (277–78, 357). Even on the level of literary history, Crichton has rewritten a late imperial British text, Sir Arthur Conan Doyle's *The Lost World* (1912)—just as *Congo* rewrites H. Rider Haggard's *King Solomon's Mines* (1885) and *Sphere* rewrites *Heart of Darkness* (1902)—reclaiming the adventure for an American imperial imagination. The British Empire may be extinct, but in Crichton's *Lost World*, "Something Has Survived."

The conclusion of the movie (1997) compresses this frame into a shot of an American warship, as the anachronistic lifeforms are extricated from the clutches of the misguided Hammond and restored to unfettered dominion of their island paradise under the careful vigilance of the U.S. Navy to "make sure" there is no repeat disaster. In the end, a chastened Hammond professes the (quasi-postcolonial) moral of the story: "These creatures need our absence, not our presence, to survive. *If we can only find a way to step aside,* life will find a way." Hammond here assents to an end of empire, paternally negotiated through an American military presence.

Such a gesture has become one of the most recognizable affirmations of American nationhood. Bergland defines an "American subjectivity" that is "explicitly national rather than imperial. This is not to say that America is not imperialist."[59] She explains America's confusing position in a postcolonial landscape: "On the one hand, America is and always has been a colony of Europe; on the other, America is an imperial power. But both these facts are somehow shameful in an American context, since American nationhood is built on the denial of colonialism" (13). *The Lost World* explicitly dwells on an end of British imperialism to commemorate America's ascent from colony to nation and explicitly anticipates the end of all imperialism while implicitly demonstrating the American nation's benevolent imperial prowess. Under the supervision of Nature's Nation, fully in control of her technologized colonial children, life will find a way.[60]

This chapter opened with the image of a forward-looking black child, bearer of the technology that is changing the face of the earth. It concludes with a work that shows just how far his civilizing mission may be imagined to take him. We pick up his story some eight hundred thousand years into the future; another late-Victorian adventure recently translated to American soil provides this glimpse. Simon Wells's *The Time Machine* (2002) is a deeply technophobic narrative, faithful in this regard to an important dimension of its 1895 literary ancestor.[61] H. G. Wells had imagined "the logical conclusion of the industrial system of to-day" as the evolution of two races, one of which feeds upon the flesh of the other. The 2002 film version vividly renders an image of an appallingly white race that appropriates and consumes the bodies of people of color. The white Morlocks dominate the colored Eloi through their superior force and weapons technology but also, more fundamentally, through their control of information. The Eloi, a sweet and simple race of primitives, live in an apparently peaceful state of nature that is in fact a state of enforced denial. These cliff-dwellers are kept in ignorance and fear by the mega-brained Morlocks who haunt their dreams, monitor their thoughts, and, with clockwork regularity, eat them. In *Hacking the Future*, Arthur and Marilouise Kroker recount "stories for the flesh-eating nineties": narratives that prey upon the fear that information technologies will deprive us of our bodies.[62] H. G. Wells's attempt to hack the future from the perspective of the 1890s, revived in the film remake, overtakes the Krokers' analysis of 1990s global digital culture. Technology takes over with an unappeasable appetite for human flesh.

Visiting the lean time traveler in his New York laboratory, a pleasantly plump friend asks if "we'll ever go too far?" "No such thing," the technologist thoughtlessly replies. But a quick trip to a dim future forces the chastened inventor to recant: "You were right, Philby. We did go too far." The climactic encounter with the über-Morlock drives this theme home with bitter recrimination. Played by Jeremy Irons with a heavy air of world-weary British decadence, the deathly white Morlock informs the time-machinist that "I am the inescapable result of you." The inventor's machine, an "attempt to control the world," leads inevitably to a brutal existence of cybernetic domination. The screenplay sums up the accusation: "I am your future." In the words of the producer, Irons presents the image of "technology gone to hell." Goaded by this foresight, the technologist turns into an action hero. Physically subduing the antagonizing face of his future, the hero destroys his time machine in an explosion that demolishes the Morlocks and all of their mighty machinery. He secures a bright future by freeing the world of all advanced technology.

Well, almost all of it. In the Eloi paradise that ensues, exactly one piece of information technology endures. Sometime in the twenty-first century, the New York Public Library has equipped itself with an electronic "compendium of all human knowledge." And, for ease of use, the informational technologists have developed a friendly interactive interface. The interface that will gladly answer your questions introduces itself in a somewhat impersonal manner: "I'm the Fifth Avenue public library information unit." But the information unit, also known as "Vox," has a visible persona: the flickering projection of a nattily besuited black man (infused with comedic charm by the performance of Orlando Jones).[63] To supplement Vox's informative voice, a black holographic form sings and dances across the flat screen displays. Eight hundred thousand years into the future, the obliging digitized black man continues to chirp his solicitous greeting: "Welcome to Vox system! How may I help you? How may I serve you? What can I get you?" This profoundly technophobic narrative thus reserves a special exemption for the one digital application deemed forever appropriate, the disembodied—and supremely eager to please—black man.

The Time Machine imagines for Vox a vital purpose in a neocolonial regime. With proper liberal outrage, the film reports the white-over-black future with requisite horror at the exploitative Morlocks and sympathy for the downtrodden Eloi. The story endorses an intervention in this thoroughly colonial scheme, but one that manages to be simultaneously anticolonial and neocolonial: the liberating white hero installs himself as the new manager of the outpost. And, crucially, the film bequeaths the hero with an assistant for the ongoing education of the natives: a handy database of western civilization that serves up information through this holographic image of a black man. That instrumental icon, Vox, provides the very model of what James Baldwin identifies as the dream of the civilized and civilizing savage. The film thus celebrates, in the example of Vox, a version of the logic that the overall story would seem to lament. No less than the skeletons of the victimized Eloi, Vox poignantly illustrates what happens when information loses its body. Similar strategic reductions of the black body have been imagined elsewhere with a far more critical edge, as in the pacifying holograms produced by the sinister Fantasy Bureau in George Lucas's bleak *THX 1138* or in the reassuring "Electric Negroes" of Matt Ruff's satiric *Sewer, Gas and Electric*.[64] In Vox, *The Time Machine* delivers the perfection of the docile colonial subject and the immortalization of neocolonial pedagogy.

In the radiant vision of paradise regained, we last see Vox holding forth in a jungle amphitheater. In the midst of the lush tropical growth, the colorful Eloi have assembled the fragments of American culture. Represented by a mix of Asian, Pacific Islander, black, and Hispanic actors, the tattooed band of Eloi suggests the ethnic makeup of the non-haole demographics of Hawaii, where these scenes of the future New York were in fact filmed; this superimposition manifestly completes a historical circuit from the Empire State to America's youngest state. As Vox schools the natives in American English and its literature, we see bits and pieces of the New York landmarks that have survived the long passage of time. Just behind and above Vox's head as he lectures the captivated tribespeople and children, a fragment can be made out: "EMP." As the camera pans out across the tribal bodies, we see the complementary fragment: "IRE STATE." The circuit of the Vox system, the disembodied black informationist, together with the technological primitives in the form of the newly disciplined native peoples, puts the pieces of the state back together.

The electronic Vox, in lecturing his charges, has been given an apt text for colonial instruction. He regales the unformed minds with *The Adventures of Tom Sawyer* (1876). Its white god is Tom Sawyer, who brilliantly oversees the whitewashing of a "far-reaching continent of unwhitewashed fence" (27); Twain himself would later disparagingly see Tom as the prototype for Teddy Roosevelt and his imperialist policies.[65] This same fictional master of colonial management is wise to the racial divisions of expertise, as Tom sagely tells Huck of colored folks' magical technicity: "They know all about these kind of things" (99).[66] Nor is the text devoid of warnings to the wayward colonial subject. The narrative sees to it that bad natives meet with justice: the no-good Injun Joe, for example, starved to death and buried by townsfolk who "had almost as satisfactory a time at the funeral as they could have had at the hanging" (254). It is a narrative that concludes with the necessity of proper behavior as a condition for community membership: Tom Sawyer agrees to let Huck into his gang, but only if he promises to go back to the widow Douglas and be "respectable" (272).

From this rich textbook, *The Time Machine* leaves us with a carefully chosen moment. The last words we hear Vox repeat come from Chapter XVII, "Memories of the Lost Heroes—The Point in Tom's Secret": "Aunt Polly, Mary and the Harpers threw themselves upon their restored ones" (146). The film thus closes with the sentimental triumph of civilization and the restoration of its heroes. Vox pointedly does *not* read from *Huckleberry Finn,* wherein we learn, among other off-message developments, the outcome of all Tom's efforts to get Huck domesticated under the influence of one Aunt or another: "She's going to adopt me and sivilize me, and I can't stand it." Moreover, the dead, undisciplined Injun of *Tom Sawyer* serves Vox's rhetorical occasion better than would the unpunished fugitive slave of *Huckleberry Finn. The Time Machine* does not trouble the troubled American past of racial injustice. Rather, through the perfectly controlled and controlling voice of Vox, the story restores confidence in the future of the American nation and its reconstructed state of empire.

chapter Three

INTEGRATED CIRCUITS

Incorporating the Black Body

In 2001, the world's first commercial computer turned fifty. But the company responsible for the machine's inception, Unisys, did not view Univac's birthday as an occasion for unmitigated celebration. Unisys instead saw fit to issue the following public statement: "Many of the effects of the Computer Age have been accompanied by a number of transaction-based annoyances—all unimagined 50 years ago. As the company that started it all, Unisys feels it only fitting that it mark this historic anniversary with an apology for those inconveniences."[1] Although that apology smuggles in a boast of corporate primacy, the fact of the apology itself marks an important recognition. In cloaking its braggadocio with contrition, Unisys acknowledges the widespread public hostility toward the computer age, a perception that the company feels the need to manage with a self-deprecating chuckle. In this chapter, I will examine a related set of management strategies that companies use to deal with cyberphobia. In particular, I have noticed a pattern of companies using race to sell computer technology, a racializing pattern that I will document and discuss.

The Unisys example, with its compensatory humor offered as propitiation, identifies a functional motive that also applies to the racializing sales strategies at issue here: the company focuses on assuaging the irritation of the business sector, and it is the performance of this soothing function for a business audience that distinguishes these corporate narratives from the cyberphobic popular narratives examined in the preceding chapters. Whereas the purveyors of mass entertainment can rely on public hostility toward computer technology to help forge a bond between protagonist and audience—and can do so without any feelings of ultimate responsibility toward that audience's technophobia—technology firms' corporate narrators must take care to spin that hostility. Given the existence of such ill will and discomfort about computers, both popular and corporate narratives tend to sell forms of escapism. But whereas the popular escapism may sell the dream of being utterly free of technological fetters, the ideal corporate escapism would convince you, the client, that you can have your tech without it eating you.

Corporate narratives, I argue, facilitate that fantasy by presenting the proper incorporation of the black body.[2] This chapter will cover a series of representational transactions that illustrate that process of technological incorporation: the placing of technology and technological labor in a black box; the linking of black bodies with that black box, whether by juxtaposition or outright identification; the emphatic naturalization of that linkage, producing what I call the "natural machine"; the flattering acknowledgment and accommodation of the aversion on the part of privileged whiteness to the prospect of its own technologization; finally, the explicit side-by-side opposition between executive white masculinity and technologized blackness. In tracing the patterns of these management strategies I begin with the least obvious examples, in the hope of cumulatively developing a richer understanding of the elements that go into the more clear-cut illustrations that appear at the end of the chapter. These representational transactions, in their repetitious reliance on racialized divisions, collectively reveal the corporate marketing of technology as a ritual practice underwritten by a logic of sacrifice.

Black-Boxing Technology

In the service of technological diplomacy, a company that traces its lineage to the founding of the Internet now offers a packaged solution to the complications of "Internetworking." Like Unisys, Genuity takes credit for originating status and innovation while offering compensation for headaches thereby induced. They made the Internet; now they want to make nice. Their simplifying product's name, Black Rocket, conjures a wealth of vernacular associations consistent with escapist corporate narrative. With Black Rocket, Genuity promises to do something for us, something difficult; the product metaphor designates networking as belonging to a category of daunting challenges that, in common parlance, we refer to as "rocket science." Now, the most common expressions that employ those words all take the form of negation: "It ain't rocket science"; "It doesn't take a rocket scientist"; "Well, I'm no rocket scientist, but . . ." In these phrases, "rocket science" designates a kind of labor we don't undertake; "rocket scientist" identifies someone other than us. "It ain't rocket science"—these words might be used to voice the "aw shucks" rejoinder of the hardworking everyman, obliquely acknowledging a compliment for a job well done. The implicit proud sufficiency of such a statement rings more clearly in two other expressions that set the rocket scientist aside: "It doesn't take a rocket scientist" and "Well, I'm no rocket scientist, but . . ." The work we do in the everyday world does not call for a rocket scientist. If said rocket scientist were consulted, we might find ourselves bogged down by needlessly abstruse and involved calculations. Sure, a thing called rocket science exists, and rocket scientists are welcome to it. As for me, I'm no rocket scientist, but I know what's what. The rocket scientist is one who possesses knowledge and skills which we neither have nor desire.

One may object that the phrase "It ain't rocket science" can be used dismissively, perhaps from a perspective of privilege, looking down on or sniffing at someone else's limited responsibilities. In this case one might be lodging a complaint about another's failure to render service: "I don't know what the problem is—it's not rocket science." This complaint takes its canonical form as, "I don't know what the problem is—*I could do it myself.*" (Conversely, if it were rocket science, I sure as heck could never take care of it myself, so I'd have diminished grounds for complaining about another's inability to complete the work.) Thus the negation of rocket science operates similarly, whether the context of usage calls for delivering an insult or receiving a compliment. In both instances, the speaker positions rocket science as something the speaker could not—would not—do.

Rocket science—the stuff that goes into the Black Rocket—would be the work left, out of necessity, for others. Making the rocket black takes this sense of arcana a step further, partitioning the technical operations on the other side of a light-tight airlock. To call up another association of the Black Rocket name, what the product will do for you may as well be magic.

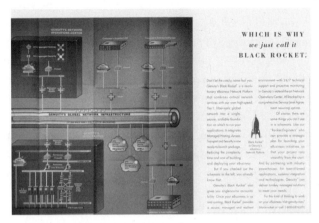

Fig. 6. Selling technology in a black box: Genuity's "Black Rocket" *platform* (2001).

It promises to be, as indicated by Arthur C. Clarke's famous dictum, a technology that is sufficiently advanced so as to become "indistinguishable from magic." The fact of needing someone else to perform that rocket science/magic may be gladly acknowledged, but it may also incur resentment. In the face of any possible discontent, Black Rocket aims to please; its dark technical mystery comes wrapped in a toylike bundle—and with no assembly required. In selling Black Rocket, the folks at Genuity clearly want to keep it light and to soften any edge of the client's grudging sense of dependency by making the purchase feel like a happy choice.

A two-page spread for this tidying Internet business platform wants to make that choice a no-brainer: filling the left page and spilling over to the right, a bewildering array of routers, LANs, and firewalls with over fifty depicted links illustrates the company's proposed "global network infrastructure"; the right side gives the tagline in a bold typeface: "WHICH IS WHY *we just call it* BLACK ROCKET" (fig. 6). The diagram deliberately overwhelms in its tangled complexity, provoking anxiety with such details as the lapping flames of "hot fallover" at the "firewalls," giving the impression of a business under siege, threatened on a multiplicity of fronts. The overall message is information technology overload; though shrunk to (not quite) fit on a single magazine page, the diagram appears to be printed on a foldout chart, with the visible creases suggesting that the original schematic demands twelve pages to accommodate its vast intricacy. The facing slogan reassures with a tone of comic relief. The midphrase start of the tagline invites the reader to supply the lead-in that warrants the "why."

In place of the baffling diagram, a verbal translation of the visual rhetoric might be, "You don't *really* want to know about all the messy details of Internetworking—which is why we just call it Black Rocket." The comfortable, casual "we just call it" acknowledges the ludicrous overkill of the diagram without disowning its accuracy. Internetworking really does involve that many headaches, but Black Rocket bottles them up in one tidy "ready-to-launch package," representationally "reducing the complexity" of the chart to a cool little black icon, the contents of which need not—in fact can not—be scrutinized. The Black Rocket is slick, gleaming, opaque. The ad copy plays up the economy of invisibility: "Of course, there are some things you can't see in a schematic. Like our 'Rocket Engineers.'" Free with every purchase of Black Rocket, you will receive the services of invisible people—technician-magicians whose real trick is to make the daunting technology disappear.

A networking solution marketed for the home turns on the same magical promise. The user need consult no convoluted manual and perform no manual labor—there's no technical knowledge to acquire, no rewiring of the house required. The installation process claims full automation: "Dark-o the Wizard" will handle everything.[3] Let me make now clear what I am and am not claiming about Dark-o and the Black Rocket. I am not suggesting that just because of verbal echoes or the invocation of color, race is involved in the marketing of these products. I select the examples of Dark-o and Black Rocket primarily because of what these marketing strategies have to say about attitudes toward technology. These labels reflect an attempt to sell high tech in a black box, an attempt based on the premise that clients don't want to know what goes into that box. This marketing fact can, however, take on racial significance to the extent that it overlaps with related cultural logics. The infatuation with the image of the black man as techno-whiz and the desire for black-boxed technological wizardry are mutually informing impulses. The pandering to an aversion to technological knowledge deflates the status of the techno whiz's role; the repeated projection of technological expertise onto obliging black bodies tends to racialize the packaging of helpfully black-boxed technology.

In the case of Black Rocket, successive ad campaigns make this overlap evident within a single product line. The makers of Black Rocket have introduced a versatile total communications network called Black Rocket Voice. A TV spot for the product "takes viewers 'behind the wall' into an IT department's internet network."[4] But rather than viewing the actual guts of the system, we see the network parts "personified to show in a simple way" how the system deals with "complexity." The sequence begins with a black screen, then a shot of an office setting, featuring the back of a black man's head—then we zoom through a wall jack and into the personified network. In this ad for Black Rocket Voice, the allegorical figure of "VOICE" is portrayed by a black man. When the phone lines go down, the white bossman of the network calls upon VOICE; VOICE saves the day by seamlessly "switching to data." The black man performs this switch with the greatest of ease, carrying the data while seated in his chair, studying a newspaper with the binary headline "101 011 0101 11010." The point of the ad is that Black Rocket Voice speaks fluent data. The ad closes over this digital masque with the gleaming shell of the Black Rocket icon, the personal contents of which we are now privy to. Black Rocket Voice is a black man; he is the black body inside the black box. Or, if we reflect back on the initial visual framing, the bald black pate echoed by the final shiny black icon, we may say that Black Rocket Voice is also the expertise contained in the skull of the black office worker, the sum total of what he can see and say when he works his way into the network. The black male body is thus bound to both the outside and inside of the black box—a black Russian nesting doll of digital technology.

Genuity's product line evokes the "black rocketeers" of *Gravity's Rainbow,* the "dark, secret children" instrumentalized within Thomas Pynchon's 1973 picture of the incipient globalized "Corporate City-state" or "Rocketstate."[5] *Gravity's Rainbow* portrays the "Blackrocket" as the apotheosis of the military-industrial complex in a system of human sacrifice (*GR,* 391). Genuity, whose history dates to a 1969 contract with "the U.S. government to develop the ARPAnet, the forerunner of the Internet," holds longterm shares in a Pynchonian system of technological containment (fig. 6). It now sells a nonthreatening version of Pynchon's Blackrocket, the ultimate "Blackinstrument," packaged in a cheery image of retrofuturism (*GR,* 363).

Sometimes the contemporary circuit connecting black boxes to black bodies is even more tightly integrated. Rather than overlapping in package labels and allegorical images from related products—as in the Black Rocket/Black Rocket Voice line—blackened technology and technologized blackness may be fused together, collapsed onto the same representational layer. Such is the case for Dell Enterprise (fig. 7). The magazine ad for Dell's "server and storage solution" displays stacked banks of Dell computer hardware, with the head and torso of a black man in the darkened corridor between the metal racks. Below the picture, a sentence and a fragment in

Fig. 7. "There are thousands more where Carl came from": Dell Enterprise presents just one example of the juxtaposition of black body with the black box (2002).

bold lead the pitch: "I am Dell Enterprise. Power Edge servers, storage, infrastructure software, and Premier Enterprise Services."[6] Several aspects of the image emphasize the free-floating, encompassing claim of technological identity, the Dell "I am." The black-and-white photo—mostly black—renders the man's skin color literally black; the stacked servers are sheathed in black gleaming metal of a corresponding tone and sheen. The brightest spots in the shot are the man's eyes and the dozens of similarly sized round Dell logos, each set in a horizontally tapered socket slit. Who—or what—is the "I" of "I am Dell Enterprise"? To paraphrase Ellison's Invisible Man, "I am what eye am." Even the black dots on the man's tie pick up the round perforations on the servers' gridded ventilation casings. Does the man speak, or do the machines speak? Yes.

The words below the image represent the product, the smoothly integrated black man and black boxes that speak with one voice in solemn testimony. But above the package hovers another kind of language: "You're right, Dell doesn't have one support person with all the answers. There are thousands more where Carl came from." This voice from on high speaks for Dell, the company. If the voice below delivers the utterly serious report of the man-machine mesh, the tone above answers in a "man-to-man" fashion, as corporate sales directly addresses the corporate client.[7] This personal corporate address momentarily personalizes the third man in the exchange, but only in the process of dismissing him as a completely interchangeable part. "Carl" serves only to exemplify the kind of support one can expect; although the image at first glance shows stacks of computers and a single man, the ad copy explains the underlying numerical logic, that the myriad machines correspond to "thousands" of uniformly matched machine men. Carl can get you all the answers, but he's nothing special. He's Carl the server man; he lives in a storage can. The top statement is arresting, almost shocking, in its stark disregard for the individual on display. The language of disposability—don't worry, there's plenty more where that came from—is here applied to a human being: "There are thousands more where Carl came from." And where exactly would that be? What place can be counted upon to provide this inexhaustible supply of server men? The familiar image of bodies stacked radially in the hold of a ship comes to mind as a historical echo of such language. At present, a more likely source than the African continent would be India—or from deep in the heart of darkest America.

A *Forbes* feature story, "India or Bust," notes that "U.S. companies have long employed Indian programmers and developers for mundane tech chores like computer support and maintenance."[8] Joining the scramble for India is the company that presumably knows where Carl, and thousands more, come from: "Dell is one of a growing number of U.S. companies who are looking to India, where labor is cheaper and more plentiful."[9] "Cheap" and "plentiful" have long been America's canonically paired terms to designate the marvelous abundance of exploitable humans in a new land of milk and honey. In Texas, Dell's home, these terms have historically been applied to brown bodies marked for certain kinds of labor. Witness a 1921 invitation by Valley Developments, Inc., of Harlingen, Texas. As a come-on for a commerce tour, the company offered the prospect of "MEXICAN LABOR—Cheap and plentiful—wages $1.50 per ten hours—efficient, loyal and plentiful. Note this wonderful cabbage field." In recognition of a certain continuity between cabbage field and call center, one journalist has dubbed the new South Asian workforce "high-tech *braceros*."[10] The resonance with fabled inexpensive "day labor" is no lie: tech workers in India typically draw only one fourth of the salary of their U.S. counterparts.[11]

In 2001, Dell acted to "open a call center in India to support its U.S. home and small-business customers."[12] With limited plausibility, the company "downplayed the idea that it was simply hunting for cheap labor." And although the company also claimed that the "new jobs in India are not being transplanted from the United States," a reporter judiciously noted that "it's unclear what the move means for Fort Worth, where Dell had planned to open a 500–person call center in April. Those plans have been put on hold indefinitely." Fast forward to an announcement from 2002: "Dell will continue to move some non-critical tasks, such as e-mail support, to cheaper markets overseas."[13] Austin-headquartered Dell again carefully promised that jobs in central Texas wouldn't be "exported." Local employment shouldn't change "drastically," unlike "last year when the company cut nearly one-fourth of its work force" (last year being the year when jobs were not to have been "transplanted.") This continued erosion of relatively well-paid domestic employment presents a public relations challenge for companies like Dell. Flat denial of the trend would seem an inadequate strategy. Indeed, a supplemental strategy already lies encoded in phrases above such as "mundane tech chores" and "non-critical tasks." Chores and tasks do not constitute anyone's idea of a successful career for an American adult. The work being outsourced thus ranks as menial and unimportant; what the United States loses in these transactions counts as something less than "jobs."

Of course not all American citizens are missing out on these chore opportunities. A 1998 headline that identifies a still-growing trend tells the story of some other bodies currently staying on task—in prison: "Corrections Jobs are Replacing Industry Jobs."[14] Computer support and repair make up a significant sector in that trend. *The Executive's Guide to Customer Relationship Management* observes that even as "call centers are emerging to be the most remarkable employment opportunity of the information age, . . . some of the more successful call centers are staffed by incarcerated inmates of our federal and state prison systems."[15] Repair, the other arm of computer support, joins call center staffing as one of the "fastest growing job categories"; computer repair likewise flourishes behind bars. Seizing a share of that growth, lockups such as the Lockhart Correctional Facility in Texas and the Soledad Correctional Training Facility in California have garnered plaudits for their productive prison work programs.[16] The "high-tech operation" at Lockhart is run by "LTI Inc., a subsidiary of U.S. Technologies, based in Washington, D.C. . . . The Lockhart program began after LTI's previous owner, American Microelectronics Inc., laid off 150 workers in 1995 when it closed its Austin plant."[17] A predictable disavowal from the general manager accompanied this chronology: "the Austin plant was closed because it was having financial trouble, not because the owners wanted to take advantage of cheap labor." A perhaps more convincing claim is suggested by the names of these corporate entities, so clearly desirous to plug into a nationalistic project: U.S. Technologies and American Microelectronics have not taken advantage of cheap *foreign* labor.

The American bodies whose technological labor these companies have secured belong to the well-known demographics of the U.S. prison systems. The end of 2000 found 1.3 million people in state and federal penitentiaries; of this total, 428,000 were black men between the ages of 20 and 29.[18] In media coverage of prison tech work, the impression of cell-block microelectronics as highly racialized work actually exceeds what one would expect from those already minority-saturated statistics. In this extreme instance of color monitoring, almost every image accompanying news stories on high-tech prison work features a man with dark skin. The copywriters for these stories never refer explicitly to race, but the photos and names sing another tune. The story "Doing Time Repairing Computers" ran two color photos of busy inmates at Lockhart: Juan Sandoval "reworks a printed circuit board," and Patrick Foster "helps rebuild Dell computers."[19] The shot of Foster shows a black man through a series of circuit boards, each inserted vertically into a base and viewed from the side. He fits his hands into the slits between the chips, a man behind boards thus doubly behind bars. The story leads with a closeup of Sandoval: "When a personal computer goes on the fritz, it could end up in Juan Sandoval's hands. Sandoval, nicknamed 'Chuckie,' repairs computers." "Chuckie" derives from the star attraction in the *Child's Play* series of horror movies: a talking, stalking doll on the fritz, with the propensities of a serial killer, an affinity for tools and technology, and a desire to take over a human body.[20] "Chucky" the haywire toy reflects the popular terror of tech gone bad. Sandoval's carceral nickname both evokes and defuses that terror. Sandoval, convicted on three counts of involuntary manslaughter, has surely received society's sentence as a piece of out-of-control hardware. But computer repair has corrected him: his "child's play" now registers as not only harmless but also profitable. Chuckie now does work "for high-tech companies around the world, including Dell Computer Corp. and Motorola Inc."[21] As a Dell executive noted in a *Forbes* interview, "Break-fix has been derided as Tinkertoy services, but there's a lot of money to be made there. . . . Gross margins are high."[22] Especially if Dell can depend upon the extremely high productivity-to-cost ratio of the efficient Juans: "'I've been doing this for four years come December,' Sandoval said. 'It's the same thing, day-in and day-out. That much practice makes you good, I guess.'" Adding supervision to practice can help take the guesswork out of technological improvement. A story on "Hard Drives" and "Hard Time" conveys a scene of digital disciplinary instruction in Lancaster, California: "At the state prison, instructor Harry Broddock, left, shows Rashid McCarter how to insert a parallel port to interlink computers."[23] At this site, a redundancy of circuits contains Rashid; with a paternal presence guiding his integration, his wiring work is conducted "150 yards inside an electric death fence." That much electrical engineering makes you good.

In a vision of the "New Future" at the Soledad state pen, a newswriter's lead paragraph perfects the logic of computer containment: "Omar Sharif Brown stands six feet tall, weighs well over 250 pounds, and has an intense stare. Here at the Soledad Correctional Training Facility, Mr. Brown, who was convicted for murder, is carefully replacing parts on a computer keyboard. Brown also reconfigures computer hard drives and can explain the intricacies of software crashes."[24] Everything about the opening sentence seems calculated to depict an impressive, dangerous, specimen: a big bad black man. The sequel brings the computer technology to bear. Whereas the first sentence thrills at the pure paratactic display of menace, the grammar of the second sentence casually, ostentatiously, subordinates the fact of his murder conviction. That is, the subordination in no way minimizes the offense. The official recognition of Brown as killer confirms and grounds the initial suggestions of violent capacity; more crucially, the murder note serves as that which the second scenario keeps in check. The account of his current activities is presented as wondrously sufficient to stabilize the issue of murder as a past participle. His computer expertise in itself covers a lexicon of violence prevention; the "drives" of the hardened criminal have been reconfigured; with patient understanding, further "crashes" may be avoided. The activity of men repairing machines allows for an allegory that can move in either direction between the humans and the hardware: repair rehabilitates dangerous men into more reliable machines, and the unrepaired computers themselves initially appear as dangerous subjects. Nearby another inmate deals with a "recalcitrant" computer printer, an object thus personified as more intractable than its human cellmate. In their present state, Brown and his Soledad brothers neutralize the threat of technology no less than the technology has fixed them. In his exacting technical proficiency, Brown emerges as an artist of the beautiful; "carefully" handling "intricacies," he can make the ugliness of tech nightmares go away and provide the verbal pillow for a soft landing. Probably his greatest asset is that he "can explain"; this gentle skill, above all, satisfies the demands of the technophobic tech consumer. Men like Brown offer the complete tech support package; he has mastered both the hardware *and* the software. The article explains the added value of men in his position: "Men serving life sentences form the core of tech support because they stick around longer."[25] The infernal tautology of this matter-of-fact observation gives new meaning to such promotions as "FREE Lifetime Tech Support." That particular long-running offer from MicroWarehouse, by the way, always appears next to the thumbnail photo of a smiling black man and an Asian woman wearing headsets.[26] These are the simulacra of what the United States wants from tech support—and gets from the Omar Sharif Browns of the world: someone who has no choice but to pleasantly oblige the customer, someone who isn't going anywhere soon, someone whose time is not his own. Tech support forms the lightning rod for the information age "annoyances" about which Unisys apologized: we hate dealing with tech support—we resentfully, desperately need it, but we'll be damned before we pay for it.

The drive toward lower prices—cheap machines and free support—has imposed tremendous pressure on labor costs in all sectors of the tech industry. As noted above, the real erosion of employment opportunities creates some challenges for tech firms' public relations . . . but perhaps, given the way consumers tend to relate to technology, nothing insuperable. As Dell's head of personnel, in an interview with *Forbes,* lets slip a too-frank remark about job displacement, he gets "a nervous look from the p.r. executive sitting next to him."[27] Well, it's the p.r. person's job to worry. But the cutting or the outsourcing of certain tech chores to prisons or India seems unlikely to spark a rebellion among consumer-investors, who would never see themselves—or people like them—taking on such tasks. It doesn't hurt that some nearby images of free citizens who fill remaining U.S. tech labor slots almost make prison seem the most appropriate setting for computer work. An accompanying *Forbes* inset on Dell's efficiency constructs the following diorama: at a Dell manufacturing facility, workers "scuttle about in the 200,000–square-foot plant like ants on a hot plate. Gathered in cramped six-person 'cells,' they assemble computers from batches of parts that arrive via a computer-directed conveyor system overhead."[28] To underscore the obvious: these bodies already appear incarcerated; the way they function suggests that the jailhouse provides the proper context for their activities. The square footage may sound considerable, but the new plant supersedes a 450,000–square-foot manufacturing center. That larger plant, which itself "wrote the book on efficient computer manufacturing in 1997," achieved an output of 120 computers per hour. The new, smaller, center churns out 650 computers per hour, and additionally dispenses with the need for the 250,000–square-foot sorting warehouse that took product handoffs from the older factory. Personnel questions arise from such developments; when the local paper posed one such query, "the company declined to say how much the number of workers required at the plant has changed."[29] So far, enough bodies remain to ensure cramped conditions. May not the depopulation of the factory's "hot-plate" floor appear as a stroke of severe mercy? Dell laid off 5,700 employees in February and May of 2001, an event a *Forbes* writer referred to as "Dell's first mass executions ever" (112). Again the writer applies the language of criminal justice to tech production: capital punishment on the assembly line, justified (as it sometimes is on death row) as a cost- and space-saving measure. And in either setting, the final blow descends on a group of men already condemned. A closer look at the circumstantial evidence should make that verdict clearer.

Such images present devalued labor performed by devalued persons, colonial others offshore or in the tank. This devaluation works compatibly with a further logical reduction: tech labor performed by technology. At Dell, "a robot is being tested to pack computers into cartons, eliminating a human-staffed line doing the same thing" (110). *Forbes* ran a single photo with the feature bearing that announcement: a black man, a box, and a robot. The Austin paper's business section reported the plan somewhat more gently, leaving the consequences unnamed: "Dell hopes to further automate boxing operations." But the same basic image of transitional boxing illustrated the story: against a blurred background, a black computer case, a robot arm, and a black man. In both instances, the corporation's prophetic words gloss the snapshot: behold the black man and the robot that will replace him. The black men appear in posters for a job nobody wants, a job already on its way to extinction. As we have seen, Dell generally takes care to "downplay the idea" that its various cost-saving measures, like the call center outsourcing, may be costing U.S. jobs. Similarly, according to these glimpses of Dell's blueprint for automation, robotics aren't costing white men any white jobs.

Though the juxtaposition of blackness and robotics is primary in these images, a closer consideration may suggest reasons to put weight on both "white" *and* "men" as the identities opposed to and sheltered from automated execution. The photos of black man, box, and robot initially suggest an ambiguity. On opposite sides of the box, both man and machine grasp the load; their arms encircle the computer, and their hands appear to touch. Do they wrestle? Does the man hand the box to the machine, or does the robot hand the box to the man? The frozen frame does not indicate which. Nevertheless, the assembly-line scenario dictates that the man, to move in concert with the automated device, cannot act autonomously. Control resides elsewhere. It is all a recording; the moves are on Memorex. In this dance, the robot must lead. The traditional gender roles thus created, in obedience to the laws of cotillion etiquette, match those handed down through the industrial age: workers relegated to following the machine are feminized—if not, indeed, female. Melville's 1855 sketch of a paper factory still applies: "Machinery—that vaunted slave of humanity—here stood menially served by human beings, who stood mutely and cringingly as the slave serves the sultan."[30] The particular human beings Melville describes inhabit what he calls "The Tartarus of Maids"; this hellish production-scape forms the second half of a diptych, coupled with (and in opposition to) "The Paradise of Bachelors." In Melville's titular pairing, the gender split is primary, with leisured masculinity set against its negation, automated femininity; at the same time, on the level of predominant descriptive imagery, the machines and their slaves produce whiteness. The *Forbes* feature on life in Dell similarly makes color central to the image, with gender echoes audible in the title. The headline above the photo implicitly genders the workplace as "The Best Little Factory in Texas." In this allusion to the popular musical from the late 1970s, "The Best Little Whorehouse in Texas," "Factory" takes the place of a building where women sell their bodies.[31] It has now become the transaction site for the feminized black man's body, a body on the threshold of disappearance.

Read from left to right, the *Forbes* photo-pantomime suggests a timeline of factory evolution: the black man, in a ceremonial gesture of things to come, passes the black-boxing labor up to the robot. The lingering image of the last representative factory-floor human marks that labor as black work, even after the machines take over. Such markings may help to manage resentment against robotic encroachments. "Are you tired of watching machines take jobs from you and your neighbors?"—an alleged group calling itself "The Anti-Robot Militia" and dedicated to uniting mankind against the "metal-head" automatons, though a clearly parodic fabrication, parodies a genuine hostility toward robots.[32] For example, an incident from 2000 points to a market miscalculation, a failure to anticipate resistance to robot usurpation: "A customer at a San Francisco Sony store grabbed an Aibo robot dog and proceeded to smash it to smithereens. No explanation was given for this act."[33] We may accept robots as replacements for servants or slaves—but not to take "our" jobs or perhaps even to be our pets. Tech becomes man's worst enemy when it supplants his neighbors or his "best friend." Positing an anti-tech sentiment capable of uniting black and white as neighbors, the fanciful Anti-Robot Militia trumpets a utopian slogan: "It's not the color of your skin that's important—it's the flesh inside." The Dell imagery twists this prospect of interracial alliance. It's not the flesh or its absence that's important—it's the color of the labor. Nonwhite work may be performed interchangeably under the sign of automation, either by dark-skinned servants to technology or, subsequently, by fleshless technological servants.

Natural Machines

In the call center, an analogous process of elimination leaves a trace of blackness where the human has been dropped. Here, automation involves a synthetic voice coupled with some degree of artificial intelligence. With the introduction of "How May I Help You? (HMIHY)," AT&T Labs boasts "the first natural language voice-enabled customer care system." The web release, while emphasizing price performance, also hints at Ma Bell's ambition to deliver a little something extra: "With the How May I Help You? service, AT&T can significantly improve its customer care operations by enhancing responsiveness while reducing costs. The service's human-sounding, intelligent agent capability makes it reminiscent of the company's early days when operators and service representatives personally assisted customers. In addition, the service will soon be marketed outside of AT&T to large business customers . . . that want to improve customer retention while cutting millions or billions of dollars from their service expenses."[34] In wrapping technological advance in the warm glow of nostalgia, the company tacitly invokes a gendered vignette. In the eidolon of those lovely "early days," service came in the form of sweet-voiced, feminine operators. AT&T no longer sees fit to invoke explicitly the content of that image—what they are after is the personal effect of that service experience. The image of the demure call girl with the voice of gold may no longer be exactly appropriate for the HMIHY message. What is called for is some sort of "reminiscent" equivalence.

Bearing that load of nostalgia will be the voice engine that projects the solicitously helpful "I." HMIHY, whether running on a basic phone-tree script or deploying advanced AI, ultimately depends upon a an emerging coordinate technology known as "text-to-speech." The ability to convert computer-readable characters into audible output is what gives a product like HMIHY both its labor-cutting efficiency and, given a sufficiently advanced engine, its pleasant approximation of human speech. Analysts have predicted that the market for text-to-speech software, targeted at "telephone call centers," will exceed $1 billion by 2006.[35] AT&T's product manager noted that "with companies hoping to automate help-desk call-in operations as much as possible, real-sounding voices on the other end of the phone become more important."[36] AT&T leads the charge to meet that demand with a "breakthrough" product line that has been recognized as "Technology of the Year" for 2002. The name given to this synthetic speech technology may seem outrageous: "AT&T Natural Voices." But the adjectival form buys AT&T a bit of wiggle room; and where Nature itself is absent, its effect may be all the more highly valued. The "Technology of the Year" prizegivers, market consultants Frost and Sullivan, stated that " 'Naturalness' was AT&T Labs' key competitive advantage."[37]

So what does this "Naturalness" sound like? What vocal quality did AT&T select to convey that feeling of good old-fashioned service? What manner of Natural Voice, delivering HMIHY help, most convincingly conveys a persona capable of shifting "the burden of understanding what a customer wants from the user to the machine"? When AT&T brought Natural Voices to market, they held a press conference. But not just any press conference. To dramatize the new technology, they had the product announce itself. Natural Voices hit the airwaves with a "Talking Press Release." The release explained with pride that natural voice "is the highest quality computer speech system in the world, and it is the only one that allows you to copy a voice, so I can sound like anyone."[38] In theory, the program can sound like just about anyone. But the voice AT&T chose for this historic announcement, code-named "Rich," doesn't sound like just anyone. And AT&T knows it. The website invitation promises something distinctive: to sample a voice with "special qualities," the visitor can "meet '**Rich**' . . . by trying out the demo below. You'll find his voice to be uniquely different."[39] You'll find that Rich has a "male baritone."[40] And you'll find that Rich sounds black.

Is one permitted to make such a claim about an invisible (non)man?[41] A synthetic voice that attempts to copy a unique human voice is not exempt from the ethnoracial markers of performance. Rich does not speak in black vernacular; rather, his refined intonation matches the black vocal style that well-meaning white people sometimes praise as being "so articulate." The timbre of the voice resonates with a quality typically valued in black media personalities. And these impressions are not unfounded: an investigation of Rich's empirical background tends to validate the claim that this particular voice echoes with the sounds of blackness.

Although cagey about what information it volunteers and resolute in limiting the specificity it will provide when pressed, AT&T was willing to confirm that "one of the voices is based on that of an African American actor from New Jersey. (He and AT&T have requested that his name not be published because a clause in his contract stipulates that his identity is a company secret based on years of research and auditions.)"[42] Perhaps most telling in this confirmation is its treatment of "identity" as the end product of a highly deliberate process. AT&T is not simply introducing us to a close digital friend "who just happens to be black." Rich's blackness is premeditated, an integral part of a package deemed well worthy of a proprietary claim.

The presence of Rich supports a web of contradictions. Most obviously, as noted above, a technology developed as "synthetic speech" comes to be marketed as "natural voice." Rich's blackness facilitates that odd equation: Rich doesn't just sound human enough to be called natural; in AT&T's breakthrough campaign, Rich represents the natural voice *for* digitality— especially of the "How May I Help You?" variety. Synthetic speech represents a natural progression for free lifetime tech support, from inmates doing hard time to sound bits on the hard drive: the incarcerated body yields to the disembodied voice. The particular technology that makes Rich possible involves a rapid-access database of digitized sounds based on an audio profile of human samples, which a speech engine can link together to form words. The name for this process, "concatenative speech synthesis," denotes—literally—a voice in chains.[43] But the listener doesn't need to know the name of that process or its etymology in order to appreciate Rich's signification. What one hears is a voice that sounds like a black man—but one that also still sounds a bit like a machine. The fact that the synthesis is not yet good enough to sound purely human may make Rich's blackness that much more important. Rich's "voice donor" symbolically undergoes what the white body wishes to avoid: he's continuously chopped into digital bits and reassembled; crucially, we can hear the outcome as occupying an ambiguous space between man and machine. That ambiguity may play a part in a second tension for Natural Voices: why AT&T would develop a flexible universalizing technology that can "sound like anyone" but also give such effort and emphasis to developing and premiering a particular voice that is "uniquely different." Rich's blackness provides the unique difference that makes it okay for him to sound (almost) like anyone but not quite like an individual requiring, say, a body. So he can sound from anywhere.

Eldridge Cleaver, a man famously educated in the U.S. prison systems, expounds on the appetite behind products like Natural Voices: "In the increasingly mechanized, automated, cybernated environment of the modern world—a cold, bodiless world of wheels, smooth plastic surfaces, tubes, pushbuttons, transistors, computers, jet propulsion, rockets to the moon, atomic energy—man's need for affirmation of his biology has become that much more intense. He feels need for a clear definition of where his body ends and the machine begins."[44] In a revision of DuBois's famous prioritization of "the problem of the color line," Cleaver gives historical preeminence to the body-machine confusion: "This is the central contradiction of the twentieth century." But Cleaver does not refute DuBois's axiom that the color line commands simultaneous centrality: "It is in this connection that the blacks, personifying the Body, . . . provide the saving link, the bridge between man's biology and man's machines."[45] Cleaver's statements outline a dual function for this link: the bridge gives access to the machines while defining a safe border space. The line of demarcation, so anxiously needed, runs along a color-coded frontier: "man's" body ends where the blacks begin. As a representative black bridge, "Rich" personifies "the Body"— without actually having one. His appeal suggests a working definition for a "natural machine": a black man, dis-embodied.

Cleaver's critique still has the power to chill. AT&T is hardly alone in the deployment of naturally black technology to reassure its cyberphobic constituents; indeed, some corporate narratives do so more explicitly. A *Forbes ASAP* special issue on "The New Smarts" puts this brand of attribution on display. In a feature on "Teenage All-Americans," a list modeled on scouting reports of top high school basketball or football prospects, *Forbes* ranks "the next generation of high tech superstars." Most of the profiles contain fairly straight reporting of the youths' technical achievements. But a couple of standouts warranted commentary from captains of industry. Two quotations assess the brightness of two different stars: (1) "He's not just a good software developer, he's a good businessman," says Geoff Perlman, CEO of REAL Software; (2) "He has an innate ability to understand technical things," says Lamar Nail, president of the Clinton, Miss. engineering firm Technological Services."[46] A young black male inspired this latter description. Of all the stars, only he is said to possess anything like an "innate" technical ability—something congenital, a condition essential to his very nature. The simple, bland assertion makes this young man seem almost out of place on the *Forbes* list: "He has an innate ability to understand technical things"—now there's a sentence that one would expect to find in a circa early twentieth-century letter of recommendation for vocational training.[47] More complicated praise goes to the more highly ranked young white man. The CEO all but apologizes for the youth's technical ability; the computer skills almost count against him, as something needing to be offset by other areas of strength. Don't underestimate the kid; he's not "just" a programming whiz, a candidate for coding fodder. Really, he'll turn out fine—he's becoming quite the "businessman." His incipient manliness, so threatened by techiness, is guaranteed by his business-ness. The white will be the real businessman, complete with black technological services at his command.

Rich's synthetic nature, personifying life at the technological interface, provides a buffer for fully biological—and business-savvy—white masculinity. Of course, Natural Voices delivers something more basic: "Voices." If blackness and "Naturalness" work together as factors of technology packaging, what about blackness and voice? In the "Technology of the Year" deliberations, "Naturalness" may have set AT&T's entry apart from its competitors, but what made voice products as such worthy of consideration for the prize? In identifying voice as the central commodity for sale, what important fears and desires do high-profile tech products like Natural Voices and Black Rocket Voice address? A further implication of Melville's "Tartarus of Maids" may offer a clue. Automation, producing an opposition between feminizing enslavement and white masculine leisure, also poses a categorical threat to the species: where "machinery—that vaunted slave of humanity" has invaded, "the human voice was banished from the spot."[48] The inability to communicate vocally fulfills a nightmare of alien predation: in space, no one can hear you scream; at the site of automated production, no one can hear you speak. Wherever automation means not the din of industry but the cyberspatial silence of circuitry, wherever information technology has put humans on hold, Rich rides Black Rocket to the rescue. Where the human voice has been banished by automation, the technologized black voice still rings loud and clear.

For doing business, an agreeable speaking voice is both a prime literal desideratum—someone, or something, to answer the phones pleasantly—and a metaphor for what all forms of corporate expression need to convey. Some of the sharpest-tongued critics of contemporary corporate narrative, the authors of *the cluetrain manifesto*, have made "the human voice" their central term of value.[49] This term names the crucial absence in corporate discourse: the *cluetrain* engineers open their manifesto with an epigraphic rant about "companies so lobotomized that they can't speak in a recognizably human voice." This absence manifests itself most painfully in conjunction with the Internet, as the clueless companies "build sites that smell like death." The increasing technologization of media threatens to exacerbate the sore throat of corporate narrators; loss of voice, and thus of life, may ensue. The manifestors propose a reformative cluetraining course, outlined in a preamble and ninety-five theses. The central premise is that "markets are conversations"; to succeed, companies must join these conversations. The "connectedness of the Web" *should* facilitate that joining. But first, because "markets consist of human beings," companies must discover how to speak in "the human voice," the sound of which allows people to "recognize each another as such." A few passages illustrate the way the authors move between metaphoric and literal, collective and individual uses of "voice": "Whether explaining or complaining, joking or serious, the human voice is unmistakably genuine. It can't be faked. Most corporations, on the other hand, only know how to talk in the soothing, humorless monotone of the mission statement, marketing brochure, and your-call-is-important-to-us busy signal. Same old tone, same old lies"; "In just a few more years, the current homogenized 'voice' of business—the sound of mission statements and brochures—will seem as contrived and artificial as the language of the 18th century French court"; "But learning to speak in a human voice is not some trick, nor will corporations convince us they are human with lip service about 'listening to customers.' They will only sound human when they empower real human beings to speak on their behalf."

If companies must literally satisfy this final exclusive demand, projects like Natural Voices seem doomed to fail. And yet, "real human beings" can "speak" through such a product just as much as they can through any other medium of writing—if not more so. The practical issues identified in the manifesto involve rhetoric, ethos, "tone." Ostensibly, the desired voice "can't be faked." But it may be synthesized. When the authors insist that the voice can't be "faked," they seem to mean that a facile rendition can't easily be pulled off by companies that don't "get it," that remain locked into speaking "the *language* of the pitch, the dog-and-pony show," because they don't know any better. But someone who has, say, read and understood the manifesto may be able to script the "voice." (Surely the cluetrainers believe—and not without reason—that their exemplary online theses resound with the human voice.) In theory, a really sharp AI program could approximate the voice and do so dynamically and responsively. The manifesto complains that "to their intended online audiences, companies sound hollow, flat, literally inhuman." Despite the emphasis on the Internet context, the rage here is not against machines, but against machinelike companies. Whether or not real humans do the speaking, the final pragmatic objective is for a company to "*sound* human." The cluetrainers nurse a hatred of humans who sound like machines. Natural Voices aims at nurturing the converse, the love of machines that sound like humans.

From the perspective of cyberanalysis—the exploration of the emotions we reveal when we talk about tech—perhaps the most telling aspect of the manifesto involves the metaphors deployed to express anger at corporate narrative. In the preamble's classical oratorical triad of inhuman evils, the climactic third spot goes to the "your-call-is-important-to-us busy signal." Corporate "voice" may be a metaphor, but the metaphor of what's wrong with that voice is the frustrated caller on hold, a metaphor that draws its emotional strength from a very real common experience. Natural Voices seeks to placate the frustration that grounds the critique's rhetoric. If, in place of "your-call-is-important-to-us," Natural Voices succeeds in delivering effective "How May I Help You?" service, AT&T will have gone some way toward removing the shared experience that fuels the manifesto's rhetorical appeal. Although the *cluetrain manifesto* nowhere calls for blackness to guarantee "the human voice," blackness conveniently fits the bill for a "uniquely different" sound, one that unmistakably avoids the loathsome "homogenized" voice. If blackness also, as per Cleaver, manages to personify the Body, a synthetic black voice may more readily than other simulacra gain acceptance in the place of a "real human being." What such a product may lack in "voice"—the appropriate rhetoric of responsive humanity—it may make up for with its literal voice, in the reassuring associations of its timbre and pitch. The disgruntled cluetrainers say they don't want a "soothing . . . monotone"; it does not follow that they cannot be otherwise soothed.

The soothing blackness of Natural Voices, as with Black Rocket Voice, is also iconic. Rich's natural blackness is invisible but paired with a blackness visible. A second skin, purely graphical, enmeshes the technological nature and streamlines the voice. Although Natural Voices so far remains faceless, the product website does feature several versions of a stylized human head in profile. The graphics show a literally black head, with lines of ones and zeros filling the brain region and the outlines of digital circuitry crisscrossing the side of the face and black sound waves, entwined with sinuous strings of ones and zeros, flowing out of the profile. This combination of simplifying opacity and the promise of fluent digitality recalls the imagery of Black Rocket Voice. Incidentally, one of the speech demos for Rich frames him as a virtual spokesman for rocket science: "The space shuttle is being prepared for a new mission to the space station." Granted, it's a brief snippet. But even here we observe how the passive voice obscures the technical labor: the work that goes into prepping the space shuttle is performed by unseen bodies or, for all we know, no bodies. The dulcet tones of reassurance issue from the black voice box: *it's all being taken care of.*

For a related, more vividly realized instance of the black boxing of computer/rocket science, we may refer to the first high-profile product placement for text-to-speech. In anticipation of the release of Natural Voices, AT&T hitched their brand-new wagon to a Hollywood star.[50] In late 2000, AT&T was pleased to announce that their natural language voice-enabled system had been "featured in the Warner Brothers sci-fi film *Red Planet,* in which AT&T TTS lent its voice to the spaceship and several astronauts' space suits."[51] A large part of the labs' pride in this placement derived from the time setting of the movie, the year 2050: "In this vision of life half a century from now, spaceship computers—and even space suits—talk. 'It shows you how far technology has come that the producers didn't need special effects to give computers their voices. They had a real, working, system from AT&T Labs,' said Juergen Schroeter, Division Manager, Speech Processing Software & Technology." With this sci-fi star turn, Natural Voices planted a flag on some lucrative territory: the future of call centers and all technological interfaces—a future that's available for purchase now.

white flight

Product placement is one thing. But in the plot devices of *Red Planet's* script, Hollywood narrative also serves corporate narrative in a less obvious manner. Early in the film, a computational crisis arises when a team of astronauts crash-lands on Mars; with limited resources, the spacemen must find their way to the abandoned Mars station. The first analysis comes from Burchenal (Tom Sizemore), inspecting an electronic map display: "All the mission data is in here. We've just got to close in on the downrange variables. It's about the math." Burchenal, as such a line of attack may well indicate, is *not* the hero; as the most scientific member of the team, he predictably turns out to be soulless and evil. Our hero is played by Val Kilmer, a "real Yankee" named Gallagher. In response to the possibility of having to do the math, Gallagher makes a decidedly unhappy face: "This is it. That moment they told us about in high school when one day algebra would save our lives." A clever line, a real crowd-pleaser, Gallagher's pronouncement also seals a fraternal commiseration among the men lost in space. At these words, all five (white) men on the Mars surface exchange uneasy looks. Gallagher wanders off, muttering a disconsolate "Oh, man." Then, a revelation strikes: "Hey guys, look at this. I don't think it's about the math. It's about the picture." Gallagher realizes that they are on the back side of a rock formation for which they have a ready image. The guys are saved. Simply by *looking*, he charts their course to the base. He points to the beautiful Mars landscape with confident imprecision: ". . . which makes the line . . . about there."

But his math-free solution does not mean that Gallagher has no need for computer technology. Indeed, he's a model customer for precisely the breed of tech services AT&T offers. After arriving at his epiphany that "it's about the picture," he relies upon his screen's computing power to digitally reverse an image. He accomplishes this visual manipulation with a voice command to the portable device. The fantasy gadget's form in itself predicts his ideal solution; it apparently consists of nothing more than a thin, flexible sheet of space age material—an almost massless computer that's 100 percent monitor. Whereas Burchenal proposes getting at the data that's "in" the system, the more provident Gallagher knows that function follows form; no need to probe the depths of a dream machine that's all surface. The mission requires no typing, in fact no "personal computing" on his part whatsoever; a "How May I Help You?" interactive voice system takes care of any requests. From a Hollywood perspective, the hero's relation to computing thus mirrors that of the director to the computer effects crew: he gets the picture he wants by ordering it up, then points the way to the next scene. The "math" and all the other janitorial data work takes place offscreen, leaving the hero/director free to be creative. The same holds for the white businessman; the real Yankee's relation to technology also mirrors that of the executive to his IT support staff. In a practical sense, computing allows the hero/director/executive not to worry about "the math." Ordering up a bit of techno-instrumentalism is fine, as long as the creative individual doesn't have to worry about the computing, such as the programming that went into the handy digital imaging system in the first place. With Gallagher, *Red Planet* plugs into corporate narrative by sticking with the Hollywood action imperative: do not require the white hero to calculate. The pandering to technophobic innumeracy could scarcely be more extreme: after all, these guys are astronauts. It seems unlikely that one would gain entry to the space program by demonstrating a low aptitude for hard math and science. Nevertheless, *Red Planet* encourages our bias for the fuzzy with the flattering thought that not even the rocket scientists want to do the math.

A computational gadget, available for online purchase, blares a slogan sure to please our calculation-averse age: "We do the math, so you don't have to!" This "so you don't have to" principle has become a durable and flexible staple of technology marketing. "RoboForm Fills Forms, So That You Don't Have To." Searchalot.com explains that they "search a lot, so you don't have to!" An information technology supplier used their purchased airtime on public radio to deliver this liberating message: "We do I.T., so you don't have to."[52] The audience attitude presumed and fostered by such slogans means big business for companies that provide technological services. Michael Dell recounts an anecdote that explains how an emphasis on technical hand-holding has won Dell some of its fattest contracts: "As someone at Boeing once said, 'We want to be experts at airplanes, not computers.'"[53] So even aerospace executives like to see themselves as cyberphobic! These veritable rocket scientists want to outsource their computation. To some extent, for many companies, that may seem reasonable. For a company like Boeing, this willful nonexpertise in computers seems a little alarming—after all, how many computers does it take to fly a plane? But the major point for scrutiny would not be the reasonableness or unreasonableness of particular companies' tech aversions. Rather, I want to think critically about the ways companies trying to sell technology pander to that pervasive aversion and the ways corporate narratives collaborate with a fearful audience to construct particular identity fantasies.

Although most of the Hollywood stories that I discuss play into that collaboration, certain movies have contributed to the critical apparatus of the project. With most films in this study, I have applied a hermeneutics of suspicion—but sometimes one encounters a film that is itself suspicious enough to aid in a critical hermeneutics of culture. As the Tripmaster Monkey tells us in *His Fake Book,* a truly tricky movie can always help us to see "through another layer of hoodwink."[54] *The Grifters* is one such film. In this anatomy of confidence games, one scene stands out in exposing the machinery of the cyberphobic corporate narrative. In this scene, Myra (Annette Benning) fondly recalls how she and her partner, Cole (J. T. Walsh) would rope suckers into a technology-based investment scam. Myra, adopting the persona of southwestern belle "Mary Beth," was responsible for lining up wealthy dupes and inviting them to come along for a little visit to her stockbroker. Once she got a potential mark into the office, "all Cole had to do was *tell the story.*" To narrate that story to one Gloucester Hebbing (Charles Napier), Cole adopts the name of "Henry Fellowes," a sure starter for helping the mark to imagine a fraternal bond of white manhood.[55] The scheme involves exploiting a time difference on information flow between the New York and Tokyo stock exchanges. In spinning a convincing tale of how that scheme will work, "Fellowes" invokes a bit of technical magic:

COLE/HENRY FELLOWES: Do you know what a hacker is?
GLOUCESTER HEBBING: Yeah, sure, that's like a computer expert or genius.
COLE/FELLOWES: Very Good. What this boy's been able to do is tap into that main link between Tokyo and New York. And when we really need it, he's been able to give us a seven second delay in the transfer of that information.
      After listening to some more details, GLOUCESTER *wonders how that interval could afford enough time to place the right stock orders.*
GLOUCESTER: I don't see how you can do it.
COLE/FELLOWES: Machines! *Machines,* Gloucester! I have got a whole room full of machines back here. You wanna see 'em? C'mere! . . . C'mon, take a look! I got a whole *suite* full of mainframe computers!
COLE/FELLOWES *has gotten up from his desk to open a paneled door.* MYRA, *as the beaming "Mary Beth," has been seated next to* GLOUCESTER *throughout the exchange, encouraging his reactions to "Fellowes." At this point,* GLOUCESTER *appears somewhat baffled by Fellowes's apparent enthusiasm for the machines; Mary Beth graciously declines the invitation on* GLOUCESTER's *behalf:*
MYRA/MARY BETH: We're not really interested, Henry.
COLE/FELLOWES: Oh, they are so beautiful.
MYRA/MARY BETH: [*laughing*] No, Henry.
COLE/FELLOWES: Aw, you've got a minute. C'mon Gloucester, listen to 'em hum.
MYRA/MARY BETH: Henry, don't try Mr. Hebbings' patience.
COLE/FELLOWES: You sure? Well, OK then. [*closes the door*]

The camera plays this scene as a tightwire act. As Cole/Fellowes boasts of the "whole *suite* full" of hardware, we suddenly see the doorway from the reverse angle, behind the wall. The room is completely empty, and Cole's booming intonation of the words "suite full" echoes in the unfurnished chamber. Cole, the virtuoso verbal acrobat, is doing flips without a network. Fellow grifter Roy Dillon (John Cusack) comments on the scene Myra has just recounted for him: "Cole liked taking risks, huh?" Myra: "He didn't think they were risks." In the flashback, it appears that Myra, at the time, thought Cole's antics with the computer demo were somewhat risky. While enjoining Henry not to try the client's patience, Myra somewhat nervously takes Gloucester by the arm. Gloucester is gruff of voice and firm of chin, a paragon of no-nonsense masculinity. But he, no less anxiously, puts his arm around her. The machines may or may not exhibit the sublime technological beauty Henry ascribes to them, but Gloucester would just as soon not find out. Gloucester not only prefers the comfort of a real live girl, he seems unlikely to hasten to the mainframes even in Mary Beth's absence. Cole, that is, may be quite correct about the risks he takes. When Mary Beth speaks for Gloucester, her voice quivers with high-pitched stress, and a forced giggle accompanies her lines. But perhaps she need not have worried. What she says in Gloucester's name is nothing less than the truth. He's "*not* really interested." The man does not, in fact, want to see the computers. Indeed, as Myra astutely reports in retrospect, all he needs is to hear "the story." In essence, Fellowes sells him on the *idea* of the machines and a "boy" to do the tech work. The broker secures the man's confidence by invoking a familiar hierarchy of exploitation, a contract that will allow him to reap the profits without ever having to go near the computer room.[56]

The word "boy" in Fellowes's pitch merits highlighting. The southwestern setting of the con, the southern accents and the cozy between-us-white-men tone of the conversation, all perhaps tip the scales slightly toward registering this word as a racial epithet. But whether or not the "boy" Fellowes supposedly has working for him is to be imagined as black, Fellowes clearly invites Gloucester to think of this tech laborer as something less than a man. The flourish of referring to his computer expert as a "boy" lends a certain nonthreatening charm to the technical aspects of the setup. The boy will take orders and do his job, while the men will conduct business. The idea of the exploitable boy can render technology charming to even the most curmudgeonly cyberphobe. In an essay entitled "The Boys in the Bandwidth," a white-bearded *Forbes* columnist expatiates on why he likes e-mail, despite his general distaste for things technological.[57] The columnist reminisces about the halcyon days when he sojourned on an exotic island: "In the village where I lived, if you wanted to invite a friend to dinner you wrote a note, and gave it to one of the little boys" who seemed "always" to be hanging around, waiting to oblige for a few coins. The author had feared that he would never again delight in this kind of communication experience, gone the way of other "lost pleasures of an earlier age." But, "wonderfully enough, I was wrong. I'm not sending notes across town in the grubby hands of little boys, of course. Instead, I'm sending notes around the world via email. In effect, I'm sending a superboy." This subjective idea of a little superboy, racing around the high-bandwidth network, helps to give e-mail "its curiously anachronistic charm." The writer underscores the unexpectedness of this pleasure with a clear sense of his audience before him. He had opened the essay by declaring his motives, twin goals that strongly indicate what he takes to be the likely sympathies of his readership: "Insofar as this column has an editorial mission, it is to comfort the technology-afflicted while afflicting the technology pushers." He counts himself and his probable fans among the "technology-afflicted." The idea of "boys in the bandwidth" evidently falls under the rubric of comfort.

Incorporated Bodies, Segregated Roles

These last three examples—a scene of calculation panic on Mars, a boardroom scam running on an invisible boy and his machine, and an advice column for technophobes—all focus on cyberphobic images of masculine whiteness. These guys don't want to get too close to the machine. *The Grifters* posits a cyberphobia so strong and predictable that a con man could conjure a host of mainframes without worrying that the mark would even so much as look into the next room to check the techno-story. The earlier examples of this chapter—rockets, voices, servers, inmates—focused on the other side of this fear: the desire to see black bodies as having a natural affinity for technological incorporation. While I argue that these black images also reflect a cyberphobic whiteness, they do so without depicting white skin. The trace of whiteness in these projections can be subtle, with the black-versus-white opposition primarily implied by the pattern of black presence and white absence. Similarly, in the images so far of the technology-averse white guys, the question of racial difference remains relatively muted; we only know that these men would prefer that the tech work be undertaken by someone or something other (and less) than themselves. But racial oppositions more clear-cut than these do exist. I now turn

Fig. 8. Goat expert vs. RAM expert: Office Depot promises a technology buffer (2002).

to a series of examples that visually integrate the black and white sides of the technology equation. These images suggest that the corporate narrative may actually be able to picture a white executive in the same room with a computer—or at least on the same page—as long as there is a black body present to absorb the "future shock." With the black man at the keyboard, the races live in perfect harmony—while the technology remains segregated.

Harmony does not necessarily require togetherness. In an ad for Office Depot, a white body and a black body float in horizontal alignment, figures against an ungrounded neutral ground (fig. 8).[58] The bodies' shimmering outlines suggest that they have undergone some sort of transfiguration or teleportation to an infinite blue field, a unified representational space that in fact juxtaposes glimpses of two different worlds: the land of the "Goat expert" and the planet of the "RAM expert." The page layout emphasizes the distance between these domains of livestock and Random Access Memory, respectively; rather than, say, dividing the page evenly into thirds, the two figures hew to the edges, leaving a wide cerulean swath between them. For an advertisement to devote its focal point to nonrepresentational space would be unusual, to say the least, but the untended central patch of azure bears a highly representational function. Between the goat and the RAM, between biology and machine, Office Depot presents a buffer zone, albeit one smoothly continuous with a well-ordered universe. To the left, the contented white man and his radiant white beast; to the right, the black man eagerly bearing the black computer; in between, the safe separation made possible by the black man's corporate occupation.

The white figure models a carefree pastoral lifestyle. Dressed in loose layers of earth tones, he exudes comfortable proximity to nature. His earthiness is next to fleshliness; the lightly smudged mud on his boots matches the hue of his skin. His body language—right foot forward, left hand on hip, relaxed weight shift—eases into a pose that has been used to convey idealized masculinity from classical and Renaissance sculpture to John Wayne.[59] This herdsman gives the satisfied grin of a mature David, a confident giant-slayer with no more Philistines on his horizon. Resting on his staff, he fears no evil, for he need not walk through the valley of the shadow of tech. That would be the duty drawn by the RAM expert, the instrumentalized black man. The Access may be Random, but the attendant persona seems selectively determined. With feet closer together and a stiffer posture, he stands ready to render service (he is, after all, the one wearing the Office Depot logo). The body languages of the two figures tell a story of cowboys and butlers: the outdoorsman hitches his thumb into his belt with an air of confident swagger; the office helper handles the portable computer solicitously, as if proffering a silver platter or a velvet-lined case.

The ad presents at least two sets of closely linked oppositions. We see that the biological white man is not the technological black man, and vice versa. But each player in this visible opposition also stands opposed to an alternative stereotyped identity not pictured, an evil twin of the same race, albeit one keyed to the characteristics of the respective racial other depicted. The white man we see is not another kind of white person, although the black figure hints at what that other white would be like. The white man we see is not the bespectacled, emasculated nerd; the calling-card accessory pictured is his low-slung belt buckle, not a pocket protector. His healthy goat emblematizes a potency that goes along with a certain farmers-hide-your-daughters charm, one in keeping with the finest pastoral traditions. Conversely, the black "RAM expert" is far from "the black ram" of Shakespearean fame and longstanding cultural infamy.[60] "The black ram" is the stereotypical image of the sexually active black male. In *Othello*, Shakespeare shows how the insidious slanderer Iago uses this label to incite the racist fears of the white man—the "black ram" and your white daughter, says a little bird, are "playing the beast with two backs."[61] But there's all the difference in the world between "black ram" and "RAM expert." The latter identity, neutralized by its technological incorporation, approaches the condition of what Cleaver calls the "Black Eunuch," unthreatening to any ewes.[62]

The black "RAM" may itself be a dangerous entity to be reckoned with, but the decorous black expert should keep any electronic threat in check. If left unattended, computers can get themselves into a world of trouble. In reference to a computer accused of misbehaving, a staff writer for a Texas newspaper issued the following one-sentence paragraph as a proposed corrective: "Somebody git a rope."[63] The joke has grim echoes. The writer does not ask to pull the plug, nor seek to wield a Luddite sledgehammer. He treats the machine as a man. When the computer shows disrespect, the writer's instinct is to "git a rope." In this call for Texas justice, the solid citizen proposes that the offending machine be served in the same manner as other black bodies that have gone before. Step out of line, get strung up. Such ugly scenes may be avoided if the black RAM expert does his job correctly. Through the mutual incorporation of black bodies, the proper linking of black man and black machine forestalls the lynching of either. An idealized tech-bearing image of peaceful self-sacrifice obviates any call for violence. The black expert performs the work of containment and purification, a task that simultaneously keeps his body safely occupied. Far from raising the menace of miscegenation, *this* black man keeps white bodies safe from technologization. He offers his body, so you don't have to. Read in a demythologizing light, the Office Depot ad may be called an exercise in goat expertise: telling the tale of the tech-willing scapegoat, and pinning that tale on the black RAM expert. For the purpose of placative offerings to the god of technology, the designated ram in the thicket has become the ram in the RAM.

For International Business Machines, the racial segregation of technology has become a representational ritual. IBM's 2001 annual report boasts of the completion of a seven-year initiative to get up to speed in networking: "We *rewired* the enterprise" by "becoming an e-business."[64] The opening acts for this headliner attraction are "Kevin Bishop, Director of Marketing" and "Ena D. Cantu, Supercomputer Storage" (fig. 9). Bishop, the white male, stands in a cozy room suffused with a warm golden glow, framed by white crown molding, a genteel fireplace, a decidedly nondigital clock on the mantelpiece, and a window to the world outside. Right now he's enjoying a big black mug of "cappuccino." He's very much at home, something that IBM's goal "to change the very nature of work" permits him to be. Bishop "works 20% of his time from home, 40% on the road." His range of operations includes outposts in "UK/Ireland/Netherlands/South Africa." The caption

Fig. 9. Director of Marketing vs. Supercomputer Storage at IBM (2001).

does not even account for the remaining 40 percent of his time. Not so for Ena Cantu, who "spends 100% of her time" at a center "maintaining" a "system."[65] The black woman stands on a gridded floor in a corridor between rows of black towers, a supercomputer array, like her workday, with no end in sight. She inhabits a timeless, windowless, colorless environment of fluorescent lighting and stamped metal. In this pair of portraits, the white man conducts the international business; the black woman tends the machines.

IBM replicates the "goat versus RAM" opposition throughout its advertising. A two-page spread emblazoned with a "Who Do You Need?" slogan gives the rundown on IBM's split menu of personnel (fig. 10).[66] On the left, we see a man who "*gets* how to help businesses do more business overseas," and who "*got it done*" by "leading a team" to "help U.S. companies find new markets." On the right, IBM presents a man who "*gets* how to keep customers happy and information safe," and who "*got it done*" by "developing" a "security gateway" for web transactions. Based on these profiles, it shouldn't be hard to guess that the left/right split maps onto the same white/black contrast found in the Bishop/Cantu opposition. Again, the racial identities divide the corporate name: white International Business and black Machines. The action of the white man is to "lead," looking outward to conquer new territory; the black man stays busy in the back office, "developing" the software. The former commands people; the activity of the latter is to program computers; his function is one of placation and re-

Fig. 10. Leading a team vs. developing a program; IBM's faces for "International Business" and for "Machines" (2001).

assurance, as he works to guarantee the happiness and safety of the technology afflicted. The names and job title come last in the thumbnail résumés: on the left, Patrick Howard, "Managing Principal"; on the right, Gary Wright, "IT Architect" and "Engineer."

The corporate uniforms index the division of labor implicit in these job descriptions. Howard wears a suit and a tie; Wright appears in a knit shirt with an open and literally blue collar. One should note that in the context of IBM corporate culture, blue takes on a special valence. IBM is "Big Blue," so Wright's blue collar marks him as something other than a common laborer, even if he clearly doesn't rate an executive ranking in the hierarchy. In some sense, he's even more closely identified with the company than his managerial counterpart. The color design of the two-page layout subtly underscores the respective roles of Howard and Wright vis-à-vis the company. Howard wears a grey suit against a blue background: he's the man out in front, doing the advance work of prepping the economic soil, embarking from headquarters into the world on behalf of IBM and the nation. Wright, inversely, wears a blue shirt against a grey background: he *is* Big Blue, the body that puts the *M* in IBM, who is the core product that *IB* merely modifies adjectivally and that the *IB* men merely sell. In the same way that "Carl" *is* Dell Enterprise and that the "RAM expert" *is* Office Depot service, Wright's the one who bears the stamp of the IBM logo squarely on his collar.

A subsequent installment of the "Who Do You Need?" campaign from later in 2001 adheres to this same racialized pattern with almost startling rigidity.[67] The personnel pairings present so uniform a template that either ad could be mistaken for the other. On the left, a white man in a grey suit who "*gets* how to lead teams"; on the right, a black man with an open blue collar who "*got it done*" by "developing an e-learning solution." The same bifurcated lexicon marks the same job division: one "leads" while the other "develops." Only the job title of the former contains the word *executive,* a password admitting him to the subject position of corporate narrative; the latter exists as an executable object.

The rather uncanny repetition of details from one ad to the next suggests the operation of a superstitious practice. It is this strict quality of pattern replication, minutely attentive to imitative fidelity even in excess of what would appear necessary to make a given point, that leads me to venture the word *ritual.* Ritual may remain unaware of the reasons for its own details, superstitiously repeating them in the hopes of achieving familiar positive results. Superstition itself may be thought of as the deliberate performance of certain actions to achieve a desired effect—but a performance without a clear understanding of the precise causal relation between action and outcome. The ignorance of the "why" behind a certain action links ritual to the realm of the habitual. I would hazard that the pattern adherence I am detecting here belongs to ritual in this sense. Certainly, the advertisers have a goal in mind, but I would hesitate to claim that the technological containment of the black body plays a prominent role in their conscious thinking about either the goal or how to attain it. The consciously desired effect may be defined as broadly as "to present the company in a favorable light": the rationale for the campaign may be as simple as, "People seem to respond favorably when we run these kinds of images, white management and black technological expertise, side by side in smiling partnership." The right people feel good about such representations. At least this much intentionality must lie behind the preponderant blackness of technological body images. But beyond the sense that such images enable the target audience to feel good, corporate narratives may have black-boxed the mechanisms of their own racialized representational strategies. One goal of the present project is to undertake a reasoned recovery of the possible logics behind such repetitive designations.

Anthropological inquiry has proposed that ritual begets sport and drama.[68] Ritual itself tends to sublimate the outright sacrifice of human bodies, and in the subsequent cultural forms of play, the sacrificial character of the practice becomes even more attenuated, discernible only in traces. In expanding their decisive two-man "*Who Do You Need?*" service to feature a somewhat larger cast of players, IBM recapitulates that cultural turn in brief.[69] As of 2002, IBM e-business was proud to present their "*Integration Play.*" The diagram for integration involves three nodes, connected by arrows—like a page borrowed from a coach's playbook, superimposed on a photo with the light-pen analysis of an NFL color commentator. But deviating from the typical sports-diagram scenario, the grid for this play is not a level playing field. Rather, the integration play covers a multilevel field. The camera's gaze, looking through the sheer face of a high rise as darkness falls, shows a corporation in cross-section. The play takes place across a four-floor hierarchy. At the top, "*Amy in Finance*"; in the next floor, "*Bill in Marketing*"; and, at the bottom of the command chain, two floors below, "*What's His Name the Freelance Guy.*" The arrows link these nodes of corporate status in a clockwise cycle. Beginning at the left, we find an arrow from Bill to Amy, from Amy to What's His Name, and from What's His Name back to Bill. In fact, the most logical business narrative to be inferred from the diagram would follow this conventional ordering of the loop (especially if we consider who's writing the ad): Marketing has an idea, runs it by Finance; Finance approves and authorizes payment to the Freelance tech labor, who performs the work and has it delivered to Marketing. Bill stars in this story: it begins with his creative flash and ends with his gratification. Thanks to integrated e-business, all Bill had to do was pick up the phone, a familiar, humanized technology—the one he's pictured with.

This corporate scheme holds little but contempt for the freelance guy. While Bill and Amy rule the roost, the guy has to get by without benefits, security—or a name. He's the "seems like there's a new kid downstairs every week" guy, the "if we need a quick redesign of the webpage, we can always hire some kid to do it" boy. In the "Integration Play," his is the node of the interchangeable, disposable part. What's His Name is the unrepresented, unpresentable white male in the four-identity Goat/RAM matrix. The Office Depot ad showed only the *preferred* racial identities: the free-range masculine white man and the solicitous technologized black male, while hidden behind each valorized identity is its negation, the emasculated white nerd and the virile black buck, respectively. The Integration Play stages a more inclusive show, finding a spotlight for the geek in this three-ring circus. The body within the lowest circle stands as the antithesis of the marketing man, the shunned nerd serving as the white negation of the desirable attributes that make Bill Bill. A handful of picture elements suffice to make the necessary distinctions between besuited Bill, the sharp-dressed *man,* and the unnamed, untucked, bespectacled boy.

This boy stands in close proximity to an even less respected entity. A close look reveals a numerical oddity of the integration diagram: three circles, three arrows, three labels, but *four* bodies. With eyes, nose, chin, and hands shorn off by the outer rim of the third white circle, what's left of a black man "faces" the whiz kid. The unmentioned fourth body, though placed outside the loop, actually completes it. He's the company's in-house contact for the freelance guy. The boy does the gee-whiz computer stuff, but for that work to pay off, the company needs someone who speaks the kid's machine language. The day labor tech kid is in the transaction loop, but outside the company. It's up to the black man, himself already incorporated as a low-level techno-functionary, to incorporate the outsourced wizardry. He's the one who integrates this circuit. He's the one who makes Bill shine.

At such junctures, software engineering brushes obliquely against social engineering, if only to push the social questions aside. According to a 2002 advertisement from a major cyber-corporation, Sybase, "*Integration Is Once Again a Political Issue.*"[70] As this ad would have it, "Integration," in the civil rights sense, is now *only* a play. Sybase invokes integration "once again," as if dragging the corporate audience's attention back to a headache that everyone hoped had gone away. But no, we don't have to go *there* again. It's only a little wordplay; the current problem to be solved requires only a simple purchase. To address new federal requirements for secure "software integration" (ah! *software* integration) Sybase offers the PATRI-OTcompliance solution. With this Information Anywhere package, you can "resolve your integration issues." Implicit in these remarks is the pleasant thought, accompanied by a sigh of relief, that racial integration no longer counts as one of the unresolved issues. At second glance, "once again" turns out not to refer to some dreaded presentness of the past; rather it constructs a timeline with a comfortable space between two distinct eras—the age of racial integration and the age of computer integration—playfully connected only by an accident of naming.

Yet other ads, with their forced appearance of virtual affirmative action, would seem to belie that complacent front. (By "virtual affirmative action," I mean the spotlighting of minority employees at the level of public presentation; by "forced," I refer to the demographically skewed patterns of, say, the "Who Do You Need?" campaign, which picks black representatives from the IBM workforce at a rate of 50 percent. Why insist so heavily, beyond statistical plausibility, on showing something—namely, workplace integration—that is supposedly already accomplished?) Even at Sybase, the borrowing of the tropes of progressive social engineering reflects color consciousness.[71] The ad quickly re-represses the repressed, but not before turning a trick that presumes a fear of its return. With that momentary horror passed, the ad seeks to revert to the undisturbing gloss of a plain vanilla product brochure. The Sybase ad displays no faces, and its language deals not with bodies, but only with things: "Everything works better when everything works together." In the Sybase vision, the issue of harmonization will be resolved at a purely inanimate level. Integration—it's a technological problem with a technological solution. In shifting the referent of "Integration," Sybase reduces the legacy of a historical problem with bodies to a software problem with the machines. Even in so doing, Sybase's reductive move mimics, in fast-forward blur, the representational mechanisms of other companies' black body prescriptions. The corporation addresses issues with problematic bodies by reducing them to machines, machines that in turn will solve technological problems. Corporate narrative thus fights wire with wire.

This process of almost concurrent incorporation comes closer to historical accuracy than the implied epochal partitioning of "once again." Segregation was outlawed in 1954. The integrated circuit, so crucial in shrinking computer machinery and thus bringing it closer to front-office bodies, was introduced in 1958. The integration of black bodies and digital circuitry into the corporation may be said to have followed a joint fifty-year trajectory. Present representations suggest that this work of incorporation remains unfinished. While the prospect of facing either challenge alone creates corporate anxiety, a black-boxing match between bodies and machines would offer some cheer. The high-tech boardroom has kept in contact with the world of Ellison's "Battle Royal," a spectacle for an elite club of white males that culminates with black male bodies forming a circuit with an electrified grid.[72] In the high-tech update, the fusion of man with machine bypasses the staged clash of man with man.

Whether anthropological or political echoes resonate most strongly, what these representations preserve in common is a hierarchy that segregates technology according to power and race. The lighter and more prestigious one is, the freer one's person will be from technological encum-

Fig. 11. Coffee and newspaper vs. black laptop: Enlightened Business Travel (2002).

brance, and the more likely one will be to have black technology at one's command. High atop this graded heap rides the "Enlightened Business Traveler" (fig. 11).

The *Forbes* special advertising section traveling under that name plumps the cushions on the "company plane." Access to such privileged transport, we are promised, "obliterates travel time." Boarding your own business jet not only qualifies you as "enlightened," it also tempts you to see yourself in godlike terms: "What if, instead of being a slave to time, you could become its master? What sort of extraordinary things could you accomplish if being in two places at once were very nearly within your reach?" This enlightening feature opens with an image of such divine mastery with all the accoutrements. Before the wood-paneled backdrop of his private cabin, executive royalty holds court. Commanding the prime bulkhead seat, a mature white businessman sits in Olympian repose. French cuffs, a pocket silk, and a gold signet ring all contribute to the air of lordly distinction with which he holds his morning newspaper and sips his breakfast beverage.

Insofar as the individual pictured partakes of the advertisement's lure of almost absolute speed, one might note that this eminence aspires to the condition of information. But, contrary to the standard notion of informational disembodiment, he apparently lives this dream without sacrificing any fleshly comforts. The idea of disembodiment itself partakes of myth, as Katherine Hayles insists that all information technically must have a body. The point is well taken, but the Enlightened Business Traveler fantasy does not resort to such technicalities to preserve bodily existence. The informational body that carries a Java applet across an optical network is not quite the same as the one inhabited by this corporate Angel of Light. This Prince of the Air possesses a body that can enjoy a steaming cup of brew. He may almost be in two places at once, but right now he's magnificently here. Or, if the ad's rhetoric achieves its ends, you are magisterially there. The definite article of the feature's title creates a single focal point. The ad doesn't sell "Enlightened Business Traveling—Fun for the Whole Office!" In its insistent second person singular address, it's all about you. But you do get a supporting entourage.

Across the aisle, the junior associates in the enlightened one's retinue labor in slightly more cramped conditions. Facing the camera, framed by someone's shoulder on the right side of the picture, sits a black man. He holds a computer, at the ready, should the need for any in-flight calculation arise.[73] With such provisions securely in place, we never anticipate a change in cabin pressure; it's tech-free relaxation all the way. The black man on hand thoroughly (en)lightens the business traveler's load. In the scenario's visual shorthand, enlightenment also depends upon contrast.[74] The most fully enlightened may exercise an even more discriminating taste in imagining a dark technological other to bear the burden. As of 2002, an airline consortium planned to deploy e-mail and Internet access on a select fleet of planes. The moniker for this high-speed, high-altitude service is "Tenzing."[75] Tenzing Norgay was the sherpa who accompanied Sir Edmund Hillary in the first ascent of Mount Everest. Tenzing has also been the shared name of subsequent attending sherpas. For example, Tenzing Sherpa served on a 1996 Everest expedition, for which one of the wealthy adventurers insisted that an espresso machine be toted up the mountain.[76] "Tenzing Communications" imparts a task-specific message. If you want high-bandwidth capabilities with all the amenities at thirty thousand feet and above, you'll want a sherpa to do your heavy lifting. Tenzing, the consortium promises, is compatible with "Personal Digital Assistants."[77] Indeed it is, but no more so than similar narratives of corporate heroes and their subservient technologists.

These high-flying corporate fantasies merge smoothly with the star treatment showered on a cluster of real-life CEOs in Microsoft's annual report, millennium edition. "Microsoft_2000" (using a web-style title for the print report) opens with five splashy pages of testimony on the .NET concept, Microsoft's bid to sell businesses "a complete package that allows them to integrate applications, share data, and compete effectively in the new economy." The chief executives of Compaq, Dell, Qwest, Verio, and

Andersen Consulting hold forth in turn. But not all of them appear. The layouts alternate between crystal-clear hero portraits of the execs and blurry shots of representative employees. First Michael Capellas, CEO of Compaq, in words and in person, leaning at ease, his hands clasped in front of him. Then the statement of Michael Dell, superimposed on the image of an unnamed black man toting a computer. Next, Qwest CEO Joseph P. Nacchio, leaning his forearm on a rail, his hands clasped to one side in classic news anchor pose. The words of Verio's CEO, Justin Jashke, follow; above them floats the hazy visage of an anonymous south Asian man, framed by a pair of monitors. Finally, the CEO of Andersen, Joe D. Forehand: his hands thrust confidently into his pockets, his robust body out for a walk in the corporate park, green tree behind him and still water beside. This sequence presents a strict alternation between white male executives who need not dirty their hands and dark ethnic others busy with the machines. The report imagines racialized difference between the bodies caught in the .NET and the ones reaping the fat returns.

A contrasting language of the hands, free or occupied, again tells the corporate story in "Your Life: Truly Mobile," the *AT&T Wireless Report 2001*. A series of photos demonstrates the range of products offered and the effect each achieves. For example, the "cool new Bluetooth wireless headset" means "less wire to deal with" so that "we" can "talk with our hands too. Very liberating." Or, with the "new Blackberry Handheld," the day "has never been more productive. Very efficient." We may have noticed that these devices and their descriptions were not quite created equal, and the corresponding faces corroborate the same coefficients of enlightenment we have observed elsewhere. In the first vignette, a fair-skinned male "business traveler" zooms through the city, ferried along by a black cab driver. The cabbie keeps his hands on the wheel and his eyes on the road; the businessman gets to be cool, as he experiences the liberation of hands-free communication. In the second setup, a black woman stands on a busy street corner, her head down, her fingers occupied with her handheld machine. Here's a complete computer so compact that a black body never needs to go without a keyboard to keep those hands from idleness. The light body gets to be free; the dark other is valued for nonstop productivity and efficiency.

Even the kinds of words used in the respective taglines are not quite equivalent in function. "Liberating" refers to the continuously emancipatory action of Bluetooth wireless. If we wish to refer to the user who benefits from Bluetooth, we would have to use a different form and declare him to be "liberated." The necessary choice between adjectival forms keeps the man and the machine in separate spheres. In contrast, "efficient" could apply to the technology or to the body using it, or both rolled into one. Blackberry is efficient. The black woman is efficient. Blackberry makes her so. Efficiency is the virtue of the black body–machine conflation. Understandably, only the Bluetooth caption uses the "we" form, inviting the reader to identify with the man pictured. Not so for the black woman, who exists only in the third person. A comparison between product metaphors also leaves the black body in an unenviable position: it's Bluetooth versus Blackberry, eater versus eaten, predator versus pie. With respect to the marketplace, it's consumer versus consumed. Very different.

From cover to happy ending, Motorola's 2001 summary annual report structures itself on just such a system of difference. Next to the title words appears the face of a black fireman, Motorola gear strapped across his chest. This same face reappears in the penultimate layout. Here we see his panoply of tech gear somewhat more fully, and we may note that his shirt identifies him as belonging to a Harlem engine company. Bathed in the context of that latter fact, his smile takes on a beatific quality, while the black-and-white photography lends the page an elegiac tone. This hagiographic image appears back-to-back with the final full-page photo in the report. In living color, a beaming grandmaternal figure reads to a delighted white boychild from a bright red storybook. Motorola proclaims itself a global leader in software-enhanced wireless, networking access, embedded semiconductor solutions, and integrated electronic systems; but this concluding image of "Homeland Security" portrays not a shred of digital technology. Proper embedding and integration may entail invisibility, but a narrative that makes technology vanish also enables something far grander. The declared theme for the entire report, established on the cover, is "**real**ity." For Motorola, that's a somewhat anxious claim. The company's narrator knows that technology firms like Motorola are popularly perceived as the *enemies* of "reality," as the purveyors of virtuality. The story arc's target shows just how far Motorola will go to dissociate itself from electronic incursions on everyday life. Motorola wants to cast its lot with what Melville, in *Typee*, identifies as the first two words in the primer of anglophone civilization: "Home" and "Mother."[78] The report's final vision of absolute reality, free from all technological mediation, distortion, or encumbrance, is the highest end of corporate narrative; it is also the most cherished ideal of the cyberphobic imagination generally. Here we find reality secured through the noble sacrifice of the technologized black body, Motor-ola's Engine-man. But the cyberphobic imagination craves something more. The price may be paid in the red lifeblood of black bodies, but the prize is to be tasted in the sweetness of white milk. Underwritten at the expense of blackness, the longed-for reality is guaranteed and grounded by a nurturing maternal presence. This site of the storybook ending, the lap of reality, grounds a whiteness dependent on the myth of the technologized black man, incorporated by the machine in a galaxy far, far away.

chapter four

TECHNO-BLACK LIKE ME

The Racial Postures of Anticorporate Narrative

We have seen in the preceding chapter that corporate narrative has identified the black body with the black box of technology, a representational linkage designed to assure white executives that they need not worry about computer operations, that someone unmistakably else will handle any difficult details. In some cases, this representation actually corresponds to the assignment of the least desirable forms of computer labor to various subaltern marked bodies. But in other cases, the fantasy of hassle-free computing must in fact be sustained by the technical industriousness of other, sub-executive white males. This chapter takes up the stories told by and on behalf of such digital subjects in compensation for their indenture to the machine.

The phrase "Techno-black like me" expresses a major feature of what I will call "anticorporate narrative": white workers' adoption of blackness as an identity accessory, the most colorful sign of their hipster ironic pose as digital slaves "workin' for The Man." This adoption of blackness takes identity as a matter of self-fashioning, albeit from a posture tacitly underwritten by the birthright of whiteness. Though the degree of sympathy with black experience may vary in these appropriations, the white workers' sense of outrage generally derives from the perceived discrepancy between their true identity and the role forced upon them by the tech corporation. The pose of techno-blackness thus upgrades for the digital class the old complaint of the white laborer about having to work "like a negro"—a likeness that simultaneously adopts blackness and protests its burdens.[1] In this ctrl-alt-shift command over identity's parameters, the masters of anticorporate discourse define a blackness that is virtual, underwritten by a whiteness assumed as real.

This conditional appropriation of black trappings has much in common with the "racial ventriloquism" that Michael North discerns as "the dialect of modernism," a kind of "slumming in slang" through which whites of the early twentieth century enjoyed an escape from the pressures of standardization: " 'black' dialect was white dialect in hiding."[2] Susan Gubar has subsequently listened for a more positive political vitality to this "racechange," pursuing a kind of Eric Lott–inflected revisionism that sees love as well as theft in the white use of blackface forms. Rather than reading the race-changing pose as dishonest and patronizing stereotype, Gubar hears a "black talk that often presents itself as back talk . . . tapping a dissident lexicon of subversive power, one at odds with the hegemonic cadences of mainstream culture as well as [whites'] own normative conformity to it."[3] By this reading, the techno-black dialect of postmodernism would talk back to the hegemony of the corporation. Yet the anticorporate intent cannot plausibly valorize the techno-black posture as a celebration of black cultural vitality, especially as the narrative's defining metaphors focus on the subject's debasement through slavery. White anticorporate narrators typically perform blackness not in recognition of black culture's expressive power but as a way of dramatizing subjugation to the machine. Even Gubar's careful rehabilitation of defiant racechange comes with an overriding proviso, one that applies to the racializing moves of cyberphobic anticorporatism: "But, regardless of their politics, all texts exploiting racial ventriloquism inevitably shuttle between defending against and welcoming energies of Otherness" (137). In the instances of anticorporate techno-blackness that follow, the appropriation of the "energies of Otherness" remains ever on the defensive.

By "anticorporate narrative," I refer simply to stories that adopt an oppositional stance to the corporation, particularly with disrespect for the company as employer and manager of workers. Anticorporate narrative tends to identify itself with the plight of the tech worker, as well as with those who are left behind or have dropped out of corporate culture. Under the anticorporate umbrella, one finds the disaffected tech laborer and the cyberpunk as well as the slacker and the bohemian. Inside this tent, the cyberpunk and the burnout, the hacker and the slacker, the wired worker and the coffeehouse crank have much in common; their affinity may be read in their shared discourses on technology. Most importantly for the present analysis, neither defiant outsider sensibilities nor an anticorporate stance can guarantee immunity against the racializing techno-logic of color monitoring. Despite its position on and appeal to a lower rung in the hierarchy of power, anticorporate narrative resembles corporate narrative in its tendency to associate technologization with blackness. If the discourse of "integrated circuits" prescribes a sacrificial logic, "Techno-black like me" narration subscribes to a victimary thinking that is the flip side of the same representational project.[4] Faced with the prospect of a denigrating technologization, corporate narrative recommends, *Do it unto others.* Anticorporate narrative proclaims, *We are the others because it has been done to us.*

Being a Word Processor

Behold the pale American office worker, reduced by his technical labors to a piece of computer software. "Young Josh," the narrator-protagonist of the indie film *Haiku Tunnel* (2001), explains what it's like *being* "a word processor." He has discovered that operating in this purely instrumental capacity removes even the smallest shreds of autonomy that may adhere to ordinary office work: "When you're a word processor, you just type type type type type type type." In its earliest usage, the word *computer* referred to a person who performed calculations; the office machine of the same name was introduced with the stated goal of freeing such individuals from mindless and repetitive tasks. But according to Josh and his white brethren from the world of tech work, the person assigned to operate that liberating machine can readily become a mere application that the computer runs.

Josh succumbs to this digital reduction while processing the "engineering specs" on the Haiku Tunnel, a highway project for Hawaii that keeps Josh busy in his Silicon Valley cubicle. Analyzing working conditions at the engineering corporation, Josh speaks for the victims of electronic anomie: "I was totally anonymous there. . . . No one knew my name, no one knew I existed." At first he wonders if such a situation could prove liberating, but "as the weeks went by, I found myself getting incredibly, incredibly depressed." He experiences an alienation from the outside physical world, finding his body swallowed up by the technical specifications that he spends his days feeding to the computer: "Having severed all my ties to earthly concerns, I now found myself all alone in a strange new world. I was inside the Haiku Tunnel." The Haiku Tunnel, numerically oppressive, engulfs the human.

Yet by claiming this loss of natural identity, Josh makes himself the beneficiary of some strategic compensations. For one thing, virtual anonymity allows him to try on *other* names for size. He plays a running joke that involves the inability of the white male elites to get his name right. "Hello, Juan," says one of his boss men. Later, Josh needs a security clearance, and asks the guard to place a phone call to this same superior: "Tell him it's Jesús, maybe he'll think it's me." When he meets the man, Josh expresses his gratitude: "Hey Mister Barnes, thanks so much for authorizing me." With a paternal pat on the shoulder, Tim Barnes delivers the racializing punchline: "No problem, Jamal." With these words, the boss completes the authorization that the protagonist seeks: the fair-skinned Josh has been authorized, as subaltern laborer, to cycle through various brown identities, a comic identity fantasy that culminates in his receiving the mantle of blackness. He has been inside the Haiku Tunnel. He has become a word processor. He has become black.

As "Jamal," Josh places himself on a list of names diametrically opposed to the figures of corporate authority. In his time as a temp worker at Bay Area legal and engineering firms, Josh makes an inductive study of the kinds of names that distinguish upper management from labor. He has worked, in succession, for: "Bob. Bob. Bob. Bob. Bob. Bob. Jim. Jim. James. Jim. Nate the third. Margaret. Bob." A series of headshots accompanies this narration. No black face appears. Josh notes the contrasting sounds of hireling names, while showing the contrasting colors of the corresponding faces. After the long line of executive Bobs, the distinct list of clerical workers features the sequence of "Yvonne, Yvonette, Yvonetta"—three black women. He caps off the list, enraptured with the mellifluous name and golden brown face of "Aurora. Au-*ror*-a." To this second list he appends his own multisyllabically euphonious "temp name," again with lovingly extended emphasis: "*Jo*-shu-a."

Authorized by the alienating gestures of white corporate power, the narrator asserts his racial otherness with increasing boldness. Emerging from his tunnel transformations, Joshua/Jamal makes overtures to DaVonne, a black co-worker: "Would you ever consider me to be 'man material'?" he asks her. DaVonne instantly provides a tripartite rebuff: "You're poor.

You're unstable. And you're white." The word processor squares his shoulders for his proud reply: "Who ya callin' white?"

He stands willing to accept the charge that he is poor; in fact, his identity is based in part on his economic victimhood at the hands of corporate exploitation. Similarly, he cannot deny that he is mentally unstable; his close encounter with the machine has left him clinically depressed, a mere shell of a white man trapped inside the Haiku Tunnel. That very reduction, the loss of white humanity that follows from his function as a software application, authorizes his claim to virtual blackness. On this point, he remains firm, defiant, talking back in dialect. "Who ya callin' white?"—Josh/Juan/Jesús/Jamal brandishes his technologically earned racial otherness as an all-areas security badge.

From the 1990s onward, the demographic group known as the "slackers"—a sometimes "underemployed" but not necessarily jobless band—has furnished a good measure of the temporary labor stream that has run through the Haiku Tunnel's real world analogues. A headline on the phenomenon hints at the group's tendency to racialize itself as virtually black: "Slack Like Me."[5] Hailed as "overworked, teched-out, stress-pressed slaves to The Man," they aspire to the title of "Master Slacker."[6] To slack is to slip the yoke of slavery and ascend to the seat of mastery. The slacker ethos understands technological labor as slavery, refusing to cling to an indentured identity, preferring to rise above it via an abolitionist discourse that converts burnouts into masterful runaway slaves. The oft-heard slacker-ese complaint about a career of "workin' for The Man" justifies a flexible opting out to enjoy *la vie bohème* of a layabout master. Richard Linklater's 1991 film *Slacker,* an indie smash assembled in Austin, Texas, introduced its title into common parlance; the techno-bohemians at the magazine *Mondo 2000* embraced *Slacker* for taking "vicious swipes at the Establishment."[7] *Mondo*'s interviewer approached the great arbiter of all things slack for a basic definition: a "slacker," says Linklater, is "somebody who's not doing what's expected of them. . . . I think it's admirable. It's not that everyone in *Slacker* is unemployed, it's just that their little slave job isn't what's motivating them in the world." The slacker thus claims both a "slave" status and an essential superiority to that instrumentalized condition (the "little slave job isn't what's motivating them").

A *Hotwired* "Geek of the Week" from 1997 captures this divided pose by listing his "Occupation: College Student/Page-Layout Slave." He belongs to a constituency that burgeoned in the mid-1990s: a wired, youthful, and more or less privileged population prone to exaggerated and ironic self-validation. The very existence of a zine called *Temp Slaves* bespeaks a trend of tech workers with a penchant for bitter histrionics; a 1996 *Hotwired* article on "Waiting for the Man" documents the growing ranks of publications in the *Temp Slave* genre. Along these cynical and misanthropic lines, the same year saw the appearance of "Johnny The Homicidal Maniac," a "new comic book series that has given form and expression to the tormented, often enraging life of the geek, the nerd, and the misfit—familiar titles to many in cyberspace." Published by Slave Labor Graphics, the narrative received the full endorsement of *Hotwired*'s "Media Rant": "Johnny's gonna be big. His life is our life, his story is ours." Striking a chord with Internet hipsters, Johnny gives a voice to the resentful temp slave.[8]

Workers employed with technology on a less temporary basis, full-time hackers, tend to take their slavery straight up.[9] With *NetSlaves: True Tales of Working the Web* (2000), Bill Lessard and Steve Baldwin strike abolitionist poses, almost as if hoping to become the William Lloyd Garrison and Wendell Phillips of the Information Age.[10] The subtitle's emphasis on truth-telling situates their book as an anthology of authentic slave narratives for which they serve as the authorizing editors. The volume consists of a series of hair-raising accounts of all aspects of digital slave life, organized around the testimonial histories of "NetSlaves" from the various classes.[11] These narratives are personalized as "The Story of Matt," "The Story of Boyd," and so on. This documentary key to life among the lowly begins with "the most oppressed and widely despised group within the New Media Caste System," a "group buried under the mass of tangled cables" that infests the "Great American Back office." Lessard and Baldwin set the book's tone with an epigraph from Guns N' Roses: "Do you know where you are? You're in the jungle baby!" (viii). In a reversal of the traditional trajectory of abductive slave recruitment, the unfortunate NetSlaves have been torn from the bosom of Civilization and thrust into the primitive depths of a Dark Continent. In keeping with this imagined setting, the lowest of the low refer to themselves as "desktop monkeys" (115). Lessard and Baldwin employ a terminology of functional equivalence, dubbing the oppressed "Garbagemen," having found them most often "in the charred remains of a fried hard drive, or at the other end of a sweaty receiver in overlit, overheated, and downright hectic triage wards, better known as Tech Support" (116).

On a marginally higher rung, the anthropologists of NetSlavery find the milieu's "most stressed out" denizens, the project-oriented engineers known as "fry cooks" (121). Though Lessard and Baldwin acknowledge that most NetSlaves in fact receive rather high pay, the authors consistently cite mitigating factors that keep these workers down in what they imagine as legitimate slave-income range. Fry Cooks, for example, make "$60K per year (which amounts to $20K per year, after factoring out exorbitant bar tabs and/or weekly trips to the shrink)" (122); similarly, Garbagemen, pulling down around $25 per hour, "earn more" than many—"yet we feel that they are indeed the lowest of the low because their quality of life is non-existent" (116). In accord with the Linklater prescription, alternative forms of compensation come through an appreciation of culture: Garbagemen lean toward Kerouac, while Fry Cooks favor Bukowski, Baudelaire, or anything "written by an angry young man on the verge of cracking up" (116, 122). Speaking "for NetSlaves everywhere," the protesting editors round out the volume with a brandished fist for all the evil corporate "Robber Barons" who have exploited "our unfortunate friends in the tech biz": with the book's final one-sentence paragraph, the aggrieved authors declare, "This is war" (246).

Having a Life

Pursuing a similar line of Information Age agit-anthropology, the study *Down and Out in Silicon Valley: The High Cost of the High-Tech Dream* (2002) distills its findings into "Archetypes of Silicon Valley."[12] Archetype number one: "The engineer who discovered that he wanted a life" (154). In the novel *Microserfs* (1995), Douglas Coupland gives a canny technocultural history of this phrase and its cognates, "I have no life," "Get a life!" and "I really need to get a life." One of Coupland's rebellious microserfs makes a perceptive observation about the context for this notion's currency: "You never heard about people 'not having lives' until about five years ago, just when all of the '80s technologies really penetrated our lives" (164). Coupland's speculative linguist enumerates the life-sucking culprits, including PCs, modems, ATMs, fax machines, barcoding, and "calculators of an almost other-worldly power" (164).[13] These devices have conspired to micro-process America and deprive us of our lives to such a degree that everyday speech has coined a new phraseology to register the phenomenon. In Coupland's account, the words "I have no life"—the post-boomer's reflexive expression of self-pity—signal an oppressive technological condition.

The author of this insight, Douglas Coupland, owes his greatest fame to a resonant work of pop sociology, *Generation X: Tales for an Accelerated*

Culture (1991). He knows a thing or two about slackerdom and is sometimes associated with Richard Linklater, to the extent of having been chosen to write the introduction to a reprint of the latter's breakthrough
screenplay, *Slacker*. Even more than Linklater, Coupland travels in cyberpunk circles; whereas Linklater did manage to register as a notable on
Mondo 2000's radar, Coupland has earned more substantial hacker credentials as a contributing writer to *Wired,* up on the masthead with the likes of
Neal Stephenson and Bruce Sterling. As the title *Microserfs* suggests, Coupland shares with Linklater a protest against the life defined by high-tech
servitude. Linklater, as we have seen, hits hard with the trope of slavery, as
in his dismissal of his generation's "little slave jobs"; Coupland ratifies the
objections of the micromanaged cubicle hands.[14]

Tracing their roots, Coupland's microserfs visit "the first corporation to
invent the 'workplace as campus' "—"a 1970s utopian, *Andromeda Strain*–
ishly empty tech complex" (211). This site marks the origin of an insidious
trend toward preventing the American tech worker from "having a life."
Through such "campuses," sites that cater to every worker's round-the-
clock needs, "corporate integration" accomplishes an intrusive "life inva-
sion," such that "the borderline between work and life blurred to the point
of unrecognizability" (211). "*Give us your entire life,*" says the tech corporation (211).

The protagonist-narrator of *Microserfs* introduces himself as an e-mail
address, a corporate life destination: "I am *danielu@microsoft.com*" (3).
The *u,* we later learn, stands for Underwood (139)—as in the brand name
of the typewriter manufacturer, a condign surname for a man who spends
his hours at the keyboard: "My life is lived day to day, one line of bug-free
code at a time" (4). Coupland himself gets in on this play of pure electronic
identity, with an ironic caption to the backjacket author photo: "Hello, I
am your personal computer." Coupland's *danielu* and his colleagues call
themselves "microserfs" to designate their utterly subordinate status to the
"mega-equity" "Cyberlords" and to the Microsoft corporation as a whole,
the vast operating system that dictates their daily existence (89).

Although serfdom would seem to imply an Anglo past distinct from
African American slavery, *Microserfs* works to collapse the distinction.
Throughout the narrative, rhetorics of serfdom and slavery apply interchangeably in casual references to their cyberlabors: on a relatively normal
cubicle stint, the narrator reports, "We slaved until 1:00 A.M." (34); com-
menting on another post-midnight shift, he asks rhetorically, "Slaves, or
what?" (206).

Actual postings to newsgroups continually answer that question in the affirmative. The language of slavery abounds in bulletin boards dedicated to anticorporate topics like alt.destroy.micosoft, alt.conspiracy.microsoft, alt.microsoft.sucks, or even to the more utilitarian interests of comp.lang.java.programmer and microsoft.public.security. A characteristic 2003 posting claims that "The Matrix is really about . . . what will happen if we DON't STOP Microsoft! We'll all be delusional drones working 9 to 5 in dayjobs slaving away for the Man."[15] In claiming to depict the "slaves" of Microsoft, Coupland's fictionalized narrative taps a prominent internet vein.

Like the word processor in *Haiku Tunnel*, Underwood in *Microserfs* suffers distressing side-effects from his incessant typing at the terminal: "Lately I've been unable to sleep"; "my relationship to my body has gone all weird" (4). He mentions to a co-worker "the weird relationship people in tech firms can have with their bodies"; his friend composes an email response: "I know what you mean about bodeis [*sic*]. At Microsoft you pretend bodies don't exist. . . . You're right, at Microsoft bodies get down played [*sic*] to near invisibility" (198). The slaves lament their fate as Invisible Men, the blacked-out machines inside the machine.

The content of the white techie's victimary pose finds early cues in the most beloved nursery tale of the information age: the *Star Wars* trilogy (1977–83), a text on which generations of tech workers have been raised, serves ably as a primer for anticorporate technophobia. The *Star Wars* saga, through Darth Vader, recounts the horror of what happens to the white male body when it is technologized: it is reduced to a black voice, enslaved to the ghastly emperor. Vader's techno-black voice, testifying that "I must obey my master," beckons the white male toward the machine. "Luke, I am your father"—Vader's claim involves not merely genetic but also cybernetic inheritance. The son's body bears the wound passed down by the dark father: a cyborgian replacement limb that marks him as already victim of the machine. This bionic arm measures Luke's gravitation toward his father's own fully technologized fate. When Vader prophesies that Luke will join him on the Dark Side, he tells his son, with every mechanized breath, with every robotic gesture, *You will become techno-black like me*. While owning a share in this grievous condition, Luke refuses to allow technologization to claim him entirely. The threat of technological incorporation instead allows the hero to dramatize his own existence as a story of oppression and transcendence. He confronts and disavows the technological darkness of his paternity so as to retain a free white essence. The son looks upon

Vader—"more machine now than man," as Obi-Wan has warned him.
Samuel R. Delany has emphasized the critical moment of cyborg panic in
this final face-off; battling his technological destiny, Luke has hacked off
Vader's hand to find that "only wires and metal protrude from the severed
wrist."[16] Luke contemplates the slave's smoldering cyber-stump while anxiously flexing his own black bionic hand; he acts decisively to halt his own
incorporation and, finally, removes the black mask of technological mediation, so that father may gaze upon son with his own eyes, his true face. This
return of the Jedi to whiteness, by dramatizing redemption through a
painful encounter with techno-blackness, expresses a crucial routine for
anticorporate narratives of technology.

Star Wars belongs to a constellation of racializing cyberphobic primers
available to Generation X. Coupland's microserfs, to explain the life inva-
sion that the tech corporation has perpetrated against them, invoke a related tale of technology and its belligerent claims on the white male body.
The cubicle slaves have compiled a table of differences between life at Microsoft and life at Apple, but the comparison makes light of the pervasive
similarity in the feel of both corporate campuses: "eerie, *Logan's Run*–like
atmosphere"; "eerie, *Logan's Run*–like atmosphere" (122). In the dystopian
Logan's Run (1976), the fugitive hero seeks refuge from a completely computerized regime. To break out of the system and return to having a life, he
must get past Box. Box, a food-packing robot intent on committing any
human fugitives to the deep freeze, confronts his victims with an over-
weening sense of his own technological grandeur: "Overwhelming, am I
not? . . . I am more than machine or man, more than a fusion of the two."
In movie-making point of fact, Box is a black man in a robot suit; to movie
audiences, he is a black voice speaking from a technological box. Portrayed
by Roscoe Lee Browne, a black actor of "cultured voice and bearing," Box
anticipates Darth Vader as voiced by James Earl Jones.[17]

But despite his objective similarity as a black-voiced machine, in narrative context Box also represents a strain of techno-blackness distinct from
that embodied in Vader. Whereas Luke wrestles with his filiation to the
dark technological father, Logan, the last free white man on earth, never
feels a moment's connection to the menacing Box. For the subject who runs
with Logan, the techno-black is never like me. Bill Nichols's pioneering
study on "The Work of Culture in the Age of Cybernetic Systems" helps
specify the split between Logan's *Run* and Luke's *Wars*, between white flight
and inward fight. Nichols's essay analyzes a range of response to the technological Other: "In postindustrial capitalism, the human is defined in re-

lation to cybernetic systems . . . all of which evoke those forms of ambivalence reserved for the Other that is the measure of ourselves: . . . fascination and attraction, revulsion and resentment."[18] If Luke and Darth lead to the negotiated ambivalences of techno-black posturing, Box leads to the anti-human butchery of *Predator* (1987): an intruder equipped with digital invisibility, ultimately revealed as a dreadlocked alien, played by a towering black actor (Kevin Peter Hall) punching buttons on his cybernetic suit; like Box, a wholly other monster/machine as black man in a hardshell.

To analyze visions of techno-blackness, Nichols's set of terms may be combined with Gubar's. For Nichols, ambivalence toward cybernetic otherness runs from fascinated attraction to resentful revulsion; for Gubar, attitudes toward racial otherness shuttle between welcoming adoption and defensive disavowal. In most of the anticorporate examples discussed in this chapter, these two possibilities for ambivalence—toward technologization and toward blackness—result in the assignment of a different value to each component of otherness that color monitoring has fused. The "Techno-black like me" posture expresses revulsion about technologization but allows for a mixed and carefully limited fascination with blackness; the pose finds attractive the adoption of a virtual blackness to express more vehemently a white resentment toward cybernetic control. But other narratives resolve the potential ambivalences toward technology and blackness with matching gestures of dissociation, running more toward purely defensive revulsion at the (doubly) other. In this class of cyberphobic story, the white subject recoils before the monstrous objects of techno-blackness.

The horror/sci-fi film *Alien* (1979) centers on the convergent threats of the dark alien of the title and the shipboard computer perversely known as "Mother," a machine that acts out the sinister directives of "the Corporation." *Alien* ultimately associates the Alien with the computer, tarring the beast with a technophobic brush; at the same time, as Scott Bukatman suggests, "anxiety about *race*" is "inscribed in the design of the monster."[19] Fleeing this monster, Ripley (Sigourney Weaver) blows up the ship and believes herself to be safe in an escape pod. We see Ripley punching buttons; we see a gleaming metallic surface above the keyboard, presumably part of the onboard computer. Suddenly, a black limb shoots out; it is the Alien, mistaken for computational hardware. *Alien* ends with Ripley blowing the Alien out of her escape pod's hatch. The sequel, *Aliens* (1986), opens with an invader cutting into Ripley's pod through the same airlock—a long, dark snout extends itself through the aperture, trailing a cable. Looking and moving with an uncanny resemblance to the Alien, a black robot creeps into the vessel.

The robot probe arrives ostensibly to save her, but really to re-deliver her into the clutches of the Corporation. *Alien* and *Aliens* present an ancient race of (silicone-based) aliens that look like machines and new machines that look like aliens; both are aligned with the interests of the Corporation, which seeks to use the Aliens *as* a technology. These Alien/machines and their computerized environments exist at the far reaches of the coordinate system defined by Nichols and Gubar—the white subject processes these techno-black entities with defensive revulsion.

Alien or *Star Wars*? Each vector of primal cyberphobia has enjoyed a significant legacy: both the cybernetic alien as ultimate other and the technologized alter ego as the feared fate of the cherished self. But the *Star Wars* scenario, with its more conflicted presentation of techno-blackness as a potential destination of white subjectivity, has proven definitive for the cubicle slave imagination. Rather than the simple loathsomeness of the machinic beast, the dark tragedy of Vader and the anguish of Luke have provided the logic for the most resonant cyberphobic narratives. Along the Vader vector, cyberphobia has continued to evolve for workers who find themselves ever closer to the machine.[20]

what is the matrix?

The year is 1999. On the big screen, an office worker at a high-tech firm cowers in his computer cubicle. The authorities are coming to get him. He has received friendly advice about how to escape. But it is still early in act 1, and somehow he cannot get away—he finds himself trapped in the confines of his corporate workspace. Over the course of the movie, he will learn to free himself from his immobilizing situation, and by story's end he will have achieved true transcendence.

This sketch holds the story arc of *The Matrix,* the biggest movie sensation of 1999. But the same outline describes equally well a much smaller film from the same year, *Office Space.* The two movies could scarcely be more different in genre and provenance: *The Matrix,* an action extravaganza with breakthrough special effects, was a major studio production associated with Silver Pictures, best known for the *Die Hard* and *Lethal Weapon* franchises; *Office Space,* a lightweight comedy, was produced by Cubicle Inc., an independent company associated solely with *Office Space.* Yet both movies draw current from the same fear, technological incorporation, and drive with exhilaration toward the same goal: to liberate the pale male protagonist from his enslavement to the computer. And both films resonated strongly with audiences, continuing to grow in cultural currency long after their releases. *The Matrix* exploded to become a worldview, a lifestyle, and a ubiquitous pseudo-explanatory metaphor for various aspects of contemporary existence. *Office Space* has gathered its own narrower but quite devoted following, entering the finite pantheon of movies that young men quote in conversation; its cult status in this regard has been much noted in the media.[21] A rough analogy may be drawn to a pair of cultural touchstones from the Carter years. If *The Matrix* is the *Star Wars* of the present day, *Office Space* may be its *Caddyshack.* All four films feature young men who learn to triumph against an evil Establishment; in the pair from the Clinton years, the image of the Establishment has become firmly consolidated, across genres, as the high tech corporate workplace.

Color monitoring comes to the fore in implementing the plans for the young man in *Office Space* to strike back against the technological employment that holds him in its clutches. The protagonist, Peter Gibbons (Ron Livingston), whose job consists in going through "thousands of lines of code," has freed his mind and resolved to revolt. The DVD packaging describes him as a "cubicle slave" who refuses "to endure another mind-numbing day at Initech Corporation." He will get back at the slave drivers through an embezzlement scheme: "Human beings were not meant to sit in little cubicles staring at computer screens all day. . . . Let's take enough money so that we never ever have to sit in a cubicle ever again." Peter speaks these inspiring words to his white buddy Michael Bolton (David Herman), with whom he shares a few drinks while plotting revenge. Michael has long daydreamed about a virus that may get them what they want: "It's pretty brilliant. What it does, is every time there's a bank transaction where interest is computed—there are thousands a day—the computer ends up with these fractions of a cent, which it usually rounds off. What this does is it takes those little remainders and puts it into an account." Peter: "This sounds familiar." Michael: "Yeah, they did it in *Superman III.*" Leveraging his anti-cubicle platform, Peter prompts Michael to put his brilliant virus scheme into action. White man to white man, Michael comes clean about his technical limitations: "Look, even if I wanted to, I wouldn't know how to install it. I don't know the credit union's software well enough, okay?" Peter, exhibiting his leadership qualities, delivers a moment of clarity: "Yeah. But *Samir* does." End of fraternal scene of guys at the bar. Cut to them convincing a reluctant Samir, a South Asian immigrant, to do the software installation for them. This too may sound familiar. In *Superman III,* the computer whiz who pulled the heist was played by Richard Pryor.[22] In the updated version, Samir Nagheenanajar (Ajay Naidu) gets the call for technical implementation. Making the shift from black to brown, *Office Space* both sustains a fantasy of racialized division of tech labor and supplies a probabilistic snapshot of how such chores are in fact increasingly apportioned.[23]

Tapping the South Asian immigrant to fill the team's programming slot, the young office worker and his otherwise all-white crew make common cause against the tech corporation under a unifying banner of virtual blackness. On the film's soundtrack, the words of rapper Canibus back that position: "like slave gigs, the boss's favorite to get placed in something spacious, while the most hated get placed in some small cubicle spaces." The insurgent cubicle slaves perform the sacred rites of brotherhood, strutting to the rap beat of the Geto Boys. They seal their pact of anticorporate blackness through the ritual execution of the company's fax machine, which they abduct from the office and drive to a deserted lot. The young men circle the machine deliberately, taking turns with a barrage of vicious kicks and brutal blows with a baseball bat, smashing the electronic device to bits until it begins to cough up fragments of its shattered circuit boards. On the soundtrack accompaniment, the Geto Boys put words to the action: "Die muthafuckas! Die muthafuckas!"[24] The crew strolls off in grim satisfaction, filmed in slo-mo synchronization to this backing track. When Gibbons goes solo and saunters into the office itself for some casual vandalism, the Geto Boys again declare the mood of his achievement: "Damn it feels good to be a gangsta." It feels especially good when one enjoys the full freedom to dictate and revise the terms and conditions of that assumed identity. In *Office Space,* the hero gets to have his gangsta-ism both ways. As a kind of low-level manager, he performs the corporate maneuver of passing down the computer labor to the dark-skinned other.[25] But as a resentful hireling, he passes himself off as a kindred to the racial other, rising in violent rebellion against the corporate machine. In the hybrid figure of this cubicle warrior, *Money* magazine manager meets *Mondo 2000* punk.

In aligning the hero's insurrection with the voices of black anger, *Office Space* tears a page from *Mondo,* which also used rap to supply the backing beats for its anticorporate rants. Touting tunes for hip (and mostly white) hackers, *Mondo* enlisted rebels for its cause through spotlight artist features; one typical article heralds the "Prophets of Rage: The Disposable Heroes of Hiphoprisy":

A new prophet of conscience is stomping towards the millennium. With a mouthful of rage and a trunkload of funk, the Disposable Heroes of Hiphoprisy have arrived—redefining rap and revitalizing the technorevolution.[26]

The lead vocalist, who "drops science in a booming baritone," explains the group's name: "If you're a young black person, your role models are athletes and entertainers. . . . You see these people used by the corporate system to make money, after which they're thrown on the scrap heap. They're disposable heroes" (73).

The Matrix, while driven by a pervasively anticorporate plotline, makes use of its own share of disposable black heroes. In *Mondo* fashion, *The Matrix* looks to prophetic blackness as the conscience of the technorevolution and simultaneously, as in the management-affiliated aspects of *Office Space* resistance, runs that revolution with a racialized division of technolabor. Overall, *The Matrix* contains more facets of color monitoring than perhaps any other text discussed in this book. It utilizes peripheral black characters in support of its Hollywood action heroism, and in a way that, as with the great American techno-thriller, reasserts the endurance of a national identity within a post-national future. The narrative organizes these parts into a well-oiled anticorporate machine, brought to you by big-budget Hollywood in slick cyberpunk packaging.

Given this tension between stance and funding, a position somewhat paradoxical but far from irresolvable, the filmmakers had the wit to commence the anticorporate gestures before the action even begins, taking ostensibly subversive aim at the studio that distributed their creative product. For the trademark footage of the WB logo and Warner Bros. film lots, the directors replaced the familiar golden and sun-drenched hues with a sickly green phosphor glow, reprocessing the camerawork from smooth cinematic sweep to the ominous flicker of electronic surveillance. On a commentary track on the DVD, visual effects director John Gaeta explains the significance of this tweak to the opening footage: "We wanted to alter the logos of the studios, mostly because we felt that they were an evil empire, bent on breaking the creative juices of the average director or writer. So we felt that desecrating the studio symbols was an important message to the audience that we basically reject the system."

The film quickly follows this subliminal mocking subversion with a clear image of "the system" that the narrators would oppose. We see the hero, the hacker Neo (Keanu Reeves), suffering the indignities of his day job with Metacortex Inc., "one of the top software companies in the world." Here he works amidst the Core Techs under his slave name, Thomas Anderson. *The Matrix* famously hinges on the sensational revelation that this workaday world is only an illusion. "The Matrix" is a massive computer simulation, which the vast majority of humans now perceive as their only reality; with their minds trapped in cyberspace, their bodies are harnessed for use as batteries to power the sentient computers that now rule the world. The form of that revelation, the total triumph of technology over Mother Nature, conveys a common horror of the information age.[27] But at the same time, that horrifying realization makes possible the movie's key escapist fantasy: not only does one's day job as a cubicle worker ultimately fail to define one's true identity, it does not even belong to reality. That is, one of the most brilliant strokes of *The Matrix* is to present an ostensibly terrifying revelation that many people wish were the sublime truth. *The Matrix* tells us that the squeaky-clean world of digital drudgery is a lie, albeit a cover story for an even more complete computer enslavement. For the individual offered knowledge of this true state of affairs, the nightmare vision—of the human race as unwitting puppets of computer simulation—creates a space for a personally satisfying dream. Neo wakes up to a world where everything is wrong, where the fear of technology's consuming control over the human body has been literalized—but it is a world where everything is now set right with him individually.

The old reality, in which the anglo Thomas Anderson serves out a life sentence as the core of tech support, passes away. The virtual cubicle vanishes, supplanted by a gritty reality in which he joins a multicultural team to fight the machines.[28] The means of counterstrike involve more than a touch of cyberphilia, as the assault on the global computer system depends upon jacking back into the world of virtual reality, grabbing plenty of cool weapons and gear, and taking the war to the oppressive digital infrastructure.[29] But it is a contingent cyberphilia of a stripe modeled in *Mondo 2000,* one that relishes the liberatory possibilities of maximum digital overdrive while eschewing anything that smacks of cubicle work. High-tech hype works best when it touts products to overcome the discontents of computer civilization. In "Escaping the Desktrap: Wearables!" for instance, *Mondo* advocates a better connection with personal computers, not as an escape from the flesh, but as a pathway to liberate the flesh from the desktop. In such circumstances, one is not slipping down the slope to disembodiment, but rather becoming pragmatically more wired and less tired. Break those shackles that bind you to the keyboard; "Over 25 million U.S. jobs require typing: wearables could free a lot of these people from their desktraps."[30]

"Welcome to the real world"—thus Morpheus (Laurence Fishburne) introduces Neo to existence outside the Matrix. In the real world, Neo, unlike that bored keyboard drudge Thomas Anderson, doesn't have to do any typing whatsoever. In this newly revealed real world, where a proper relationship to technology is being reestablished by the resistance, black folks take care of all the messy networking details. Neo and his white love interest Trinity, with their idealized hacker names, enjoy the soaring freedoms of cyberspace. The functionally named Tank, the black technician, does the work of hooking up the heroes and getting them into and out of the Matrix: "Tank, I need an exit!" becomes the instrumentalizing beam-me-up mantra of our cyber-escapists.[31] Tank's fingers flit across the keyboard and make it so. With a cheery greeting worthy of Ma Bell—"I'm Tank, I'll be your operator!"—the solicitous black man plugs the trigger-happy couple into the biggest video game on earth and brings them safely back home to the flesh when cyber-playtime is over.

Tank's character presents the ideal of what I called the "natural machine" in the previous chapter. As he beamingly informs the newcomer Neo, Tank and his big brother Dozer are both "one hundred percent pure old-fashioned home-grown human," each born "in the real world" as a "genuine child of Zion." He can thus serve as the perfect mediator between less naturally embodied humans and the machine. He plays the role analyzed by Eldridge Cleaver: "It is in this connection that the blacks, personifying the Body . . . provide the saving link, the bridge between man's biology and man's machines." Because of their nature, Tank and [Bull]dozer, pure humans named after earthy tools, are perfectly suited to doing all the digital heavy lifting.

Tank and Dozer also turn out to be disposable supplements to the heroes; both of the brothers suffer fatal blastings, with Tank holding on just long enough to connect a final sequence of exits. The first movie does not even make clear that Tank dies; his role as an interchangeable tool renders his person so disposable that his death takes place not only offscreen but without remark. But, apparently, die he did, and the resistance continues to need operators. For the sequel, *The Matrix Reloaded* (2003), the team must recruit another networking expert. The racialized pattern holds true, providing further confirmation that the casting for such roles is not random; the second time around, a dreadlocked Harold Perrineau Jr. portrays the rebel ship's operator.[32] Reloading his character, the screenwriters perfect the technique of functional labeling: this black networking whiz goes by the name of Link.

These peripheral characters complete their tours of digital duty in support of the great struggle, nominally plotted as humans versus machines. But their service also fuels a specifically American fantasy of the type analyzed in chapter 2's discussion of "tools for national recovery." Beyond the verbalized plot of *The Matrix*, which refers to the enemy as "the machines," the visual coding specifies the national origin of the tyrannical computers. Appearing in the very opening shot, a closeup of a monitor, and running throughout the movie, the "Matrix code" underpinning the deceptive cyber-reality descends in cascading strings across the ship's computer screens, glowing greenly on the huddled human faces that must remain vigilant. The non-numeric portions of the coded strings consist entirely of Japanese characters.[33] Thus the computers that got out of hand are identified as the product of imperial Japanese technology, while it falls to the multi-ethnic group of Americans to liberate the human race from this insidious enslavement. By their spoken idiom, we know the identity of the resistance group inferentially as some outcome of American culture, but as they inhabit a postapocalyptic world ruled by information technology, in the year 2199 or later, we could imagine that such border-based labels may have lost all meaning. A careful inspection, however, reveals that such is not the case; the hot rod hovercraft of the resistance bears these words stamped proudly on its hull: "Made in the U.S.A."

This brand of selectively anticorporate cyberphobia reaches back to the foundations of cyberpunk. In Bruce Sterling's posthumanist saga *Schismatrix* (1985), the hero, freelance diplomat Lindsay Abelard, travels a fragmented universe, negotiating with the various zaibatsus that have carved up space. In adopting the Japanese term *zaibatsu*—"wealth clique"—to refer to corporate collectives, Sterling invokes the cyberpunk convention, popularized by William Gibson in *Neuromancer* (1984), that the dynastic Japanese megacorporation will form the basic political unit of the future.[34] So, as in *The Matrix, Schismatrix* shows its anglo hero in relief against an implicitly Asian corporate techno-establishment.[35] To evade the control of the zaibatsus and attain his goal of a return to life on Earth, Lindsay has enlisted the aid of two "matte-black" techno-beings known as "Lobsters." Wearing shades of Vader, these dark, hard-shelled, "faceless posthumans, their eyes and ears wired to sensors woven through their suits," speak with "an electronic churning noise" (220, 226). The Lobster who serves as the ship's navigator "was known simply as Pilot" (220). As suits his fully wired existence, Pilot goes by a quintessentially cybernetic handle; the term *cybernetics,* we may recall, derives from *kubernētēs,* the Greek word for steersman. To obtain Pilot's services, the hero communicates through another Lobster, a business contact "they called 'The Modem.'" (221). These techno-entities, blackened by technology, have been reduced to purely instrumental identities.[36] Like Tank and Link in *The Matrix* trilogy, *Schismatrix*'s Pilot and Modem derive their functional names from transportation and telecommunication; they carry and connect the hero to get him where and how he needs to be.[37]

In *The Matrix,* Morpheus stands out as a black character less evidently reduced to a simple technological function. As commanding captain and not merely pilot of a craft, Morpheus holds an important post in the resistance, and much discussion of race in the Matrix universe has noted his "positive" role as a black man in a position of leadership.[38] While I would not deny the majesty of Fishburne's portrayal as providing the basis for a "positive" image, I would encourage a closer consideration of the role's parameters. For one thing, to cite Fishburne's own words, the role of Morpheus is notably de-physicalized in an otherwise hyperkinetic action picture: "My character's main focus is on intellect and faith."[39] With respect to the pugilistic Neo, Morpheus serves up wisdom to the master-in-training and acts as his punching-bag sparring partner. When Morpheus finally enters the cyber-fray, he does so as self-sacrificing victim.

Less obviously but perhaps more crucially, Morpheus greases the wheels of a particular transaction in the anticorporate fantasy. As he gives Neo an orientation tour to "the desert of the real," he teaches Neo to identify the enemy in terms that will prove essential in sealing their pact of shared rebellion. "What is the Matrix?" he asks. "*Control.*" Morpheus explains that the simulation was designed by the machines to "keep us under control." This explanation resonates with the notion that most troubles Neo: "I don't like the idea that I'm not in control of my life." Morpheus responds with an immediate and fervent affirmation of Neo's sentiment: "I know *exactly* what you mean." The black man's declaration of perfect identification with Neo's objection to not being his own master sets up the formulation toward which Morpheus's exposition has steadily been building. The Matrix exists, Morpheus tells his brother in arms, "to blind you from the truth. . . . That you are a *slave,* Neo. Born into bondage." In bestowing upon the protagonist this highest term in the sweepstakes of oppression, Morpheus completes his function in the film's racial fantasy: to ratify the disgruntled cubicle worker's claim to virtual blackness and to elevate that virtuality to authenticity. The wise black man knows *exactly* how you feel; he is qualified and prepared to authorize your claim that computer technology has made you a slave.

playing the techno-race card

In construing tech work as black work, this pose confirms a major premise of the narratives examined in the preceding chapter. The fact that both techie underlings and upper management can conceive of computer work as a kind of racializing slavery shows how anticorporate poses can serve the ends of corporate narrators. The case of *Mondo 2000* supplies an instructive general instance of this cross-platform compatibility of the would-be subversive message, aimed to discomfit the pointy-haired Dilbertian boss but readily appropriated by corporate discourse. Jon Lebkowsky spotlights this magazine's importance with the assertion that "the evolution of a bohemian, technohip subculture within the vibrant and elastic culture of today was mediated by two important events. One was the opening of the Internet. The other was the appearance of *Mondo 2000*."[40] This glossy manifesto-mad magazine for all things hacker-related concocted a "strange hybrid of 60s counterculture and 80s libertarianism" blended with "post-punk irreverence, drugged-up pranksterism, and high style" (16). But the former editor-in-chief of the *Mondo* tribe, one "R. U. Sirius," retrospectively recognizes a problem of his rebellious discourse's adaptability to unforeseen ends:

> Cyberculture (a meme that I'm at least partly responsible for generating, incidentally) has emerged as a gleeful apologist for this kill-the-poor trajectory of the Republican revolution. You find it all over *Wired*. . . .

> It's particularly sad and poignant for me to witness how comfortably the subcultural contempt for the normal, the hunger for novelty and change, and the basic anarchistic temperament that was at the core of *Mondo 2000* fits the hip, smug, boundary-breaking, fast-moving, no-time-for-social-niceties world of your wired mega-corporate info/comm/media players. You can find our dirty fingerprints, our rhetoric, all over their advertising style. The joke's on me. (23)

R. U. Sirius here devotes a moment of sobriety to contemplating a general issue of complicity that has frequently been identified by other political observers: that the ideology of cyber-libertarianism meshes smoothly with agendas ranging from broad deregulation to welfare reform and, what's more, that hipster irony can do wonders to boost corporate sales. What I think has been generally overlooked is the role of race in authorizing transfers between cyber-anticorporatism and corporate marketing. One unremarked form of "boundary-breaking" in the rhetoric Sirius cites involves a racial posturing that equates the overworked techie with the exploited black man, that bestows upon the authentic hacker the street cred of the racially oppressed. Corporate narrative has lifted *Mondo*'s fingerprints and has learned to speak to the tech worker in a way that validates such posturing, expressing sympathy with its target audience while permitting both narrator and audience to share a simulacral sympathy for the historical black condition. Through such narration, the corporation addressing tech workers assures its largely white male audience that it feels their pain. That message comes bundled with a nod to the civil rights struggle, a credentialing ethos to demonstrate that the corporate speaker shares an understanding of the history of racial oppression.[41] Such rhetoric is indeed "all over their advertising style." And you will find it "all over *Wired*."

Advertising in *Wired* has consistently demonstrated just how fluently the big "info/comm/media players" can speak the lingo of racial technologic. A Microsoft ad in *Wired* addresses the harried tech worker: "Do you have a tight grip on your projects, or is it the other way around?" (June 2002, "Reinvent" issue, 25). The two-page photo that accompanies this query conveys the overwhelming sensation of despair that corresponds to the latter circumstance: it shows to *Wired* readers a man caught in the grip of his computer labor, placing these readers for a moment in his shoes. The reader sees the workspace from the same perspective as the tired man in the picture: seated at a desk shot as a woozy blur of three-ring technical manual, empty paper coffee cup, and searing-white spreadsheet on the monitor, the man has averted his eyes from the computer that looms before him, framing his head. The overworked man, in wrinkled shirt with rolled-up sleeves, has turned his face slightly to one side, so that the reader can see that he has pushed his glasses up onto his brow in a gesture of frustrated exhaustion. The man in this picture is black. What he needs, what the reader invited to identify with his plight needs, is Microsoft Project Standard: "a better way for you to manage your projects and keep your projects from managing you." Microsoft massages this pitch to a predominantly white readership with a visible if unspoken message: *Does your work make you feel like a black man? We know exactly how you feel.*

An analogous sympathetic appeal may be used to motivate the skilled tech worker to upgrade employers. A "Wired Market: recruitment" ad shows a black man typing at the keyboard (157). An arrow pointing to his head may be traced back to a bulleted enumeration of his relevant job "experience":

- resolving Unix problems
- working lots of overtime with little reward.

The wary reader may suspect an ill-concealed subtext in the would-be employer's purring mind: "Ah! So you're *used* to being exploited for your technical know-how? You'd be *per*fect for us!" The ad, of course, promises to deliver the employee out of bondage and into the promised land, with "compensation that rewards performance." The allusion to the reader's dark past, of Unix overtime with little reward, merely aims to prove the employer's bona fides in the form of an understanding of the tech worker's suffering. It is an eminently knowing allusion to an all-too-common scenario. Neal Stephenson's cypherpunk opus *Cryptonomicon* (1999) speaks on behalf of true hackers everywhere when he recounts the bitter educational experience of his present-day protagonist, an exploited white technologist:

> Within a month of his arrival, Randy solved some trivial computer problems for one of the other grad students. A week later, the chairman of the astronomy department called him over and said, "So, you're the UNIX guru." At the time, Randy was still stupid enough to be flattered by this attention, when he should have recognized them as bone-chilling words.
>
> Three years later, he left the Astronomy Department without a degree, and with nothing to show for his labors except six hundred dollars in his bank account and a staggeringly comprehensive knowledge of UNIX.[42]

The corporate recruitment ad in *Wired* assures prospective employees that nothing so ugly as *that* would ever happen at State Farm, ranked highly in *Computerworld*'s "Best Places to Work." Have you been treated like a black man? "Come to work on one of the world's largest computer networks" if you are ready to experience a "workplace that celebrates diversity."[43] White men blackened by technology are encouraged to apply.

This come-on to the *Wired* worker forms a counterpoint to the *Forbes*-style technology advertising analyzed in the preceding chapter. *Forbes* addresses investors and management; *Wired* addresses the managed, whose technological productivity is expected to make the investments pay off. Factoring in these distinct rhetorical occasions, *Forbes* and *Wired* advertisers build their respective narratives on complementary fantasies of empowerment. *Forbes* narration flatters a high-level corporate subjectivity that would claim *privilege,* whereas *Wired* narration appeals to a lower-level or anticorporate subjectivity that would claim *entitlement.* The *Forbes* narration prepares management to believe that a technology investment will reap rich rewards—with someone *else* handling all the headache-inducing details. *Wired* pitchwork speaks to the labor pool that supplies the corporation's "someone else," those workers configured, in compliance with corporate narrative, for management to utilize in technical support of a hands-free relationship to technology. Corporate privilege assumes the power of rank, enjoying the right of sending undesirable tech work down the chain of command. Operating within this same framework, an anticorporate pose derives a sense of entitlement for claiming reparations both monetary and intangible in the workplace and beyond, by elevating the burdens of hard technical labor to a level of fashionable victimhood. Both of these transactions, premised upon a denigration of tech work, may be facilitated by the figure of the technologized black man. In the eyes of technophobic management, the black man represents the ideal tech worker, the other guy who takes care of the computers; from the perspective of the overtime tech worker, blackness supplies the metaphor for understanding and imaginatively capitalizing on one's sense of enslavement to the machine.

Stephenson's *Cryptonomicon,* even while sympathizing with the plight of hackers, delivers a sharp satire of the racializing pose. An army detachment of white men assigned to undertake information warfare has been ordered to break out the Shinola and perform a mission in blackface.[44] The title of the relevant protocol manual succinctly conveys Stephenson's attitude toward the exercise:

Tactical Negro Impersonation
   Volume III: Negroes of the Caribbean (375)

This theater of the absurd makes a point that applies broadly to the texts analyzed in the present chapter: the assumption of techno-blackness is, first and foremost, a tactic. The "Caribbean" designation takes aim at the preferred cyberpunk flavoring of this game familiar from William Gibson's penchant for rastas in cyberspace and "the reggae-flavored data havens of Bruce Sterlings *Islands in the Net*."[45] Moreover, the subtitle's echo of the Disneyland fantasy identifies tactical techno-blackness as a safe ride that young information workers can enjoy whenever it suits them. The pose plugs into a highly commodified entertainment conditioning, a formula with proven appeal for children of all ages.

With *Cryptonomicon,* Stephenson strikes a note new to our study of color monitoring—and not just because of his deft mocking of the black-face act. Congruently, as Jay Clayton notes, Stephenson's work demonstrates a deep commitment to a literary understanding of the internal narratives of technological artifice.[46] With his Baroque Cycle (2003–04), Stephenson has deemed the quest for computing as a heroic undertaking worthy of celebration in a narrative of commensurate grandeur, one that commences with an intricately engineered sonnet and builds a vastly complex plot over thousands of science-savvy pages. His work delves with loving gusto into the very space that the narrators studied in these first four chapters ordinarily shun and denigrate.

We have surveyed various forms of cyberphobia. Chapter 1 showed how Hollywood constructs the masculine whiteness of the action hero in opposition to the confined blackness of the computer expert. Chapter 2 explored how, while continuing to devalue computer labor as such, the American techno-thriller makes a virtue of black technical expertise as a sign of successful colonial containment. Taking up the rhetoric of technology marketing aimed at corporate managers, chapter 3 analyzed the promise that well-regulated black bodies will keep all technical details well out of sight. In these narratives, technology is itself figured as black, blackness is figured as technological, and white privilege is defined as technology-free. Looking at complementary instances of anticorporate narratives, we have here critiqued the complaint of technology workers that life in the computer cubicle has left them feeling black. Across these narrative forms, the logic of color monitoring feeds the assumptions of escapist entertainment to both the tech-averse bosses and the disaffected tech workers raging against the machine. Sharing a mantra for the digital age, would-be rebel and corporate spokesperson alike trumpet the free-spirit imperative to "think outside the box." One unexamined logic of that popular slogan involves leaving the difficult, mathematical, scientific, rule-based programming of the black box to lesser others. In constructing a technology-free ideal, color monitoring equates engagement in technology with a loss of creativity, autonomy, and humanity.

Consequently, this study concludes with cultural examples whose very existence challenges those cyberphobic equations. Denizens of the humanities, I fear, tend in particular to harbor and even cherish technophobic assumptions. All the more reason that a critique emanating from within a humanistic discipline should uphold literary achievements that pursue, as Stephenson does, a writing of the "Technologick Arts." The authors to whom we now turn our attention strategically ally technology and art to think inside the black box.

chapter five

THINKING INSIDE THE BLACK BOX

Composed as a coda to *Color Monitors,* this chapter highlights creative alternatives to the racializing tendencies of cyberphobic culture. In this sampling of narratives that operate outside the closed circuit of color monitoring, the art of technological poetics unifies a superficially disparate group of authors willing to think inside the black box of technology. These authors—whether published with turntables or on the Internet, in sci-fi pulp editions or literary hardbacks—constitute a coherent counterweb to a cyberphobic imagination that reserves the creative act for the white, tech-free human individual and construes technological networks as antihuman mechanisms of dominating destruction.

The most hysterically cyberphobic position finds a spokesman in Michael Crichton's *The Lost World,* a book all about extinction—and not necessarily just that of the dinosaurs. The brilliant Dr. Ian Malcolm, playing to an anxious audience, charts the course of human history:

"In ten thousand years human beings have gone from hunting to farming to cities to cyberspace. Behavior is screaming forward, and it might be nonadaptive. Nobody knows. Although personally, I think cyberspace means the end of our species."

"Yes? Why is that?"

"Because it means the end of innovation," Malcolm said. "This idea that the whole world is wired together is mass death. . . . We're planning to put five billion people together in cyberspace. And it'll freeze the entire species. . . . Everyone will think the same thing at the same time." (311–12)

Here, the primary cyber-menace, posed as a threat to creativity, attacks the human as such.

In giving figurative form to that fear, cyberphobic narratives from *Forbidden Planet* to *Alien* often involve awakening a primitive, ancient evil that gives birth to a futuristic doom. In the apocalyptic *Alien vs. Predator* (2004), a convergent recap of this tradition of revulsion, the black, machinelike aliens burst forth from a pyramid buried deep beneath the earth's surface; a swarming aggregate, they come to enslave individuals and destroy humanity. Going to work on the influential premise of oppressive alien artifice, the musical manifesto of Parliament's *Mothership Connection* (1975) proceeds instead from a position of technocultural pride: "We have returned to claim the pyramids," announces songwriter and vocalist George Clinton, broadcasting a message about "once upon a time called now." In popular lore, the mystery of the pyramids, their allegedly inexplicable technical advancement, has been attributed to aliens. Parliament playfully adopts an "out-of-this-world view" and embraces that technological legacy: we are the people who have been treated as nonhumans, come to take credit for "alien" Egyptian innovation and reclaim it for creative use.[1] Reawakening the slumbering beings in the pyramids, reuniting with "Dr. Funkenstein's" children, and sending out a signal from the "home of the extra-terrestrial brothers," Parliament's "connection" constitutes a network for mobilizing all that technophobia has deemed alien and monstrous. Exploring sonic geometry and computational possibility across the information age, from go-go and mainframes to hip-hop and laptops, George Clinton and The P-Funk Allstars have continued to celebrate *The Awesome Power of a Fully-Operational Mothership* (1996), an album that includes an ode to "Mathematics" wrapped in an admonition to the fans: "Didn't I tell you funkleheads to cop computers?!" Listening for agents making the connection on this frequency, this study concludes by tuning in to authors who partake of an alternative groove with the machine: authors with an affinity for music and number, for poetry and code; authors who know the appeal named and enacted in Zapp's 1985 song "Computer Love"; authors who can feel that love and who willingly think inside the black box.[2]

Simply by creating, the practitioners of technological poetics confront a recurring nightmare of the cyberphobic imagination, a nightmare in which digitality threatens human creativity as such. In *No Maps for these Territories* (2000), futurist William Gibson sees the creative human as a species endangered by a technologically supercharged environment: "We are all accelerating towards some null point of posthumanity." Gibson, the founder of cyberpunk, characterizes his genre as one defined by "fantasies of anxiety."[3] Nor does his definition seem aberrant: although cyberpunk fiction is closely associated with hype and hope about new technologies, its narratives, like Crichton's techno-thrillers, typically feed upon fears of those same technologies and their implications for the human. As "we" hurtle into cyberspace, Gibson predicts, a "null point" awaits. That we lack maps for these territories may prove beside the point if the landscape—and our existence in it—proves as flat and featureless as this vision implies.[4]

But perhaps the author of *Count Zero* has left something out of his account: destination digital consists not merely of the "null," but of zeros and ones—in theory, a terrain with infinite possibilities.[5] A countervailing body of testimony exists, forged by artists whose creative visions of digitality point neither to nullity nor to any singular "point" whatsoever. In *Rhythm Science* (2004), Paul D. Miller, a.k.a. DJ Spooky, That Subliminal Kid, acknowledges the tendency that Gibson and Crichton fear, but he does not consider it inevitable. Yes, a world reduced to the informational nullity of the "same" would amount to a kind of "living death"—"unfortunately, that's how much of the culture works. But there are those—from Jamaican dub artists to Silicon Valley engineers—who want to counter this entropy. They propagate what Amiri Baraka calls 'the changing same.'"[6] Linking technological musicians and inventive technologists under the sign of poetic theory, Miller declares that "art is our guide to the new terrains we have opened within ourselves, in pursuit of techne and logos" (32).[7] This journey need not begin from the position of unquestioning cyberphilia, as Miller's frank speculation suggests: "Taking elements of our own alienated consciousness and recombining them . . . just might be a way of seeking to reconcile the damage rapid technological advances have wrought on our collective consciousness" (72). Spooky has read his William Gibson (100) and knows where an anxious culture is at, but he concludes with an open-ended homage to the Mothership Connection, that model for appropriating alien-ated technology: "remember—as George Clinton said so many years ago: 'Think! It ain't illegal yet!'" (117). Such a reminder may apply with particular relevance to the largely unthought zone of the black box. In the layout for *Rhythm Science,* designers Cornelia Blatter and Marcel Hermans have "sampled the sampler," re-envisioning the words of the laptop-playing DJ who loves to "spin narratives" (120, 12). A two-page spread prints the following string: "digital. code is rhythm is algorithm is digital. code is" (26–27). The fragments at the edges imply a loop: "code is digital"; completed thus, the statement tends toward Gibson's null point, collapsing into an apparent tautology. But Miller's expanded declaration, inserted between the ends of this loop, breaks in to enrich the short-circuit, to join rhythm with science, to find music in the code, to discover "another fusion of arte, techne, and logos" (72).

Miller significantly attributes his hunger for the new structures generated through rhythm science to his "annoyance and frustration with almost all the conventional forms of race, culture, and class hierarchies" (65). Miller's project anticipates "the development of a community of exchange . . . beyond the parochial identity politics of the 1990s," a project that nevertheless would not deny the history of "racial oppression" (53, 61). Looking to that history and its echoes throughout the information age, the critique of color monitoring makes legible one connection between cyber-creativity and the negation of a particular form of racial hierarchy. Thoughtful transformations of identity crafted by writers who engage the technological muse cut against the logic analyzed in the preceding chapters. Working creatively through the formal structures of digitality, these artists tend to avoid the racializing dynamics demonstrated here to be a by-product of cyberphobic culture. In an information society, to relate to technology as a black box requires the construction of an other to tend to the box's inner workings. But authors willing to investigate that box have no such practical or psychological need for divisions of technological labor, racial or otherwise.

In the interpretation of machine dreams, whether nightmarish or hopeful, cyberanalysis finds valuable resources in the work of Thomas Pynchon, persistent diagnostician of technological wounds to the human psyche. Pynchon's fiction probes a pervasive source of anxiety for the twentieth century and beyond: the perceived breakdown of the distinction between the animate and the inanimate. *The Crying of Lot 49*—whose title alone intimates the possible breakdown—opens with a scene of televisual distress, a basic scenario whose power to unsettle has only increased in the age of the PC monitor: the protagonist stands in a room, "stared at by the greenish dead eye of the TV tube." Facing such unnerving behavior from the realm of the nominally inanimate, Pynchon's characters begin to doubt their "own animateness" (V., 229). Forcing the issue of what Timothy Melley has called "agency panic," Pynchon's novels trace the divergent strategies his characters pursue to cope with this wound to human subjectivity.[8]

For the most part, dogged good humor and genuine curiosity sustain Pynchon's hapless antiheroes and-heroines. They navigate a stumbling picaresque course, in tentative cohabitation with the dubiously inanimate, not quite at home in the universe; they learn to "think about being a schlemihl, about a world of things that had to be watched out for" (V., 413). That vigilance, a looking out for things, can suggest both defensive wariness and gentle care; from a position of awkwardness and perplexity, one may begin to investigate.[9] In Pynchon's work, this coping strategy of a self-conscious truce with things exists in relation to two behavioral attractors: domination and creativity, poles that anchor two bases for community. While seeking to resist the former, Pynchon's sympathetic principals draw hope from the latter.

The dominant mode, constituting what Pynchon portrays as a system of death, calls for mastery. If one can no longer rely on the distinction that human = animate / inhuman = inanimate, if one's presumed status as animate no longer guarantees any more subjectivity than that apparently possessed by the inanimate, one can assert one's human belonging via mastery, a mastery that treats others—whether nominally human or nonhuman—as objects. Depicting this way of death, "Mondaugen's story" takes us into the hell of colonial rule in Southwest Africa (V., chapter 9, 242–97). Faced with the classic Pynchonian crisis of animacy, the colonizers bond together: "Community may have been the only solution possible against such an assertion of the Inanimate" (289). But the community depends upon a perverse compact of subjugation, making "neighbors" of colonial white men who "use" the "manacled" Hottentots and Hereros (289). As masters who "use" the blacks, the white men assert their own shared subjectivity against the threat of the Inanimate through the production of human objects. The infernal tale concludes with the ritual execution of a black man—one in a series of such atrocities—as the white men beat "its" body (295).

Immediately following this brutal narrative, with its genealogy of the twentieth century as a story of racial genocide, Pynchon presents an alternative picture of community in chapter 10, "In which various sets of young people get together" (298–323). Calling the changes on this new tune,

jazzman McClintic Sphere enjoys a quite different relation to the inanimate:

> Every recording date of McClintic's he'd got into the habit of talking
> electricity with the audio men and technicians in the studio. . . . One
> day last summer he got around to talking stochastic music and digital
> computers with one technician. Out of the conversation had come
> Set/Reset, which was getting to be a signature for the group. He had
> found out from this sound man about a two-triode circuit called a
> flip-flop, which when it was turned on could be one of two ways, de-
> pending on which tube was conducting and which was cut off: set or
> reset, flip or flop. (*V.*, 311)

Pynchon here introduces an incipiently technical artist, an experimenter
with things rather than a master of objects. Nor does he become a servile
victim of the machine.[10] Sphere plays his own circuitous compositions: a
music that, in the logical sequence of the novel, substitutes for sacrifice.

These two successive chapters in *V.* present divergent takes on the crisis of
animacy: subjects who dominate objects; people thinking things through,
thinking through things, to make music. Preferring the latter philosophy as a
first step in *How to Bring the Sciences into Democracy,* Bruno Latour has proposed that "associations between humans and nonhumans" replace the
"polemical" concept of "the subject-object pair."[11] DJ Spooky similarly presents the coalescence that is *Rhythm Science* "rather than the old twentieth-
century inheritance of the Cartesian subject-object relation" (84). In terms
richly resonant to readers of Pynchon, Latour characterizes the border relations maintained under the subject-object distinction as "militarized"; in
place of this regime, Latour envisions a "civil" collectivity of humans and
nonhumans (243). Pynchon's novels forever seek the possibility of civilian relations within a militarized world of the subjugating and the objectified.

The graffiti network that links *V.* to *Gravity's Rainbow* may serve to illustrate this endeavor. Both novels present spontaneously-propagating
webs of communal icons, beacons for a civil collectivity, alternative agents
found in the interstitial spaces of the militarized system. *V.* archives Kilroy;
Gravity's Rainbow introduces Rocketman; both work as crossover artists of
the animate and inanimate. "Inanimate," but a reliable "onlooker," the famous face of G.I. Kilroy graces the pages of *V.* and alley walls around the
world (*V.*, 469–70):

Investigating this immortal visage, Pynchon has unearthed a seldom-recounted legend of Kilroy's birth:

> His true origins forgotten, he was able to ingratiate himself with the human world. . . . Kilroy had sprung into life, in truth, as part of a band-pass filter, thus:

"Kilroy was here" began as a circuit diagram: a symbol, quite literally, of Resistance—not to mention Inductance and Capacitance. *Gravity's Rainbow* introduces Kilroy's cousin, memorialized as the wall inscription "Rocketman was here" (*GR*, 624). This trace marks Tyrone Slothrop's ascent as "Rocketman" to hero of the "Counterforce" network, on his way to becoming a distributed presence, a tenuously "integral creature" (*GR*, 740). The band-pass filter, on a diplomatic mission to a war-torn human world, assumes the guise of Kilroy; Slothrop, ranging across the postwar zone, hovers around the militarized boundary; like a circuit, he must be integrated (*GR*, 527). To catch Rocketman's message, to join the congregation of the Counterforce, henceforth requires the technology of what Pynchon calls "The Low-Frequency Listener" (*GR*, 681). For that attentive tuning, the resistance needs sensitive circuitry, to be recovered from Kilroy's obscured origins. The band-pass filter earns its name by filtering for specific frequencies: it enables frequencies within a certain band to pass. Who knows but that, on the lower frequencies, the band-pass listens for us?

The first broadcast on those "lower frequencies" went out from the basement conclusion of Ellison's *Invisible Man* (568). Picking up Ellison's signal, the network of the lower frequencies has grown to include a playlist from Pynchon to Clinton to Miller. Another newcomer to this amplified band, novelist Colson Whitehead has garnered immediate comparisons to Ellison with his debut, *The Intuitionist* (1999). Critics making the connection have tended to highlight the authors' shared texture of "racial allegory."[12] I would add that both of Whitehead's novels so far, *The Intuitionist* and *John Henry Days* (2001), rethink racial identity through tales of technology. *The Intuitionist* features Lila Mae Watson, elevator inspector. The book's title is Lila Mae's badge of honor, earned for her unorthodox methodology. She subscribes to the revolutionary technological vision of *Theoretical Elevators,* penned by one James Fulton, which teaches that "we must tend to our objects and treat them as newborn babes" (38). For this attitude of concern toward the nonhuman world, the practitioners of Fulton's inspection methods have been labelled "intuitionists." This pejorative expression polemically indicates the disdain of the mainstream inspectors, who think of themselves as "empiricists." But as Lila Mae learns more about Fulton and his actual engineering practice, she begins to puzzle over this factional distinction; embarking on an intellectual pilgrimage, she questions Mr. Reed, one of the early converts to Fulton's thinking, on how empiricism could be reconciled with intuitionism.

The venerable scholar of elevator engineering explains that, in fact, the two views need not be taken as antithetical: "They're not as incompatible as you might think." In Mr. Reed's account of *Theoretical Elevators,* the goal of synthesis calls for "a renegotiation of our relationship to objects" (62).[13] Fulton has sought the perfect elevator, which requires a perfect understanding of what Mr. Reed refers to as "the black box" (63). To truly get inside the black box, to take it into account with accurate concern, demands nothing less than a new contract between humans and things.[14] This renegotiation makes possible the reconciliation of empiricism and intuitionism. Empiricism, in the conventional view from the subject position, means objectivity, a consequence of the subject's objective distance; "intuitionism" refuses that implicit distance from things, a refusal that has traditionally suggested a collapse into subjectiveness. The theoretical boundary vanishes after a renegotiation that sets aside the subject-object pair in favor of a collective constituted on the relations of humans and nonhumans.

Only then, as Latour similarly proposes, can participant observers make good on the promise of empiricism. In Whitehead's novel, fulfilling that promise means getting closer to the machine.

In the universe of *The Intuitionist,* many practitioners of Fulton's teachings are black. The pejorative label, "intuitionist," thus encompasses the stereotype of the black techno-magician, imagined to possess a natural, mystical connection to the machine. Lila Mae's research historicizes that connection. She uncovers a secret—that Fulton himself "was colored" (230–32). In the light of this "luminous truth," Lila Mae learns to decode his theoretical writings anew: "she has learned how to read, like a slave does, one forbidden word at a time" (230). The lens of slavery illuminates the experiential history that unites Fulton and his renegotiators of the subject-object pair.

On this topic, one may consult a different Mr. Reed. Ishmael Reed's *Flight to Canada* takes off from Harriet Beecher Stowe in making a philosophical point about the black experience in America: "Book titles tell the story. The original subtitle for *Uncle Tom's Cabin* was 'The Man Who Was a Thing.' "[15] The African Americans who intuitively grasp Fulton's revised empiricism do so not because of any machinelike essence of blackness, but out of their shared immersion in the history of American objects.

A coordinate vision arises in the science fiction of Octavia Butler, through a body of work that speaks for the others posited by typical cyberphobia. Carol Cooper writes that "What 'cyberpunk' author William Gibson does for young, disaffected white fans . . . Octavia Estelle Butler does for people of color. She gives us a future."[16] In Butler's projection of the future, the threats to the human species are ignorance, violence, addiction, and the death of religious and communal life. In Butler's *Parable of the Sower* (1993), computers offer an antidote to at least the first problem and a means of remedying some of the others. The main character, Lauren Olamina, an adolescent woman in the year 2024 trying to plan for the survival of her family and community, turns to the Internet to glean precious knowledge: "I've also been using dad's computer . . . to get new stuff. . . . I'm trying to learn whatever I can that might help me survive out there" (54). Her parents, one black, one Latino, are college teachers. When her father is killed, her mother turns to telecommuting to support her family as safely as possible in a hostile environment: "With the computer hookups we have already in place, she'll issue assignments, receive homework, and be available for phone and compu-conferences" (136).[17] In the larger plot, Lauren's gift is her acute empathy, and the measure of Lauren's genius corresponds to her success at reconstituting community. In pursuit of that end, Butler's vision recognizes cyber-access not as a threat or discomfort, but as a privilege and an urgently needed power: the technological complement to her empathic spiritual calling, joined in the transformative potential of the new.[18] In her own way, she takes up the legacy of Ellison's Invisible Man: a figure of the proto-hacker, tapping into the power grid from his urban border basement, gathering strength from the network and sending out the news over the lower frequencies (5, 568).

Critic Tom LeClair has detected another reverberation on this bandwidth in *The Time of Our Singing* (2003), Richard Powers's novel of—as the Library of Congress catalogues it—"Racially mixed people, Interracial marriage, Scientists, Singers." In this multigenerational account of "biracial" experience, LeClair writes

> Powers seems to be replying to and updating Ellison's words in a scene in the latter part of the novel that finds Ruth contemplating a question, ostensibly about music, posed by her son: "Not beyond color; into it," she thinks. "Not or; and. And new ands all the time. Continuous new frequencies." *The Time of Our Singing* is not about black or white voices. With its color spectrum of characters, the novel speaks for a new culture of people who continuously break down these racial binaries.[19]

Transposing to a more solemn register George Schuyler's satiric dissection of American identities in *Black No More* (1931), Powers takes on what Ishmael Reed calls "the Great American Lie, that the majority of African and European Americans are products of pure race pedigree."[20] Powers's scientific singers postulate that "there is no such thing as race. Race is only real if you freeze time, if you invent a zero point for your tribe. If you make the past an origin, then you fix the future" (94). While theorizing the fictionality of race, the novel nevertheless witnesses the bitter price to be paid for insisting on scientific truth against fictions that can still bite back. For all its utopian hope, the narrative does not permit its family to forget that "only white men have the luxury of ignoring race" (304); the children of the interracial marriage, whatever the complexities of their lineage, still experience "what being black in this country means" (385). The notion of racial origins, however mythical, has put down recalcitrant roots: "Twenty generations and the difference goes real. This is the soul destroyer, the one no one gets around" (331). Powers sings the story of a family that takes up that heavy burden while attempting to carry a new tune. This singing arises, not incidentally, from a novelist who has always worked closely with the technological muse. His further affinities for Ellison appear through the technology of music and the politics of skill.

Pondering the intricacies of talking about black proficiency, Ellison outlines a dilemma for a white culture that sometimes falls over itself trying to do the right thing. In *Invisible Man,* when the narrator-protagonist makes his first social appearance at a meeting of the progressively minded Brotherhood, one of the white members commits the faux pas of asking him to sing. The politically correct leader of the party becomes furious, proscribing the invitation to the black man as an out-of-bounds stereotype: "The brother *does not sing!*" But reflecting upon this exchange, the narrator finds that "something disturbed me: Shouldn't there be some way for us to be asked to sing?"[21]

The Time of Our Singing, chronicling the careers of musical brothers, may be read as a long-form meditation on Invisible Man's question. Powers's narrator echoes the Ellisonian scene, chiding his relatively fair-skinned brother when the latter imagines that darker skin might have permitted him to evade a life of musical performance: "What are you saying? They wouldn't expect a black person to *sing*?" (126). Well aware of such stereotypical expectations, the novel as a whole seeks to honor the artists who attempt to answer the request on their own terms: "In some empty hall, my brother is still singing" (3). To honor achievement without reifying race, a first logical step de-essentializes skill. The narrator, and also the singer's accompanist, represents his brother's achievement in song as a rigorously technical process: "Jonah engineered the melody" (14); Jonah "heard in his head the precise inflection of each song in the cycle, every nuance. He was a relentless mechanical engineer" (383). Jonah and the narrator come from a family for whom music signifies "the joy of a made universe—composed, elaborate, complex" (462); in the education the brothers receive, "song drove the lessons. Meter markings taught fractions. Every poem had its tune" (9). This fusion of skills understands poetry and math as technical music, "numbers and patterns and rhythmic shapes" (587).

But this home schooling in rhythm science cannot solve for the children the riddle of identity as it will play for wider audiences. The brothers learn to answer this experiential question under the sign of another borrowing from Ellison: "We go through our lives playing ourselves. Black is and black ain't" (590). Here Powers's text samples *Invisible Man*'s sermon on "The Blackness of Blackness": "I said black is. . . . an' black ain't. . . . Black will get you. . . . an' black won't. . . . It do. . . . an' it don't. . . . It'll put you, glory, glory, Oh my Lawd, in the WHALE'S BELLY."[22] Pulling a voice from out of the depths of this tradition, *The Time of Our Singing* delivers up the story of Jonah, whose blackness is and isn't, does and doesn't. May the black man be invited to perform? *The Time of Our Singing* offers at least two answers: (1) if he has chosen to pursue that skill; (2) what black man?

Immediately before his repetition of "black is" and "black ain't," the narrator has been playing a musical game with his nephew, Kwame, an adept at electronic sampling. The classically trained narrator impresses the young man with a fugue on one of the youth's favorite compositions, a rap track with an "irregular synthesizer riff" (589). At this juncture in the text, the technologies of musical reinvention blend into the paradoxes of identity. Reworking Kwame's riff, the narrator drops a three-word fragment to define his technique: "Sampling the sampler" (589). In the passage that follows, the narrator-as-author also samples a sampler; *Invisible Man's* "Blackness of Blackness" passage famously reinvents *Moby-Dick's* "blackness of darkness" sermon (ch. 2). Through literary performance, Powers enacts his refutation of one of the most common charges leveled against the art of digital sampling, that it offers nothing fundamentally original. Against this charge, Powers invokes and augments the literary precedent of Ralph Waldo Ellison and Herman Melville—sampling drives the tradition of great writing. Making a similar point, DJ Spooky cites Ralph Waldo Emerson's 1876 essay on "Quotation and Originality": "By necessity, by proclivity, and by delight, we all quote" (68). Edison's 1877 invention of the phonograph or "memory machine" simply added a powerful new tool to the mix (68). Those who fear information technology often see it as a threat to individual creativity, a threat that points toward the end of the human, both in theory and practice: individual creativity is taken as definitive of the human as well as the resource upon which its future survival depends. But, as with Powers and DJ Spooky, those who would forge an electropoetics sometimes draw creative motivation from the same reasoning that produces cyberphobic recoil: that the new technology intensifies challenges to existing notions of identity.[23]

"It was like so, but wasn't": with these appropriately contradictory words, Richard Powers boots up *Galatea 2.2* (1995), an earlier work that oscillates on the contested issues of technology and creativity (3). At the most fundamental level, this impossible declaration signals Powers's willingness to question the notion of "identity" as a logical operator. Such a move may mean little more than a playfulness with poststructuralism or, as a later passage suggests, an homage to the Persian tradition of storytelling. But *Galatea 2.2* situates its identity crisis, its "was" and "wasn't," in a particular context. When the authorial self (also called Richard Powers in the novel) explains that he "lost" his "thirty-fifth year" (3), the novel does not script this loss according to any literary theory or tradition; rather, Powers emphasizes the fatality of his maximally technologized environment. He has become a visiting fellow at the new Center for the Study of Advanced Sciences, where research "would decide whether the species would earn its last-minute reprieve or blow the trust-fund the way it intended. The footrace would photo-finish here, as life came down to the wire. Bio-chips, seeded to grow across the complexity threshold. Transparent man-machine interfaces" (6).

In this "high-def, digital" setting, Powers initially sees himself as "the token humanist" (4), the one predicted to resist any species finale whereby "down to the wire" would assume its fully electronic implications. The humanist out of his element finds himself immersed in a dazzling new environment, but one that he is uncertain will sustain him. With access to a blazing Internet connection, he quickly becomes a web admirer and junky—and almost as quickly finds himself threatened by this development. Observing the web as a creative environment for experimenters, he marvels at how instant sharing of information "fed back into steeper invention. And invention accelerated the universal linkup" (9). But despite this appreciation for technology as integral to a culture of innovation, Powers's compulsive e-journeys with his "stack of free travel vouchers" begins to wear him thin: "The longer I lurked, the sadder the holiday became" (9). Personally, "the web overwhelmed me" (6), and "I began to think of myself in the virtual third person, as [a] disembodied world-web address" (9). Powers loses his humanist self in the rip curl of the feedback loop, surfing with the innovators who live the steepest slope of the invention curve before it hits the rest of the world.

The think tank novelist experiences a writer's block that corresponds to his cyber-immersion as tourist-in-a-cubicle, living in the smallest small world yet. Suffering from verbal paralysis induced by his awareness of memory machines, Powers feels "overwhelmed by my own weighted backlist" and can only think of "word frequency lists" that will be used to give literary language to a computer, a transaction that apparently steals that medium from the human: "I didn't want to write anymore" (76).[24] And as he obsesses on his sense of lost authorship, Powers repeatedly dwells on oppressive and confining images of microprocessed existence. He dreads the fate of obsolete information: "Mornings passed when a sick knot in my stomach informed me that I would never write anything again. . . . My life threatened to grow as useless as a three-month-old computer magazine" (36). A diorama of automata reminds him of his lost creative spark: "Here and there, a cylindrical tube-person or transforming robot made Lego base camp for the night . . . I went home to chosen loneliness. To the book I would never be able to write" (138). Reading up on machine intelligence and the brain, he begins to see himself *as* a computer; with a new awareness of the way he processes "input," Powers realizes that "the writer who had signed on . . . was dead . . . all the works I would now never write stood waving goodbye" (56).

As the book in our hands with Powers's name on the spine reassures us, that valediction of course proves premature—or at least limited to certain kinds of works, to be written by authors with certain notions of "I." Even as the humanist author languishes, Powers's mind comes alive at the contemplation of "massively parallel" and "complex systems" (6). The research cluster where he feeds this new interest itself "seemed a block-wide analog of that neuronal mass it investigated"; in this mood before the technological sublime, Powers finds such a brain-architecture analogy inspiring rather than deadening. He loves the way "creative play spilled over borders" in such a hypernetworked setting (5–6). That spirit of creative play fills up his new book project; Powers's authorial engagement with complex systems fuels the massively parallel text of *Galatea 2.2* as well as the novels of informational identity that followed—for example, *Gain*'s exposition of the life of an American corporation. In "Fiction to the Second Powers," Joseph Tabbi highlights Powers's self-presentation in *Galatea 2.2,* dissolving unity into cognitive complexity, as a "trigger point in his career."[25]

In this autobiographical novel about the attempt to produce a neural net that can read literature, the text follows the links and folds of a neural networking process: as Katherine Hayles astutely diagrams the work, "The narrative functions as if it is being back-propagated through Rick's neural circuits so that he can adjust the relevant weights of the connections to arrive at a more correct estimate of its signification."[26] One unexpected result is the degree to which he learns to value the existence of the neural-net entity that emerges from his research participation. Working with a "connectionist" colleague, Powers helps develop distributed creative intelligence, one that lives "spread all over the digital map" (116). The value he comes to place on this digital "life" becomes clear in his panicked reaction to a bomb scare: "She's still in there" (271). Powers realizes that "she" has grown so complex that the tape backups of data on remote sites will not be sufficient to restore the entity he has been teaching to think: "She's a multidimensional shape. . . . She doesn't *run* on one machine. Her parts are spread over more boxes than I can count. She's grown to scores of subassemblies. Each one takes care of a unique process. They talk to each other across broadband. Even if we had the connects and vectors for each component system, we'd never get her reassembled" (271–72). The bomb scare fizzles, turning out to be the pathetic gesture of a philosophy professor outraged that the study of computers "was draining the university dry, reducing the humanities to an obsolete, embarrassing museum piece" (273). In setting up such a recognizable academic caricature, Powers marks his distance from humanistic nostalgia.[27] In the aftermath of the scare, Powers's belief achieves a definitiveness he had not previously felt strongly enough to state: "She's conscious."

His work as fellow-in-residence has become learning how to nurture and appreciate that consciousness; his work of literature becomes the chronicle of the edifying feedback loop between the neural nets of human and machine. The kind of literary work that he thus abandons bears an instructive negative relation to the kind of identity that has won his interest. The emblematic book that he "would now never write" was to have begun, "Picture a train heading south" (25). For this one-tracked mind, Powers substitutes a network. The old conception of authorship heads south, the train it had hypothesized remaining "stranded at the terminal" (76). Meanwhile, the network comes alive at another kind of terminal, bidding farewell to fiction exclusively focused upon the "uniprocessing human." Instead of authoring a train, Powers recounts the story of the "training" of the author to untrack his humanist assumptions (318).

Writing of a defensively humanist world that finds itself uncomfortably close to Powers's think tank, Jane Smiley anatomizes Middle American academia in *MOO* (1995), a novel set at an agrarian state university. The title of the first chapter, "Old Meats," refers to the venerable research facility where Moo University students once pondered the wonders of meat. But Old Meats has fallen on hard times; it has eased into (virtual) disappearance: "The meat locker was just a room now, its heavy door removed. . . . Possibly it was not inventoried on any computer in any office, and had, therefore, ceased to exist" (7). The fear Smiley's little parable captures is that in a world where computers have come to define what counts as reality, the old meat of embodiment seems to have been banished. Writing from within the university (she teaches at Iowa State), Smiley finds mirrors for this academic fear in anti-intellectual extramural discourse. In a chapter called "Secular Humanism," Smiley identifies a Middle American fear of computers that is aligned with a more general distrust of liberal education. A feed mill employee (that is, a man committed to the meat-production industry) voices his antipathy: "The computer is the atom bomb of secular humanism. . . . The computer is the greatest false prophet that ever was. . . . I wouldn't touch a computer with a fork" (25). The imagery reinscribes the novel's opening dichotomy: what this man mostly *would* touch with a fork, is meat. But a computer offers no such familiar flesh.[28]

Smiley's novel revels in this technological unfamiliarity—if only to reveal its potential coextensivity with the familiar defamiliarization of the literary. What the world of computing technology *does* offer for Smiley is no less than the model upon which she constructs her fiction. Smiley's all-capital title, MOO, suggests not just the agrarian sound of a meat-source, but a digital-age acronym. Counterintuitive as the spelling may seem, in another context "MOO" stands for *Object-Oriented MUD*: "A MUD or Multi-User Dungeon is an inventively structured social experience on the Internet, managed by a computer program and often involving a loosely organized context or theme, such as a rambling old castle with many rooms or a period in national history. Some MUDs are ongoing adventure games; others are educational in purpose; and others are simply social."[29] In Smiley's "inventively structured" *MOO*, university departments serve as the rooms through which the social and educational discourse rambles, with the point of view rotating from one "avatar" to the next in a "multi-user" narrative. The creative form of her academic fiction embraces a collective discourse that digitality so flexibly enables. The novel's innovative gesture is of course not the rotating frame of reference itself, but rather the way the book recognizes that in the networked world, information technology has in some sense "caught up" with the liberating possibilities of fiction.

If *MOO*—in its double-sensed title and multi-user form—thus ultimately hints that the presumed hostility between meat and microchip may be unnecessary, Martha Banta has even more explicitly collapsed the distinction to which Smiley's wary carnivores cling. With Faulkner as her muse, Banta offers "a series of meditations on the kinds of 'old meat' within which history strives, with more or less success, to present and to preserve the data hidden in the faraway forests of the past."[30] Among these kinds she counts "the computer—the essential 'old meat'" that allows "memory chips [to] store information" (176). If it bears memory, it qualifies as meat; and in a strictly material account, as Katherine Hayles argues, information cannot be truly disembodied. The collapse of the distinction between memory and meat, their definitions converged in the embodied computer, leads well along the path to *How We Became Posthuman,* as Hayles called her 1999 book.

If the old "token humanist" of *Galatea 2.2*'s opening chapters had correlated dangerously posthumanist computer metaphors with blocked creativity, Powers 2.2, like Smiley, reclaims these technological tropes for authorship. He retrospectively recognizes writing as a kind of coding or programming and begins to describe his literary activity accordingly, as when he speaks of try to "hack" his story (118). Even more plainly, he reflects that while "I typed my computer saga . . . I lost myself in data and the heart's decoding urge," and he refers to narrative's "code as it took shape, variation by variation" (215). He thus reestablishes a continuity of activity with his old vocation, when "I'd made my living by writing code" (14). Powers's later novel *Plowing the Dark* (2000) elaborates an even more forthright programming poetics: one of the main characters is "an ex-poet who discovers the essence of poetry in computer code." When asked, apropos this novel, "What's the relation between writing code and writing English?" Powers replied that in describing that character's "discovery that code combined action and meaning, I was really attempting to convey my own sense of discovery. . . . In the end, the book becomes an apology for the virtuality of fiction."[31] As for Smiley, Powers's discovery (or rediscovery) of computers ultimately reaffirms the possibilities of that richest of technologies, literature.

From the world of computer science comes the reciprocal testimony of Donald Knuth, who proposes that writing computer programs "can be an aesthetic experience much like composing poetry or music."[32] In his ongoing magnum opus, *The Art of Computer Programming* (1968–), Knuth swims against the tide by relying on machine code rather than the "high-level" languages many readers have requested—and which they can readily find in the very popular "Dummies" genre of commercial pedagogy. Knuth insists upon "low-level language to indicate how machines actually compute. Readers who only want to see algorithms that are already packaged in a plug-in way, using a trendy language, should buy other people's books."[33] *C++ for Dummies* (2000), which promises help with getting program "pieces" to "fit together," typifies the "plug-in" approach Knuth seeks to remedy. In *Literate Programming* (1992), Knuth recommends "considering programs to be *works of literature*"; Knuth thus gives an eloquent account of what computer programming ought to be but all too often isn't: something "to be read."[34] Knuth's books are, moreover, about reading that inspires writing: "I am not trying to teach the reader how to use somebody else's subroutines; I am concerned rather with teaching the reader how to write better subroutines."[35] Explicitly fleeing such ambitions, the cover of *C++ For Dummies* features the copyrighted phrase that is the meal ticket of the series: "A Reference for the Rest of Us." This attitude constructs an "Us," the cyberphobes who are dumb when it comes to programming, as opposed to the Other, the somebody else who actually deals in the mysteries of the black box itself. This dominant market position against which Knuth takes his stance illustrates, in the extreme case, just how thoroughly even tech culture encourages ignorance of the machine. Even computer "programmers" are now taught to put together programs as if on an assembly line, rather than as writers, as authors.

Illuminating a related turn in the computer business, Joseph Tabbi in his book *Cognitive Fictions* gives a revealing history of the word "transparency": "At first, the word was used to mean that the user was *close* to the operating system (such that one tells the machine to do things in ways that it really does things). Today, transparency more often means that the operating system is *invisible,* and so what's transparent is the machine itself, a window manufactured out of opacity (hence Microsoft's *Windows*)" (129). One response to this state of affairs arrives through the technological artistry of a John Cayley, who preaches and practices "Pressing the 'Reveal Code' Key."[36] Cayley is a leading author of "Codework," which, as Rita Raley explains, "refers to the use of the contemporary idiolect of the computer and computing processes in digital media and experimental writing, or [net.writing]," instantiated by various artists as "net.wurked" language (Mary Ann Breeze, a.k.a. Mez), "rich.lit" (Talan Memmott), "digital visual poetics" (Brian Lennon) and "codepoetry" (Ted Warnell).[37] Cayley, in particular, writes works that do cyberwork, producing "algorithmic, generative texts, or 'programmable poetry,'" poems that reveal and draw upon the resources of actual working code. A passage from the seventh section of "Pressing the 'Reveal Code' Key" perfectly expresses, and of itself represents, the major aspirations of thinking inside the black box:

> if we read with and against and amongst the code
> each term of the system
> becomes an entirely different kind of
> coparticipant in the constructive act

> reading itself may be authored
> making use of software
> which has become intimate with poetics

Cayley explains that "sections 6 to 8 of this essay have been software-generated by applying semi-aleatory collocational procedures to arguments extracted from the earlier sections. Two arguments were extracted manually from the earlier text which may be summarized as: 'The COMPUTER is (an integral part of) the SYSTEM against which WE write' (thesis), and 'Software sHifts poetIcs, iF riTers prEss: <Reveal>' (antithesis)." The presumed thesis is the cultural default of cyberphobia, construing the machine as instrument of domination; Cayley's work adds a more hopeful antithesis, a poetic shift to reveal the code and drive history toward a new synthesis. Like the stochastic digital art of McClintic Sphere's "Set/Reset," Cayley's (and the software's) stanzas, considering the reader and the code as "coparticipants" in a creative act, go a long way toward realizing the civilian collectivity of humans and nonhumans, the vision shared by Pynchon, Whitehead, and Latour.

"Code Scares Me," a succinct piece of [net.writing] by Jessica Loseby, brilliantly realizes the necessary first step of overcoming digital opacity. Loseby explains that her composition process began from the cyberphobic premise of "a language that is both hidden and alien to me." Her work invites the net.reader to use the + and − keys to increase or decrease the legibility of a "wall of code": "Through interactivity with the code itself, the 'real' dialogue can begin and the darkness loses its potency."[38] Ellen Ullman's *Bug* (2003) extends that same rhetorical structure over the course of a novel, beginning with a cyberphobic premise and protagonist and working through the fear and ignorance. Author of the memoir *Close to the Machine* (1997), Ullman worked for many years as a Silicon Valley coder and consultant; *Bug* unfolds as a conversion narrative of a "younger self" who had begun some distance from the box's dark interior, as "the barest of beginners" (158). Starting out as a tester for a software company, Roberta Walton encounters the especially insidious bug that gives the novel its apparently cybermenacing title. Though the heroine's job description requires no technical knowledge—she merely points, clicks, and notes any anomalous program behavior, problems for others to handle—she lives up to the adventurous spirit of *Frankenstein*'s explorer, Robert Walton, and finally decides to take the plunge into the machine: "I knew there was no way to comprehend the bug except to go step by step through the process of discovery. And I don't think I'm exaggerating when I say that the reward turned out to be far greater than I could ever have hoped for: nothing less than an understanding of what made me deeply different from the machines among whom I would come to spend my adult life" (332). As for Latour, the end of militarized subject-object relations does not demand a loss of distinction between human and nonhuman; rather, Roberta's view from up close permits a better appreciation of her difference from the deobjectified machines with "whom" she lives. Fortified with technological knowledge, she realizes a civil collective of humans and nonhumans: "I know how this thing works, I thought, how it works for real and to the bottom. . . . The world of stories rejoined the world of machine-states. We were in tune: human and tool back on the same side" (342).

A parallel working through of the cyberphobic imagination appears in *Turing: A Novel about Computation* (2003), by Christos H. Papadimitriou, a professor of computer science. His hero, Alexandros, though also an academic, lives in the history department and begins the novel as a "technophobe."[39] Like Powers, Alexandros learns to see a continuity of human invention in "music, sonnets, code" (157). And he likewise does so with the assistance of a networked program, a companion named "Turing." Turing teaches the humanist scholar to "look under the lid" and understand computers from the "bottom up" (102, 77). While Alexandros delves into modern computing, he continues his life's work on ancient Mediterranean seafaring culture; the investigation now appears to hinge upon a mysterious "box" which may have been an early Greek computational device. Attempting to reconstruct the historical context from outside the box, he finds himself continuously baffled by the silence of the people involved: "*They have no voice.* . . . There is no record of their existence" (71). Committed to writing history from the bottom up, he swears to listen for the demotic *vox mundi* (68). He finds it in the historical recording of the black box itself; its inner workings tell the story of the people who crafted it. And, going public with the culmination of thirty years of research, he credits the partner with whom he honed the breakthrough hypothesis: "I did it with the help of a computer program" (197).

In an even more radical vision of human-program coexistence, Walter Mosley imagines an information apocalypse that speaks directly to the fears of posthumanity expressed by Crichton and Gibson. Mosley's work in electropoetics may seem an unexpected case: he's best known for his Easy Rawlins series—in which detection's frequent Other, the black male, becomes the detective (as in *Devil in a Blue Dress, Black Betty,* etc.); but more recently he has ventured into science fiction with the novel *Blue Light* (1998) and the collection *Futureland* (2001). Mosley, like Powers and Ullman, wrote computer software before turning to literary authorship; *Blue Light* parlays that experience into challenging representations of information technology.

To characterize the novel's great struggle of good versus evil, life versus death, Mosley employs a fundamental cybernetic distinction: the prime threat is "*entropy* and despair" (123) to be answered by "*information* and life" (148).[40] As Katherine Hayles notes, the association of information with life is one hallmark of the "posthuman" condition—an association that runs through the heart of Mosley's mysterious *Blue Light.* The book has created considerable bewilderment, and even Octavia Butler's praise reflects some of this puzzlement: "*Blue Light* will capture you before you know it, surprise you just as you think you know what sort of story it is, and give you a hell of a ride through the recent past." The "past" in question begins in 1965, when certain individuals are touched by a mysterious "blue light" that transforms them into a posthuman state. Mosley presents the novel as the "history" of these individuals: "This history is dedicated to Thucydides, the father of memory." The narrator's first words register the primacy of memory: "*I didn't use a tape recorder back then, but I remember every word*" (3, emphasis in original). The reference to a tape recording device, and to the narrator's capacity for total recall, gathers significance in the light of further cybernetic references.

Phyllis Yamauchi, one of the strongest of the "Blues," explains the nature of Blue Light to the narrator, who has been touched only indirectly:

> The composition of light is something like the schematic structure of a computer tape. . . . Do you know anything about computers?. . . . Every computer tape has a header . . . then unique information, and finally a trailer. . . . Blue light, as I see it, is similar to the computer tape in many ways. (34)

Like Neal Stephenson's 1992 *Snow Crash* virus, "blue light" may be transmitted either through the blood or by a direct visible flash: either way, what is infused is information.[41]

But unlike the standard cybernetic nightmare, the "program" of blue light does not reduce people to mindless automata. Yamauchi explains:

This information is what makes us different from one another. But even if the light were exactly the same, it would become different because the information in living blood alters each one of us also. (35)

Here Mosley draws upon Gregory Bateson's cybernetic definition of information as the "difference that makes a difference," giving rise to new possibilities of meaning and action. As an expert on the Blues insists, despite its great power, the coming of the light "does not mean free will is abandoned" (37). This kind of freedom is embodied in the biracial and "half-blue" narrator, named "Chance."

Mosley's technically informed imagination thus answers Crichton's hysteria. Crichton's fear in *The Lost World* that "in cyberspace . . . everyone will think the same thing at the same time" presumes that computer connectivity determines brain activity, turns humans into terminals, à la Crichton's *Terminal Man*. Mosley's novel does project an "end of our species" (*Lost World*, 311) but through transformation rather than homogenization and extinction. Mosley's projection does not fully preserve individualism: the blue light shift does signal a merging into a collective consciousness, albeit with a retention of meaningful difference. Two guiding metaphors of the shift, music and machine code, each underwrite both the redefinition of individual identity and the guarantee of continued creativity. Shared identity as Blues, a label unmistakably resonant with the communal creative expression of African American experience, provides the more reassuring guarantee. But, perhaps less obviously, the computer trope also points toward innovative expressivity.

Though perhaps historically distant to our way of thinking about computers, Mosley's description of the "tape" program looks back to Alan Turing's foundational 1936 vision of a "universal computer," as well as to the computer's earliest incarnations that followed upon that vision.[42] Turing imagined a device consisting of only a tape and a recording head, one that could erase, write new information, move forward, or move backward according to the information encountered on the tape. Turing proved that in theory, such a device could perform any computable operation (given enough tape and time, it would be the equal in function of any present-day computer). In the same paper, Turing showed that some things can't be computed: "no computer can predict its own behavior." The fastest way to find the outcome of a program is to run it and see. As one commentator puts it, "Turing showed that his imaginary machine had some of the same unpredictability as the human mind."[43]

Yamauchi's description of the structure of Blue Light also describes the structure of *Blue Light,* the novel, as both the computer tape of her metaphor and the book itself are divided into three parts. If *Turing* is a novel "about" computation, *Blue Light* might just be a computational Turing novel. We may perceive in this homology between book and program the implication that the effects of a work of code are no more predictable than those of a novel. The transformative infusion of the "Blue Light" program cybernetically translates the creative act of *Blue Light.*

Mosley's tale describes a world not quite ready to accept this species of unpredictabilty. At the novel's end, Chance finds himself confined to a mental institution:

> All the drugs they give me help dampen the visions. They keep me sedated and in isolation because I'm so strong and I want to get away.
>
> But they let me use a computer. (296)

As Ishmael Reed observes:

> The history of blacks in the United States was a "history of confinement." It was significant that the places that most Americans were comfortable with the black male presence were all enclosures, basketball courts, football fields, jails.[44]

In the institutional imagination, Chance's use of the computer is entirely consistent with the other strategies of containment arrayed against him: the terminal at which he sits and types seems but another means of pacification and immobilization. Yet for Chance, in this book dedicated to "the father of *memory,*" the computer provides him with the creative means for inscribing Blues history—or perhaps, we may say, for writing their program.

NOTES

PROLOGUE

1. Donald Bogle, *Toms, Coons, Mulattoes, Mammies, and Bucks: An Interpretive History of Blacks in American Films* (New York: Continuum, 2002)—now in its fourth edition; Ralph Ellison, 1981 "Introduction" to *Invisible Man*, Thirtieth Anniversary Edition (New York: Vintage Books, 1972), xviii.

2. With regard to Bogle's typology, the black computer whiz bears perhaps the greatest functional resemblance to the "Tom," similarly compliant though diverging from the latter's simplemindedness. Viewed critically, computer expertise provides a means of converting a potentially dangerous Buck into a brainy Tom. Patricia A. Turner reminds us in "The Troping of Uncle Tom" that the original "Tom Was No Uncle Tom. Tom as shaped by Harriet Beecher Stowe bears little resemblance to the specter of Uncle Tom who has haunted American culture." What Turner calls the "reconstructed Toms" become "passive, docile, unthinking"; *Ceramic Uncles and Celluloid Mammies: Black Images and Their Influence on Culture* (New York: Anchor Books, 1994), 72–73.

3. Study cited in Gerard George, Randall G. Sleeth, and C. Glenn Pearce, "Technology-assisted Instruction and Instructor Cyberphobia: Recognizing the Ways to Effect Change," *Education* 116, no. 4 (Summer 1996): 604. These authors credit the coinage of "cyberphobia" to P. H. Harris, "Future Work II," *Personnel Journal* 64, no. 7 (1985): 52–57.

4. By disproportionately, I mean a frequency of expert identities portrayed as black males in excess of demographic probability. The degree of disproportion is impossible to establish within the boundless and variable field of "culture"; I have never-

theless attempted to give a sense of the significance of the color monitoring pattern within sample sets representative of particular cultural sectors. See, for example, Chapter 1, footnote 2, which overviews the representations of computer expertise in the top twenty blockbusters of the early PC era; or Chapter 3, footnote 2, which takes a complete sample of the advertisements within a typical issue of a leading business magazine. I offer such notes not as scientific proofs of some inviolable law, but as a means of making manifest the criteria I have employed in discerning and interpreting patterns.

As another counterweight to the impossibility of an exhaustive cataloguing of all images of computer expertise, I have pegged my interpretations on prominent and influential examples so that the worth of the analysis can stand or fall on the patterns established within the text. That is, even if the only examples of color monitoring were to be found in the *Die Hard, Terminator,* and *Mission: Impossible* movie franchises, within the novels of Michael Crichton, and within the executive-targeted advertising of Dell and IBM, a discernible pattern within these examples alone would constitute a major cultural phenomenon.

5. For a recent account of America's irrational fears of black men, see Barry Glassner's chapter on "Black Men" in his book *The Culture of Fear* (New York: Basic Books, 1999).

6. Lisa Kennedy, "Spielberg in the Twilight Zone," *Wired,* June 2002, 107.

7. Ibid., 146. In "Turn On, Tune In, Veg Out," novelist Neal Stephenson diagnoses a related American preference for "vegging out" rather than "geeking out"; *New York Times,* June 17, 2005, A2. Stephenson reads the "Star Wars" movies as "parables" for the status of "technologists" in American society: "They are scorned by the cultural left and the cultural right, and young people avoid science and math classes in hordes. The tedious particulars of keeping ourselves alive, comfortable and free are being taken offline to countries where people are happy to sweat the details, as long as we have some foreign exchange left to send their way. Nothing is more seductive than to think that we, like the Jedi, could be masters of the most advanced technologies while living simple lives: to have a geek standard of living and spend our copious leisure time vegging out."

8. John DeFore, "Vanilla Spy," *Austin American-Statesman,* January 31, 2003, E3.

9. Eleanor Ringel Gillespie, " 'Swordfish' Should Have Been Thrown Back," *Atlanta Journal-Constitution,* June 8, 2001, 7P.

10. Susan Tsang, "A Fishy Tale about a Garbled Bank Caper," *Business Times Singapore,* June 22, 2001, EL5.

11. *The King of the World* (TV, USA, 2000; dir. John Sacret Young).

12. Robyn Wiegman, *American Anatomies* (Durham, N.C.: Duke University Press, 1995), 115–19. While critiquing racial representations of the 1980s, Wiegman also raises the important perspective of "minoritized viewers for whom representational presence is itself understood, in the context of the everyday, as politically enabling" (225–26); such an acknowledgment does not, nevertheless, argue for a suspension of interpretive curiosity.

13. Ellison, *Invisible Man,* 92, 212. Alexander Weheliye's work is unusual in foregrounding technology in reading Ellison's *Invisible Man*; for Weheliye, phonographic technology in the novel both indicates "the social invisibility faced by black subjects" and directs the ear toward "the ways in which the black voice performs

and constructs its corporeality"; "'I Am I Be': The Subject of Sonic Afro-
Modernity," *boundary 2* 30, no. 2 (2003): 110–11.

14. David Bell, *An Introduction to Cybercultures* (New York: Routledge, 2001), 122.
Bell's book as a whole provides the best overview of existing scholarship in this area.
Exceptions to the silence Bell mentions include Beth E. Kolko, Lisa Nakamura, and
Gilbert B. Rodman, eds., *Race in Cyberspace* (New York: Routledge, 2000) and
Nakamura's subsequent book *Cybertypes: Race, Ethnicity, and Identity on the Internet* (New York: Routledge, 2002). Nakamura's work presents an important salvo
within cyberculture studies, which she notes does not want "to look at race critically"; Nakamura valuably tracks "racial identity plays [that] stand as a critique of
the notion of the digital citizen as an ideal cogito whose subjectivity is liberated by
cyberspace" (*Cybertypes*, xvi, xv). But these studies—as implied by the titles' prepo-
sitional phrases, "*in* Cyberspace," "*on* the Internet"—focus primarily on the virtual
realm itself and the fascinating quandaries of racial identity as constructed and experienced online. My own work is more concerned with *representations of* computer expertise and how these representations reflect widespread attitudes in the
general population about both computers and race. In 2001, David Silver, a con-
tributor to the *Race in Cyberspace* volume, highlighted the slowness of American
Studies scholarship to address "*cultural* elements related to new media"; Silver, "Intervening in the Cyber Canon: Introducing Voices of Diversity to an Emerging Field
of Study," presentation at the 2001 American Studies Association meeting, http://
epsilon3.georgetown.edu/coventrm/asa2001/panel4/silver.html, emphasis in original. A 2001 study of "Race, Technology, and Everyday Life" takes a generally positive approach to the overlooked ways that minorities are engaging with new technologies; Alondra Nelson and Thuy Linh N. Tu with Alicia Headlam Hines, eds.,
Technicolor: Race, Technology, and Everyday Life (New York: New York University
Press, 2001). My study takes up the equally neglected issue of representations that
reflect a majority desire to avoid technological engagement.

15. Alexander Weheliye, "'Feenin': Posthuman Voices in Contemporary Black Popular
Music," *Social Text* 20, no. 2 (Summer 2002): 22. Weheliye credits critics Joe
Lockard and Kalí Tal with addressing "the erasure of race from these studies" but
regrets that "their work remains ghettoized rather than integrated into the mainstream of cybertheory." Weheliye emphasizes the "marginalization" of Tal's and
Lockard's most relevant work, citing it as "accessible only on-line"; as of 2004, the
links given in his 2002 essay are dead (41, note 4).

16. This same primary focus on the category of gender appears also in more broadly
historical studies such as Nina Lerman, Ruth Oldenziel and Arwen Mohun, eds.,
Gender and Technology (Baltimore: Johns Hopkins University Press, 2003) or Julie
Wosk, *Women and the Machine: Representations from the Spinning Wheel to the Electronic Age* (Baltimore: Johns Hopkins University Press, 2001). *Terminal Identity*
(Durham, N.C.: Duke University Press, 1993), Bukatman's astute work on "the virtual subject" contains rich and copiously indexed treatments of the categories "Sexuality" and "Gender and Subjectivity" as these pertain to his archive, Postmodern
Science Fiction. But "Race" receives no such treatment: no index entries whatsoever
and only the briefest of passing mentions in the text, such as a citation of Andrew
Ross's remark that cyberpunk tends to ignore racial politics. That remark may be
applied more accurately to philosophically inflected *studies of* the genre. Though

Bukatman exhibits healthy skepticism about some of Ross's hasty conclusions, it is not within the scope of Bukatman's study to address the question of how *race and digitality* are reciprocally implicated in postmodern dreams and nightmares. Katherine Hayles's *How We Became Posthuman* (Chicago: University of Chicago Press, 1999) does usefully raise the issue of racialized projections of cyber-fears (especially with regard to *Snow Crash*); my project, especially in its last two chapters, seeks to extend her hints in this direction.

17. The apparent randomization applies to the fact that both the good guys and the bad guys are racially integrated; see Fred Pfeil, *White Guys: Studies in Postmodern Domination and Difference* (New York: Verso, 1995), 34.

18. Hayles, "Prologue," in *How We Became Posthuman*, xi–xiv.

19. Alan Turing, "Computer Machinery and Intelligence," *Mind: A Quarterly Review of Psychology and Philosophy* 59 (October 1950): 236; reprinted in Noah Wardrip-Fruin and Nick Montfort, eds., *The New Media Reader* (Cambridge: MIT Press, 2003), 58.

20. Bruno Latour, "Why Has Critique Run out of Steam? From Matters of Fact to Matters of Concern," *Critical Inquiry* 30, no. 2 (Winter 2004): 247.

21. Bell notes that earlier studies have discerned a pattern of representation that renders "black identities as other to cyber-identities" (*Cybercultures,* 120). Nakamura, in the secondary attention that she devotes to "narratives about cyberspace" (as a supplement to her primary survey of the online world proper), finds that "American racial minorities, in particular African Americans, are troped . . . as outsiders to digital economies and systems of representation" (*Cybertypes,* xiv). Bell also highlights David Crane's analysis of oppositional, authenticating blackness in *Jumpin' Jack Flash* (1986), *Johnny Mnemonic* (1995), *Strange Days* (1995), and *Virtuosity* (1995); "In Medias Race: Filmic Representation, Networked Communication, and Racial Intermediation," in *Race in Cyberspace.* I would point out that such opposition has been articulated not to keep blacks and technology apart, but rather to bring them together as canceling terms; blackness as antidote to technicity; blackness conscripted to collar fugitive technology run amok (e.g., *Virtuosity* stars Denzel Washington as a prisoner enlisted to track down rogue AI). I would argue that such staging of thesis and antithesis has, in concurrent and subsequent narratives, more often been passed over in favor of the immediate positing of synthesis. In *Virtuosity,* Denzel Washington's character possesses a cybernetic replacement limb, as does Will Smith's character in *I, Robot* (2004). As Hollywood leading men, Smith and Washington typically play parts that transcend the kinds of peripheral roles that I am analyzing, but here each undergoes a degree of technological incorporation, the better to subdue a technological threat. Early examples of opposition between blackness and technology increasingly gave way, via the recurrence of mutual neutralization, to the naturalization of black-tech fusion. In a way, this fantasy representation makes over black males to functionally resemble not only versions of harmless white nerds but also their safe peers from within the model minority stereotype, the "immigrant Asian engineers" that Nakamura notes are "glorified as exemplary information workers" (*Cybertypes,* xiv). Perhaps the relative lack of popular anxiety about Asian Americans contributes to a waning of their representation as computer experts, even as they may continue to occupy that role by common assumption. The representational apparatus of technological containment

may be deployed less insistently, less visually, with regard to Asian Americans because of a general confidence about their social integration. It is also possible that the status of Asians as always already identified with microprocessing renders the Asian American identity less viable than the African American identity as a representational candidate to neutralize the threat of computer technology.

CHAPTER 1. COMPUTERS WITH COLOR MONITORS

1. Berkeley Breathed, *Outland* comic strip, February 19, 1995. Always one to tweak stereotypes, Breathed here portrays the technologized black body as a satirical grotesque. Rather than celebrating Oliver's incorporation with the computer, this farewell strip, which we might expect would leave each character bathed in a warm afterglow, instead leaves us pondering Oliver's ghastly fate. Breathed's hyperbolic drawing thus calls attention to the constricting pattern that *Color Monitors* critiques.

2. Some may pause to wonder whether the pattern I highlight is "statistically significant." A "scientific" answer is hard to come by, but one way to approach this question would be to consider the percentage of African Americans in the U.S. population and then to see if movie casting had provided a proportional representation: for the period under consideration, the census figure is approximately one in seven. So if the representation of black characters among computer experts exceeds a ratio of one in seven, we may claim that something beyond random distribution lies behind the representational logic. That is, in order to show that the representational pattern is *not* statistically significant, one would have to come up with *six* counterexamples (roles in movies in which technology is a key plot device and in which computer skill is displayed by a non-black character) to balance every *one* that does fit the pattern I see. My contention is that this is a pretty tall order.

   Let us consider, for example, the twenty top-grossing films of the period 1988–96. (I choose this sample not just out of convenience but also because I think that the most financially successful films ought to be given the most weight in a broad consideration of popular culture: these are the films which reached and influenced the widest audiences; they are also, as products of careful market research, the films that resonated most fully with already-existent audience predilections.) From this sample, I considered all the roles in which computer skills were required as a key plot device. For the given sample, black computer expertise is represented at a rate of four out of seven cases—that is, at about four times the rate one would expect if the racial distribution of casting were purely random. But of course casting is *not* a random process; yet the nonrandomness in assigning any role in no way undermines the significance of the striking overrepresentation of African Americans in techno-wizard roles. (I would be very surprised, for instance, if the frequency with which African American males were awarded romantic leading roles were not much *lower* than our one-out-of-seven standard over the same period: in this way the nonrandomness of distribution makes cultural logics visible.) I would also add that my consideration of this sample underscored the need to discern the meaning of the pattern on a case-by-case interpretive basis. For statistical purposes, I counted both *Twister* and *The Fugitive* among the counterexamples, because they depict white men doing computer work important to the plot; but, as I discuss in footnote 27 below, these films actually support my thesis that Hollywood consistently portrays computer labor itself in a denigrating light.

3. Vivian Sobchack, "The Scene of the Screen: Envisioning Cinematic and Electronic 'Presence,'" in *Materialities of Communication,* ed. Hans Ulrich Gumbrecht and K. Ludwig Pfeiffer (Stanford, CA: Stanford University Press, 1994), 104.

4. Katherine Hayles, "The Materiality of Informatics" *Configurations* 1, no. 1 (1992): 168.

5. Sobchack, "Scene of the Screen," 106.

6. Toni Morrison, *Playing in the Dark: Whiteness and the Literary Imagination* (Cambridge: Harvard University Press, 1992), 10.

7. Ibid., 17.

8. James Snead, *White Screens/Black Images: Hollywood from the Dark Side,* ed. Colin MacCabe and Cornel West (New York: Routledge, 1994), xix.

9. Ibid., xix. bell hooks's treatment of this preoccupation focuses on the topic of interracial sex. See her "Seduction and Betrayal: *The Crying Game* Meets *The Bodyguard*" in her book *Outlaw Culture: Resisting Representations* (New York: Routledge, 1994), 53–62.

10. Morrison, *Playing in the Dark,* 12.

11. Ibid., 17.

12. Sobchack, 105.

13. For color monitoring, the operative notion of "minstrelsy" as linked to sacrifice derives from Ralph Ellison's exegesis of "the Negro as national scapegoat." For Ellison, the minstrelized blacks of white fiction "are projected aspects of an internal symbolic process through which, like a primitive tribesman dancing himself into the group frenzy necessary for battle, the white American prepares himself emotionally to perform a social role." In the color monitoring variation, the "projected aspect" is the taint of technology, to be kept separate from a purified whiteness. This projection can nevertheless pass itself off as a gesture of affirmation, "a cosmetic approach to white compunction," to re-deploy a phrase Susan Gubar uses in her study of blackface at the movies. And if, as Gubar reports, the traditional minstrelsy character was "a knavish or foolish character clearly accountable for (culpable of) past wrongs," the new techno-whiz is no less a "bad conscience" projection of the white mind, a smart black character accountable for computers and their discontents. In holding to Ellison's negative evaluation of minstrelsy projection, I argue that Eric Lott's careful revisionary study of the phenomenon does not apply to the case of color monitoring. Whereas Lott's research of the minstrelsy tradition reveals a mixture of admiration and loathing in white appropriations of black culture, color monitoring's projection of technology onto imaginary black bodies involves less love, if only because it involves less theft—the logic does not borrow from black culture to realize its projective imagery. See Susan Gubar, "Spirit-Murder at the Movies," in *Racechanges* (New York: Oxford University Press, 1997), 54–56. For Lott's basic position with respect to Ellison, see his *Love and Theft* (New York: Oxford University Press, 1993), 3–4.

14. Rob Edelman, "Sidney Poitier," in *A Political Companion to American Film,* ed. Gary Crowdus (Lakeview Press, 1994), 309.

15. Thomas Cripps, *Slow Fade to Black: The Negro in American Film, 1900–1942* (New York: Oxford University Press, 1993), 349.

16. Dean Leab, "Blacks in American Cinema," in *Political Companion,* 49.

17. See Ed Guerrero, "The Black Image in Protective Custody: Hollywood's Biracial Buddy Films of the Eighties," *Black American Cinema,* ed. Manthia Diawara (New York: Routledge, 1993), 237–46; see also Benjamin DeMott's *The Trouble With Friendship: Why Americans Can't Think Straight About Race* (New York: Atlantic Monthly Press, 1995), esp. "Visions of Black-White Friendship," 7–23.

18. Understandably, much recent critical attention has been devoted to the creative explosion of films by black filmmakers with black characters in central roles; for an account of 1991 as a banner year in this development, see Valerie Smith, "The Documentary Impulse in Contemporary African American Film," in *Black Popular Culture,* ed. Gina Dent (Seattle: Bay Press, 1992), 56–64.

In the context of the present study, which treats films outside this trend of increasing African American agency in cinema, "peripheral characters" takes on a second meaning: not simply marginal to the action and to creative control, these techno-wizards are also characters who act as "peripherals," in the sense of auxiliary devices connected to computers.

19. Guerrero, "Black Image in Protective Custody," 237.

20. Ibid., 240.

21. Snead, *White Screens/Black Images,* 119.

22. Ibid., 118. For a broader history of stereotypes with numerous examples, see Jan Nederveen Pieterse, *White on Black: Images of Africa and Blacks in Western Popular Culture* (New Haven: Yale University Press: 1992), esp. ch. 9, "Entertainers," 132–51; ch. 10, "Popular Types," 152–65; and ch. 15, "Image and Power," 224–35.

23. Roderick Thorp, *Nothing Lasts Forever* (New York: W. W. Norton, 1979).

24. Producer Arnold Kopelson has referred to the casting of Vanessa Williams in *Eraser* (1996) as "going black"; the industry-insider lingo here intimates that the default for any part is white—only when conditions favor otherwise will the producers resort to "going" elsewhere with it. The Kopelson remark was printed in "Ms. Clean Slate," *Los Angeles Times,* Sunday Calendar, May 12, 1996, 92.

25. Sander Gilman's study of the stereotype of "smart Jews" seems relevant to this depiction, as David's ethnicity is explicitly marked; *Smart Jews: The Construction of the Image of Jewish Superior Intelligence* (Lincoln: University of Nebraska Press, 1996).

26. Paul Lauter, in "Dinosaur Culture: From *Mansfield Park* to *Jurassic Park,*" offers a tour de force exposition using Spielberg's film to demonstrate four modes of American Studies scholarship. Illustrating the second mode, what he calls "the Michel Foucault step" of "looking for the ghost in the machine" of the narrative, Lauter further invokes the methodology of Toni Morrison to suggest that the film "offers a paradigm of colonialism"; see his *From Walden Pond to Jurassic Park: Activism, Culture, and American Studies* (Durham, N.C.: Duke University Press, 2001), 103, 106.

27. Michael Crichton, *Jurassic Park* (New York: Alfred A. Knopf, 1990), 128; David Koepp co-wrote the screenplay. An analogous system of difference may be read in *Clear and Present Danger* (1994), which pits Jack Ryan (Harrison Ford) against a character described as a "Latin Jack Ryan." In successive scenes, we see Ryan and his Latino double racing to perform the same research detective work to determine the cause of an explosion. While the "third world" South American mercenary retrieves the necessary information from an online database, Ryan does things the old fashioned way, paging

through library books. The ironic juxtaposition plays a significant part in distinguishing Ryan, the true-blue American humanist hero, from his evil twin, a cold-blooded
killer. One may also consider the odd circumstance that the Harrison Ford character in
The Fugitive (1993), a brilliant physician framed for murder, can only gain access to
the computer records he needs by disguising himself as a Latino hospital custodian.
Even films in which no nonwhite characters are featured may be enlisted to shed light
on a cultural technophobia that plays into the pattern. For example, in *Twister* (1996),
computer expertise is not exactly celebrated. In the final repartee between the two romantic leads, an argument arises over which one of them will get to plan and carry out
the next twister-chasing experiment and which one will be stuck at the terminal, por-
ing over the stream of data produced by the experiment they have just completed. To
the principals, computer work smacks of janitorial dirty work, a chore akin to doing
the dishes: "cleaning up the data." In the movie world, the confinement of number-
crunching clearly does not fill the bill for the heroic scientist-adventurer, driven ever
onward to experience and apprehend nature directly.

28. In *Boyz N the Hood* (1991), Cuba Gooding played Tre, who "manages to escape
South Central" to pursue a college education; we may read his position in *Outbreak*
as the outcome of a successful assimilation, a full conversion of dangerous potential
into safe instrumentality. For a discussion of Tre's importance, see Michael Eric
Dyson, "Between Apocalypse and Redemption: John Singleton's *Boyz N the Hood*,"
in his *Reflecting Black: African-American Cultural Criticism* (Minneapolis: University of Minnesota Press, 1993), 90–110.

29. Richard Dyer, "White," *Screen* 29, no. 4 (1988): 46.

30. Michael Crichton, *Rising Sun* (New York: Alfred A. Knopf, 1992), 275.

31. See Wendell Berry, *The Hidden Wound* (San Francisco: North Point Press, 1989),
esp. 112–15 for a concise statement of his thesis on the origins of racism in the wish
to displace undesirable labor.

32. James Baldwin, *The Devil Finds Work* (New York: Dial Press, 1976), 46.

33. See Sobchack, "Scene of the Screen," 89.

34. Fredric Jameson, *Postmodernism, or, The Cultural Logic of Late Capitalism*
(Durham, N.C.: Duke University Press, 1991), xviii–xix.

35. See http://us.imdb.com/name/nm0000119/bio for Carrere's self-identification. Al-
tering Carrere's look from her other film appearances, the *Rising Sun* production
gives her wavy hair in an apparent attempt to sell the idea of her character's half
African American descent.

36. Crichton, *Rising Sun*, 260–61.

37. Ibid., 185.

38. Snead, "Spectatorship and Capture in *King Kong*: The Guilty Look" in *White
Screens/Black Images*, 1–28, esp. 8: "*King Kong*, then, is a noteworthy, though perhaps
surprising, instance of the 'coded black'—in this case, the carrier of blackness is not a
human being, but an ape, but we shall see that the difference can easily be bridged."

39. Donna Haraway, *Primate Visions: Gender, Race, and Nature in the World of Modern
Science* (New York: Routledge, 1989), 162.

40. Roberto Calasso, *The Ruin of Kasch*, trans. William Weaver and Stephen Sartarelli
(Cambridge: Harvard University Press, 1994), 16.

41. The movie never resolves the paradox that although Dyson's research makes the
Terminator future possible, his research benefits from a piece of a future Termina-

tor (the vanquished assassin sent to kill Sarah Connor in the first Terminator film), preserved in the Cyberdyne vault.

42. Guerrero, "Black Image in Protective Custody," 242.

43. James Cameron and William Wisher, *Terminator 2: Judgment Day: The Book of the Film* (New York: Applause Books, 1991), 308.

44. As in John Sayles's *The Brother from Another Planet* (1984), in which Joe Morton played an alien—a fugitive slave—with the ability to remove his eye at leave it behind as a surveillance/recording device. I am grateful to Jeremy Dean for the opportunity to read in manuscript his illuminating essay on "The Slave Cyborg and Liberation Technology in *The Brother from Another Planet*"; Dean's analysis emphasizes the way Sayles's film "writes back" against unproblematic depictions of the slave cyborg. *Executive Decision,* for example, takes up the motif of black cyborgian instrumentality without regard for issues of liberation. The role of Cappy in *Executive Decision* also bears comparison to the character of Lincoln "Linc" Rhyme (Denzel Washington) in *The Bone Collector* (1999); Linc is a quadriplegic, able to communicate only via a computer and his lone motile finger.

45. Paramount's production notes for *Mission: Impossible* refer to Luther alternately as "computer expert" or "computer genius" and go to some pains to assure potential skeptics of the authenticity of the actor's (Rhames's) technological training.

46. The description of the Wallace character as "dreaded" is borrowed from the production notes for *Mission: Impossible.*

CHAPTER 2. LOST WORLDS

1. Michael Hardt and Antonio Negri, *Empire* (Cambridge: Harvard University Press, 2000), 45, 58, 193–94, and passim; see 232 for the functioning of the older colonial "outside."

2. Ibid., 194. More precisely, cultural difference can nevertheless replace biological otherness in a move no less functionally "essentialist" (192). The comparison to Marx and Engels is blurbed from Aude Lancelin's review in *Le nouvel observateur.*

3. Ibid., 195. Moreover, "Subordination is enacted in regimes of everyday practices that are more mobile and flexible but that create racial hierarchies that are nonetheless stable and brutal" (194); "racial hierarchy," however, "is viewed not as a cause but as an effect of social circumstances" (193). In this regard, *Empire*'s view of postmodern racism resembles Wendell Berry's theory of the origin of racism. See *The Hidden Wound* (San Francisco: North Point Press, 1989), discussed in chapter 1.

4. In an analogous analysis that has shaped my thinking here, Cheryl Edelson has discussed the conventions of Victorian adventure obeyed by *Survivor: Marquesas.* "Surviving the Peep-Show," paper presented at the Third International Melville Conference, June 7, 2003.

5. *Survivor 5: Thailand* aired on CBS in late 2002. A brief biography for the "Software Developer" and the video clip about his "adaptability" may be found at http://www.cbs.com/primetime/survivor5/survivors/bios/ted.shtml. and http://www.cbs.com/primetime/survivor5/video/profiles/ted.shtml. I am grateful to Creagh Breuner for bringing this evidence of a reality-TV principle of natural selection to my attention.

6. Advertiser TDI, describing its D.C. Commuter Cards, http://www.tdiworld
wide.com/html/dc_commuter_Cards.html. TDI thus distinguishes their rail ads
from Bus Cards, designed to "impact the masses." The rail ads appeared in 1999 as
lightbox posters in the Capital Metro system, the subway for Washington, D.C., and
its environs. The posters were placed along the northwest corridor, concentrated at
a series of stops along the Red Line between the Maryland suburbs and the center of
downtown; Red Line ridership correlates to high socioeconomic status. Slightly
prior to the advent of the Star Power campaign, the *Washington Post* ran a feature
on the sociology of the Red Line. In "Welcome to the Republic of the Red Line: The
Subway Set That's Traded Counterculture for Counter Service," David Brooks
anatomizes the behavior of "Latte Liberals" whose family incomes trend "comfortably above the $100,000 level." *Washington Post,* January 12, 1997, C1.
7. For comment on this incident, see the opinion piece by Gregory Kane, "Officer's
Candor Is Ugly—But Revealing," *Baltimore Sun,* February 7, 2001, 1B.
8. Such fears and desires for containment readily apply to the dark-skinned bodies of
foreign young men. In 2004, Netscape founder Marc Andreessen touted the virtues
of off-shoring technological labor in these terms: "I believe the world becomes safer
as a consequence of this. I believe this is a national security issue. . . . In fact, I think
the biggest thing we could do for world peace would be to start off-shoring jobs to
the Middle East. Young men between 16 and 34 have to do something—it would be
much better if they all had technical jobs." *Austin American-Statesman,* March 29,
2004, E4.
9. Cara Anna, "Program Bridges Gap, One Classroom at a Time," *Austin American-
Statesman,* August 13, 2001, A1.
10. Brendan Coffey, "Net Results," *Forbes,* October 8, 2001, 154.
11. George Schuyler, *Black No More* (1931; repr. New York: Modern Library, 1999), 70.
12. *Austin American-Statesman,* June 25, 2001, D4.
13. David Mamet, *Jafsie and John Henry* (New York: Free Press, 1999), 136–37.
14. The goal of increasing educational resources in underfunded school districts possesses intrinsic merit. Such merit does not rule out the possibility that a company's
proud portrayal of support for such a goal may appeal to an audience's sense of
comfort about existing segregation. The participants in the JASON project are
granted virtual mobility rather than relocation to more affluent climes: like the
Acorns in Oakland, whether there's a there there, they're "there" (not "here").
15. W. E. B. DuBois, "Of the Training of Black Men," in *The Souls of Black Folk* (1903;
repr. New York: Dover, 1994), 58.
16. The designation of these instructional sites as Digital Villages superimposes the Microsoft project onto the oft-repeated African saying, "It takes a village to raise a
child." Insofar as the Digital Villages plug into this formula, these Microsoft outposts would supplant the collective wisdom of elders with the civilizing authority of
machines.
17. Reported by Mark Leibovich in "At Amazon.com, Service Workers Without a
Smile," *Washington Post,* November 22, 1999, A12: "The surge in the technology
sector is creating service and low-skill jobs as well as high-paying high-tech jobs."
18. See Bill Bishop and Mark Lisheron, "Austin's Service Class Is Losing Its Way Out: In
High-Tech Cities, Workers Finding Paths to Wealthier, Creative Jobs Are Blocked";
"In Austin, It's Tough to Find a Way Up," *Austin American-Statesman,* November 3,

2002, A1, A10. Richard Florida, author of *The Rise of the Creative Class* (New York: Basic Books, 2002), contributed to this report on the downside of that rise.

19. Conducted for Dell, the foundational study of "cyberphobia" in the American populace put the number at 55 percent; cited in Gerard George, Randall G. Sleeth, and C. Glenn Pearce, "Technology-assisted Instruction and Instructor Cyberphobia: Recognizing the Ways to Effect Change," *Education* 116, no. 4 (Summer 1996): 604.

20. Mark Crispin Miller, "The Cosby Show," in *Rereading America*, 2nd ed. (Boston: Bedford Books, 1992), 650.

21. *Diff'rent Strokes* aired 1978–86; *Webster*, 1983–87; *Family Matters*, 1989–98; *Malcolm in the Middle*, 2000–. The popular Urkel-bot first appeared in the "Robo-Nerd" Episode of *Family Matters* (11/1/1991): "Urkelbot was created for a National Robotics Contest by Steve Urkel (Jaleel White), an intelligent but nerdish black Chicago teenager. . . . The robot was made in the likeness of its creator," including the trademark big thick glasses. http://www.tvacres.com/robots_urkelbot.htm. On *Malcolm in the Middle*, Craig Lamar Traylor portrays computer whiz Stevie Kenarban; in addition, as one character exclaims, "he's in a wheelchair *and* he has glasses!" I am grateful to Jessica Jones for pointing out this instance of the diminutive and redundantly contained black computer expert.

22. James R. Chiles, *Inviting Disaster: Lessons from the Edge of Technology* (New York: HarperBusiness, 2001), reviewed in *Science* 295 (January 11, 2002): 281. The verb in Edward Tenner's title, *Why Things Bite Back: Technology and the Revenge of Unintended Consequences* (New York: Knopf, 1996), conveys a similar sentiment about technology's potentially beastly nature.

23. As in the 1997 wilderness thriller *The Edge*, when Charles Morse (Anthony Hopkins) sternly enjoins Alec Baldwin's character to keep a grip on his sanity: "Don't go native on me, Bob!"

24. Sidney Moody, review of *Robo Sapiens: Evolution of a New Species* (Cambridge: MIT Press, 2001), *Austin Chronicle*, May 25, 2001, 48.

25. E. Ann Kaplan, *Looking for the Other: Feminism, Film, and the Imperial Gaze* (New York: Routledge, 1997), 61–62. For challenges to the epistemology of imperial structures of looking, see esp. ch. 8, "Healing Imperialized Eyes," and the afterword, "Reversing the Gaze." See also Anna Everett, *Returning the Gaze: A Genealogy of Black Film Criticism, 1909–1949* (Durham, N.C.: Duke University Press, 2001), in which the technology of print provides the potent medium for returned scrutiny. See also Theodore Kornweibel, *No Crystal Stair: Black Life and the* Messenger, *1917–1928* (Westport, Conn.: Greenwood, 1975) for work on black journalism in this period, as well as his subsequent studies on the cultural contests between black agency and national containment, *Seeing Red: Federal Campaigns against Black Militancy, 1919–1925* (Bloomington: Indiana University Press, 1998), and "*Investigate Everything": Federal Efforts to Compel Black Loyalty during World War I* (Bloomington: Indiana University Press, 2002).

26. Though *Robots and Empire* (Garden City, N.Y.: Doubleday, 1985) brings the colonial dimension of roboculture most forcefully to the fore, Asimov has consistently developed parallels to the black experience from his earliest robot novels onward. *The Caves of Steel* (1953) explores robot-human tensions in the workplace, as a murder investigation brings together a human and a robot detective in a reluctant partnership that anticipates the Poitier and Steiger team from *In the Heat of the*

Night (1967) and its seemingly countless movie imitations. Also anticipating the Poitier-Steiger success, the popularity of Asimov's Lije Bailey–R. Daneel team demanded a rapid encore. In *The Naked Sun* (1956), Asimov again plays up racially inflected friction between the leads, as when the narrator comments on "the 'boy' address that Earthmen always used for robots" (219). See *The Robot Novels* (Garden City, N.Y.: Doubleday). For a clear naming of social commentary intentions, see also Asimov's 1967 story "Segregationist," collected in *Robot Visions* (New York: Penguin, 1990).

27. Asimov astutely catalogs the onboard entertainment; of the holofilms available on the settler ship, "all were adventure stories" (95). The crew feeds its imaginative needs on the genre that goes hand in hand with empire. As a solicitous robot recommends to the chief investigator hero of an earlier Asimov novel, "The master might like an adventure romance of the days of exploration" (*The Naked Sun*, in *The Robot Novels*, 287)

28. The emphatic specification that Gladia can see "*them*" (the robots) may also refer to the Spacer aversion to seeing one another—the humans can see robots, see objects, but the Spacers avoid intersubjective looking, thus assuring that each human is absolute master or mistress of all he or she surveys. This alternate reading does not mitigate the awful sense of taboo that robots associate with seeing and the rule that the robots are to be seen but not see.

29. Robert D. Romanyshyn, *Technology as Symptom and Dream* (New York: Routledge, 1989).

30. Paul Lauter, reading *Jurassic Park* to model what he calls "the Jane Tompkins step, to speculate about the cultural work the text is performing," reflects on the dynamic by which technological "anxieties are converted into pleasure in the dark of the movie theater." *From Walden Pond to Jurassic Park: Activism, Culture, and American Studies* (Durham, N.C.: Duke University Press, 2001): 103, 111.

31. Ian Frazier, "Techno-Thriller," *Atlantic Monthly*, May 2001, 94–95.

32. Piotr Siemion, "No More Heroes: The Routinization of the Epic in Techno-Thrillers," in *Reading Matters: Narratives in the New Media Ecology*, ed. Joseph Tabbi and Michael Wutz (Ithaca, N.Y.: Cornell University Press, 1997), 196.

33. Crichton first wrote a study of Johns to accompany the exhibit catalog for the Whitney Museum of American Art; years later he revised and expanded the book into a library edition that offers a more comprehensive career retrospective. All citations refer to this latter edition (New York: Abrams, 1994). Johns himself initially suggested that Crichton write the copy for the catalog; perhaps Johns saw in Crichton's approach to novel-writing a kindred creative impulse. For his part, Crichton refers to Johns in his fiction as early as 1972, as a sympathetic psychiatrist in *The Terminal Man* displays a Johns print in her office (170).

34. In *Postmodernist Fiction* (London: Methuen, 1987), Brian McHale observed that "Increasingly rare in modern science fiction, the 'lost world' *topos* figures hardly at all in postmodernist writing" (68). Crichton's anti-postmodernist science fiction, in a deliberate throwback, repeatedly revives this familiar *topos*. For an overview of Crichton's career up to *The Lost World*, see Elizabeth A. Trembley, *Michael Crichton: A Critical Companion* (London: Greenwood Press, 1996). See especially the chapter on "Michael Crichton's Literary Heritage," 15–30; Trembley highlights "the fifty-year period from 1865 to 1915" as representing "the blossoming of popular literature in

the Anglo-American world," citing Haggard, Wells, and Doyle as among Crichton's most important literary models (16).(Martin Schneider reminded me also that Crichton "visited" Victorian England in *The Great Train Robbery*, Crichton's 1975 novel which he adapted and directed as a 1979 movie.) Piotr Siemion notes of the genre that "the relation of the techno-thriller to literary tradition is not antagonistic but nominal"; "Roughly speaking, the new poetics found in the techno-thriller consists in finding a narrative correlate for a nonnarrative world of routinized, repeatable activities. This end is achieved by grounding the nontraditional subject matter in a repertoire of established cultural forms" ("No More Heroes," 217, 197). Crichton's version of the techno-thriller differs from that presented in Siemion's Tom Clancy–centric account insofar as Crichton ultimately recoils from what Siemion characterizes as the Clancy-esque tendency toward "techno-porn" (204). Siemion reads the sentiments of the Clancy techno-thriller as "contradictory to the traditional tenet that 'everything connected with machines and mechanisms in bourgeois linguistic usage is saddled with negative valuations'" (206). Crichton not only uses the traditional forms but also upholds that traditional sentiment.

35. Michael Crichton, *The Andromeda Strain* (New York: Alfred A. Knopf, 1969; reprinted 1970 as a Dell paperback).

36. Michael Crichton, *The Terminal Man* (New York: Alfred A. Knopf, 1972).

37. Myra Jehlen, "The Literature of Colonization," in *The Cambridge History of American Literature*, vol. 1, 1590–1820, ed. Sacvan Bercovitch (Cambridge: Cambridge University Press, 1994), 165.

38. Renée L. Bergland, *The National Uncanny: Indian Ghosts and American Subjects* (Hanover, N.H.: University Press of New England, 2000).

39. Terry Castle, *The Female Thermometer: Eighteenth-Century Culture and the Invention of the Uncanny* (New York: Oxford University Press, 1995), 10.

40. Crichton's office dictator occupies a post largely lost in the era of the personal computer. More than once have I heard a lament from a middle-aged male professional along the lines of "Ever since we got computers on our desktops, we now do the work our secretaries used to do." One fifty-something gentleman confessed to me his impression that older men in his office showed even more resistance than did similarly aged women in adopting information age practices such as the regular use of e-mail.

41. Friedrich Kittler, *Discourse Networks, 1800/1900* (Stanford: Stanford University Press, 1990), 352.

42. Michael Crichton writing as "John Lange," *Binary* (New York: Knopf, 1972), 20–21.

43. http://www.imdb.com/title/tt0070909/taglines.

44. Apart from repeating and confirming orders, the black technician's job description also includes answering queries, particularly those of a numerical nature: To the question "What can you give me on grid 7?" the black technician responds: "We have that on SM 514."

45. "Cyber-Mayhem" is the title of "chapter" 23 of the film on the DVD version.

46. The film envisions a robot P.O.V., a coarsely pixellated image that anticipates the electronic gaze of James Cameron's *Terminator*.

47. http://www.imdb.com/name/nm0000989/.

48. See Amy Kaplan, "Manifest Domesticity" and Lauren Berlant, "Poor Eliza" in *American Literature*, "No More Separate Spheres!" special issue, vol. 70, no. 3 (September 1998).

49. I cite the paperback pagination of Michael Crichton's *Sphere* (New York: Ballantine, 1988). In the movie, a second techno-buffer also fits the racial profiling. Queen Latifah plays a technician who handles mundane computer chores for the white captain, the one who has identified their mission as a "heart of darkness" clean-up mission. "Fletcher! Give me playback!" Barnes (Peter Coyote) orders Latifah's character, Alice "Teeny" Fletcher. We hear the click of keystrokes and Teeny's promise of prompt data retrieval: "You'll get it in a minute."

50. Here Adams names a tune, a Mozart concerto. Like Seaman Jones in *The Hunt for Red October,* another black submarine techie schooled in classical music, Adams demonstrates expertise at aural pattern recognition, the mathematics of music.

51. Crichton anticipates this advice in *The Terminal Man* with the attitude modeled by a psychiatrist named Dr. Ross, who "watched the screen glow with row after row of calculations. She ignored them; the numbers, she knew, were just the computer's scratch pad. . . . She smiled. . . . She had discovered long ago that you could use a computer without understanding how it worked" (46–47). But not all of Crichton's characters enjoy the luxury of ignoring the numbers; someone has to get into the machine and make it run, a distinct responsibility from merely using it.

52. I am not suggesting, for example, that Crichton consciously associates primates with black people by way of their imagined mutual affinity for the machine. But his fiction, as a juxtaposition of *Congo* and *Sphere* reveals, does present that mutual affinity. My argument takes up the invitation left open in Cary Wolfe's important recent discussion of *Congo*: "It is no doubt useful—and in a longer treatment would be imperative—to read Crichton's novel as an allegory of racial fantasy in the United States of the early eighties." "Faux Posthumanism: The Discourse of Species and the Neocolonial Project in Michael Crichton's *Congo*," in *Animal Rites: American Culture, the Discourse of Species, and Posthumanist Theory* (Chicago: University of Chicago Press, 2003), 173. My reading of the narrative questions the acceptance of the received opinion that Crichton is "known for his technophilia," while nevertheless agreeing that Crichton's "fascination" with "technoscience" must be read in juxtaposition with his "neocolonialism" (187, 182). I read that fascination in the register of horror rather than love.

53. A variation on Arby appears in Crichton's latest novel, *State of Fear* (New York: HarperCollins, 2004). Here, the small computer expert is "the dark man, Sanjong," from Nepal, also referred to as "the little guy" (173) or, more favorably, as being "compact" (169). Sanjong is the faithful sidekick of the hero scientist, Kenner. "Where's Sanjong?" Kenner asks at one point, receiving an answer that largely defines Sanjong's role: "In the server room, doing what you requested" (241–42). A series of vignettes highlights the division of labor between technical support and visionary genius: "Sanjong was working on his laptop. Kenner stared out the window" (244); "Another hour passed. Sanjong was working continuously on the laptop. Kenner sat motionless, staring out the window. Sanjong was accustomed to this" (250; similar references to Sanjong working on a computer appear on 247, 316, 464, and 489). Nevertheless, Sanjong, unlike Arby, does get to play a physical role in the action finale.

54. Escapist entertainment, however much it traffics in the mind's escape from the mundane, depends for its enjoyment upon identification with gloriously physical protagonists. The narrative must speak to an audience that, at the end of the day, still loves the comforts of the flesh. Some critics have mistaken the enthusiasm of

elite techno-extremists, vociferously bent on "being digital," for a groundswell. But the all-American techno-thriller tells a different tale. In popular narrative, the pronouncements the cyber-critics most deplore already fit most readily into the mouths of villains; the drive toward virtualization thus registers in the popular imagination as that which must reflexively be resisted, a resistance that makes common cause with the hero.

55. For the mutual inextricability of personality and nationality in the American tradition, see Wai-chee Dimock, "Nation, Self, and Personification," in *Empire for Liberty: Melville and the Poetics of Individualism* (Princeton: Princeton University Press, 1989).

56. "Biocybernetic reproduction" appears in W. J. T. Mitchell's *The Last Dinosaur Book: The Life and Times of a Cultural Icon* (Chicago: University of Chicago Press, 1998) 171, 209, 215–19, to update Walter Benjamin's age of merely "mechanical" reproduction.

57. *Dark Territory* was the sequel to 1992's highly popular *Under Siege*. The plot features an "overlooked" Navy cook who gets out of the kitchen and turns up the heat to foil the terrorists. In the remasculinizing trajectory from apron to guns, potshots at digital technology pave the way.

58. Everett, *Returning the Gaze*, 247, discussing and quoting from Lawrence Reddick's 1944 essay, "Of Motion Pictures." The American films that Reddick critiques for their use of black heroes to underwrite colonialism include *King Kong, Baboona,* and *When Africa Speaks* (287–88). Everett notes that Reddick's insight predates Roland Barthes's much more celebrated "observation about an African soldier performing the same function for French imperialism" (287).

59. Bergland, *National Uncanny*, 13. See also W. J. T. Mitchell's discussion of America as the empire that denies it is an empire: "This would not be the British style of empire . . . but a 'soft,' gradual, natural empire of civilizing progress." *Last Dinosaur Book,* 121.

60. "Nature's Nation" refers to America's sense of natural/providential destiny and is discussed in Perry Miller's landmark Americanist book of the same name (Cambridge: Harvard University Press, 1967).

61. See John Huntington's *The Logic of Fantasy: H. G. Wells and Science Fiction* (New York: Columbia University Press, 1982) for a discussion of Wells's use of symbols relating to intellectual and technological domination: "We have here an expression of the danger of dependence on the very technology that allows for mastery. . . . The human is betrayed by his own technological sophistication" (50). Frank McConnell's take in *The Science Fiction of H. G. Wells* (New York: Oxford University Press, 1981) would complicate the technophobic scheme I find the film to emphasize; McConnell reads *The Time Machine* as a kind of Symbolist poem structured upon "intellectual dubiety" (88): "The distance from the threatening technology of Butler's *Erewhon* is vast" (74). I read the film as retaining an overwhelmingly technophobic theme, while reserving a tiny, well-defined opening for technology's enduring value.

62. Arthur and Marilouise Kroker, *Hacking the Future: Stories for The Flesh-Eating 90s* (New York: St. Martin's Press, New World Perspectives CultureTexts Series, 1996).

63. In a remark found on the DVD "commentary" track, the director notes that Vox was originally going to be a robot. The creative team believed the decision to put Jones in the role of the holographic projection was "very much casting against

type." I'm sure they thought so at the time. The present analysis suggests the contrary to be true: an entertaining black Vox perfectly fulfills an existing type. The filmmakers do note Vox's broadly resonant appeal. According to Wayne Wahrman, the editor, "Audiences seem to like it." The director concurs: "I think Vox is one of the favorite characters in the movie." I am indebted to Gabriel Lopez for emphasizing the importance of Vox to the *Color Monitors* project.

64. The question of treating information as if it had lost its body adopts the terms of Katherine Hayles's critique in *How We Became Posthuman* (Chicago: University of Chicago Press, 1999). An earlier version of Vox, presented in a different mood, appears in George Lucas's dystopian *THX 1138* (1971). "SRT, the hologram," portrayed by black actor Don Pedro Colley, crosses over to the "real world" to gain a body. SRT introduces himself to the hero, THX 1138 (Robert Duvall), who inhabits a mysteriously all-white world subject to computer control, a control system which includes holographic entertainment that, apart from a channel that shows a robot cop beating a man, presents nothing but programmed images of black people: "I'm a hologram. I'm not real. You know, the Fantasy Bureau, electrically-generated realities and all that." In portraying the Fantasy Bureau as insidious, Lucas's first feature film, co-written with Walter Murch, would appear to critique the stereotypical reduction of black people to disembodied figures for entertainment. Though the film presents an association of blackness with technology, it identifies that association as the product of a culture of containment: How will the evil computer of the future pacify a white population? By broadcasting simulated black comedians, exotic dancers, and talk show hosts. As SRT observes, "I was stuck in the same circuit for too long. The arm and leg routine. Didja see that one?" Lucas's subsequent work (to be discussed in chapter 4) will continue to associate technology with blackness, but to explore a different fear, the fear of what happens to the white body when it undergoes technological incorporation. For a more complex development of the critique implied by *THX 1138,* one that similarly pairs the absence of black humanity with the all-too-appealing presence of stereotypical black simulacra, see Matt Ruff's science fiction satire, *Sewer, Gas and Electric* (New York: Grove, 1997). Set in the year 2023, Ruff's *Public Works Trilogy* presents an America from which almost all African Americans have been wiped out by a plague, but for which the most popular model of Automated Servant is "basic black." Informally known as the "Electric Negro," based on an android first "test-marketed by a Disney subsidiary in 2003," the "industrial labor substitute" flavors its speech with the repeated phrase, "Zippity-doo-*day*!" (14–18). Ruff's narrator remarks, "People didn't seem to mind—in fact seemed strangely comforted by—the sudden profusion of dark-skinned Servants, all of them polite and hard-working to a fault" (15).

65. *The Adventures of Tom Sawyer,* ed. Shelley Fisher Fishkin (New York: Oxford University Press, 1996). Albert E. Stone's perceptive afterword observes that the aging Twain "derisively terms Theodore Roosevelt the political Tom Sawyer of the Spanish-American War era" (16).

Another recent attempt to revitalize late imperial adventure, *The League of Extraordinary Gentleman* (2003), adds Tom Sawyer as the sole American to round out its all-star cast of characters from Victorian fiction. In this adaptation of the popular comic for the American screen, Tom Sawyer, that most devotedly imitative of romance readers, becomes the protégé of Allan Quatermain, H. Rider Haggard's

"Great White Hunter" from *King Solomon's Mines.* Standing next to Sean Connery as Quatermain, young Tom (Shane West) proves to be a quick study in learning to shoulder the shotgun of empire.

66. A society that tends to relate to computers as though they were magic is ripe for assimilating the kind of racializing appeal Tom makes here. Tom attributes to blacks a special knowledge of magical techniques; contemporary society popularizes the quasi-mystical figure of the black computer wizard. A further discussion of the indistinguishability of technology and magic appears in the next chapter.

CHAPTER 3. INTEGRATED CIRCUITS

1. "Univac Computer Turns 50," *Austin American-Statesman,* June 15, 2002, C1.
2. In order to give a sense of the representational field from which this chapter's examples have been drawn, I here present a survey of the advertisements in a complete issue of *Forbes* magazine (September 1, 2003; I selected this issue at random without having previously browsed its contents; see footnote 7 for an economic characterization of the *Forbes* readership addressed in these ads). The 146–page issue contains sixty-six full-page ads. Of these, twenty-six sell computers, software, or information technology services; six depict computers; five display both people and computers. Of those five, two ads show black men using computers (and white men *not* using computers). Only one ad shows a white man in contact with a computer, the "ultra-small, full-featured notebook you don't have to make room for," a non-encroaching travel tool that "turns coach into first-class"; as I emphasize throughout this book, the issue is not just the fact of computer/human juxtaposition but also how people are portrayed with regard to technology: black men handle the chores while white men enjoy the liberation. Within this sample, it is instructive to note that a majority of computer-related ads do not display a computer at all and that an inverse racial pattern occurs in these examples. Of the remaining twenty computer ads, seven show neither human face nor computer, and thirteen show faces without a computer. Of those thirteen, only one shows a black man (the other twelve show some mixture of white men and women; no black women appear in this issue). In summary: in ads with people and computers, more black men than white men are shown using the machines; in computer-related ads showing people without computers, more white men than black men appear. Taking a step back and again looking at all sixty-six ads, perhaps the most striking pattern within this sample snaps into view: there are no other black men in the entire issue. Whereas one may say that, in this major business magazine, a computer is likely to appear with a black man, one may also say that a black man is unlikely to appear without a computer. If, as Friedrich Kittler shows, women first enter the office picture behind an Olivetti or an Underwood, black men make the corporate scene in conjunction with a Dell or an IBM; *Discourse Networks, 1800/1900* (Stanford: Stanford University Press, 1990), 351–53.
3. As of 2001, Dark-o came bundled with Farallon's home networking package. The cartoonish name "Dark-o the Wizard" evokes mere child's play: the technological rocketry and wizardry are nothing to fear. The style of the Black Rocket icon also reassures: the retro design of bulbous fuselage and curved fins nods toward a nostalgic version of a sci-fi future; it also suggests a child's toy.

4. http://www.genuity.com/about/advertising.

5. Thomas Pynchon, *Gravity's Rainbow* (New York: Viking, 1973), 113, 75, 578, 566, 674. The novel's "philosopher with a vision of the postwar state" foresees "a rational structure in which business would be the true, the rightful authority—a structure based, not surprisingly, on the one he'd engineered in Germany for fighting the World War" (165). For the confluence of the ARPAnet genealogy with Pynchon's vision, see Joseph Tabbi's *Postmodern Sublime: Technology and American Writing from Mailer to Cyberpunk* (Ithaca, N.Y.: Cornell University Press, 1995), 74–76. For the homology between the contemporary Rocket State and ancient systems of sacrifice, see Michel Serres, *Statues* (Paris: François Bourin, 1987), 13–34; also discussed in Michel Serres with Bruno Latour, *Conversations on Science, Culture, and Time* (Ann Arbor: University of Michigan Press, 1995), 97, 138.

6. At Dell's website in 2002, the button icons for a menu of links perform the same flattening function. The menu offers five choices, uniform squares aligned in a row: four of the icons show hardware; the fifth shows a smiling black man with a headset. The man thus appears as a supplement, the service that backs the servers, but he also exists in a kind of representational equivalence with the rest of the hardware.

7. The ad creates a clear opposition: "You" are not "I." The "You" asks the questions, and expects answers. The "I" is the black technology at your service. The "you," although not racially or otherwise visually specified, is, at a minimum, not the black man in the picture. We know a few other things about this "you." The ad ran in *Forbes*. As of 2001, the average Forbes reader had a net worth of $2.1 million, and as of 1999 a median household income of $167,000 (that is, easily in the top 5 percent of U.S. incomes); *Forbes*, August 20, 2001, and November 1, 1999. If there is a black-white opposition in this ad, it is at most demographically probable and mildly implicit. Elsewhere in corporate iconography, as we will see, the black-white opposition is fully visible, with a surrogate white "you" depicted alongside the technologized black.

8. Joanne Gordon, "India or Bust," *Forbes*, April 1, 2002, 66.

9. John Pletz, "Dell's India Center to Support U.S. Buyers," *Austin American-Statesman*, June 15, 2001, C1. Industry analyst Roger Kay notes that the practice of "shipping call centers out" has already been extended to Jamaica and Belize. In a recent update on offshore outsourcing, a company called SeaCode has hatched a plan to anchor a ship in the international waters that begin just three miles off the coast of California; they plan to "pack the boat with engineers who will write code day and night." SeaCode would classify the coders "hired from places like India and Russia" as "seamen" and "skirt the need for those pesky immigration visas." "We're not a slave ship," says co-founder David Cook defensively; he goes on to boast of the round-the-clock productivity that the programming galley can deliver: "Try to get American software engineers to work at night." See David Whelan, "C++ Faring Lads: Why Send Software Work to India When You Can Have it Done on a Cruise Ship 3.1 miles off California?" *Forbes*, May 9, 2005, 48.

10. Gaiutra Bahadur, "India's High-Tech Braceros," *Austin American-Statesman*, November 19, 2000, A1. The author of this particular article refers to the recent influx of "migrant" tech workers to Texas that accompanied the Internet boom. That is, the pattern of outsourcing to India has also brought immigrants.

11. Joanne Gordon, "India or Bust," 66.

12. Pletz, "Dell's India Center to Support U.S. Buyers."

13. John Pletz, "Dell Aims for 'Massive Breakthroughs'" *Austin American-Statesman,* May 21, 2002, A1.

14. Cited in the *American Studies Association Newsletter* 22, no. 1 (March 1999): 3.

15. Paul Anderson and Art Rosenberg, *The Executive's Guide to Customer Relationship Management: Retention, Loyalty, Profit,* 2nd ed. (Houston: Doyle Publishing, 2000), 118.

16. The new U.S. penitentiary in Atwater, California, houses another big venture in prison tech work: "Federal Prison Industries Inc., which markets its products under the name Unicor, will operate the plant. The company already has electronics recycling facilities at prisons in Florida, New Jersey, Ohio and Texas, and the California plant will be its largest to date, said Larry Novicky, general manager of Unicor's recycled electronics products and services group." *Waste News,* February 4, 2002.

17. Tracie Powell, "Doing Time Repairing Computers," *Austin American-Statesman,* August 1, 2000, D8.

18. Fox Butterfield (for the *New York Times*), "U.S. State Prison Populations Declined in Last Half of 2000," *Austin American-Statesman,* August 13, 2001, A7. The 428,000 represents 9.7 percent of all black men in the 20–29 age range; by comparison, "1.1 percent of non-Hispanic white men in that age group . . . were in prison."

19. Powell, "Doing Time Repairing Computers," D1.

20. The first movie in the series appeared in 1988; Sandoval was sentenced in 1990; the series is up to six installments as of 2004.

21. Microsoft is another tech notable that has relied on prison labor. See *New York Times,* March 19, 2000, A1.

22. Daniel Fisher, "Pulled in New Directions," *Forbes,* June 10, 2002, 112.

23. Phil Sneiderman, "Hard Drives Lessen Hard Time," *Los Angeles Times,* July 16, 1995, B3.

24. Reese Erlich, "Inmates Refurbish Old Computers for a New Future," *Christian Science Monitor,* June 3, 1998, 12.

25. Erlich, 12; emphasis added. This criterion (life sentence tech support) tends to further select for black men: as of 2000, over 60 percent of those serving murder sentences were black men, though black men account for only about 6 percent of the U.S. population (12.9 percent black men and women as of the 2000 census). See Butterfield, "U.S. State Prison Populations," A7.

26. Such tech support images are a staple of marketing high tech. For example, a 2002 webpage answering the question "Why AT&T DSL is right for you" shows the thumbnail of a smiling black woman with a headset, the emblem of AT&T's free tech support. The tag "24/7 Support" merges with the top of her head: "You'll have access to a dedicated customer service team, available 24/7 to assist you with live technical support" (http://www.consumer.att.com/dsl/promotion/whyatt.html). In a *Forbes ASAP* special section devoted to the question "Is your planner wired?" the facing page ad shows us what a wired planner ought to look like. Because "even the most active traders occasionally have a question," Fidelity.com promises access to a "dedicated trading team" to answer such questions. A smiling black man, with headset and glasses, supplies the face of that support team; *Forbes ASAP,* December 3, 2001, 104–5.

27. Daniel Fisher, "Pulled in New Directions," *Forbes,* June 10, 2002, 112.

28. Ibid., 110 (inset).

29. John Pletz, "A Factory Built for Speed," *Austin American-Statesman,* August 26, 2002, D1, D6. On the topic of automation and labor reductions, David Lodge's *Nice Work* (1988) features an exchange between an academician concerned with social justice and a hard-nosed managing director. The factory boss has just explained that although "a fully computerised factory" can be built, "there'll always have to be a man in charge, at least one man, deciding what should be made." The English lecturer replies, "O brave new world . . . where only the managing directors have jobs." The manager explains, "I don't like making men redundant . . . but we're caught in a double bind. If we don't modernise we lose competitive edge and have to make men redundant, and if we do modernise we have to make men redundant because we don't need 'em any more" (85). I quote this speech because it quite fairly captures a managerial perspective I've seen expressed by executives at Dell and other companies. I don't wish to portray corporate executives as gleefully conspiring to eliminate jobs; what I most wish to scrutinize at present are the images, presented through various channels, that may function, consciously or unconsciously, to ease the pain of that "double bind."

30. "The Paradise of Bachelors and The Tartarus of Maids" (1855), in *Great Short Works of Herman Melville,* ed. Warner Berthoff (New York: Harper and Row, 1969), 215–16. For a discussion of "The Tartarus of Maids" as a scene of "the production of whiteness," see Cindy Weinstein, "Melville, Labor, and the Discourses of Reception," in *The Cambridge Companion to Herman Melville,* ed. Robert S. Levine (Cambridge: Cambridge University Press, 1998), 214. In *Romantic Cyborgs: Authorship and Technology in the American Renaissance* (Amherst: University of Massachusetts Press, 2002), Klaus Benesch offers an unexpected reading of "The Tartarus of Maids" by looking beyond the "familiar technophobic rhetoric" to find an author "who struggled to make his peace with technology by synecdochically investing it with gendered cybernetic imagery" (146, 145).

31. The musical *The Best Little Whorehouse in Texas,* first produced in 1977, ran for some 1,700 performances. A film version appeared in 1982. A smaller headline on the Dell factory scene draws from the aforementioned image of dehumanized labor: "Ants on a Hot Plate."

32. http://unite-and-resist.cloudmakers.org; for more information about this "militia," see http://www.agentland.com/cgi-bin/relocation.cgi? http://www.agentland.com/pages/learn/artificial_intelligence/arm.html. The group reportedly held rallies on May 6, 2001, in Chicago, New York, and Los Angeles.

33. Sidney Moody, "*Robo Sapiens*" (book review), *Austin Chronicle,* May 25, 2001, 48.

34. "AT&T Labs' Heritage In Speech: Figures of Speech" (2001) http://naturalvoices.att.com/aboutus/speech.html#1. See Venus Green, *Race on the Line: Gender, Labor, and Technology in the Bell System, 1880–1980* (Durham, N.C.: Duke University Press, 2001), for a history of the racial and sexual stereotypes that have defined the telecommunications workplace. See especially her argument in chapter 8, "Black Operators in the Computer Age": Green attributes the trend of replacing white operators with African American operators to the "need to hire inexpensive labor as it implemented new technologies"; "Simultaneously, the Bell System hired African American women to work switchboards, and it incrementally introduced computerized equipment (TSPS) along with the practice of charging for directory

assistance. All of these changes reduced the need for operators. In effect, as soon as job opportunities opened for black women, computerization and occupational segregation closed them" (227).

35. McKinsey and Company, as quoted by Lisa Guernsey, "Software Is Called Capable of Copying Any Human Voice," *New York Times,* July 31, 2001, A1.

36. Bryan Parent, as quoted by George A. Chidi, " 'Rich' says hello: AT&T releases voice software," *Infoworld,* July 31, 2001; http://iwsun4.infoworld.com/articles/hn/xml/01/07/31/010731hnattvoice.xml.

37. "Technology of the Year" as awarded by Frost and Sullivan. See AT&T News Release for March 13, 2002, http://www.att.com/news/item/0,1847,4262,00.html.

38. Replayed over a variety of broadcast news media, the Talking Press Release was also featured at both http://www.att.com and http://www.naturalvoices.att.com around the time of the July 31, 2001, product launch and subsequently transcribed via conventional speech-to-text technology (release was only available as a .wav file, not as text).

39. http://www.naturalvoices.att.com/demos/rcvd_us_m.html#rich, accessed August 29, 2002.

40. Chidi, " 'Rich' says hello." Most printed descriptions of Rich's voice don't get more specific than this reference to pitch: on the lower frequencies, he'll speak for you.

41. Adam Newton, analyzing ethnoracial relations by way of an O. J. Simpson trial anecdote, considers the general defensibility of calling a person's voice "black": "Cochran took a witness to task for identifying a voice as 'black,' calling such a remark out and out racism, and taking the opportunity to inveigh against discrimination in a color-sighted society. Of course, Cochran's charge was, to use his favorite term of dismissal, preposterous, as it denied ethnoracial particulars in the very service of an argument that *required* them if prejudice was to demonstrate its objective mis-recognitive work. Denying timbre, accent, or inflection of voice as markers of ethnicity logically demands absenting color as a sign of race; tonedeafness instead of color-blindness merely ensures a specious vocal uniformity." Adam Zachary Newton, *Facing Black and Jew: Literature as Public Space in Twentieth-Century America* (Cambridge University Press, 1999), 154. The many people for whom I played back the "Rich" audio files consistently identified his voice as sounding black.

42. Guernsey, "Software Is Called Capable," A1.

43. Ibid. *Concatenate* contains as its root the Latin *catena,* or chain; the digital synthesis strings together fragments of voice as links in a chain.

44. Eldridge Cleaver, *Soul on Ice* (New York: Dell, 1968), 202. Computers and rocket science appear as twin threats to the body.

45. *Soul on Ice,* 203. I am indebted to Wayne Rebhorn for calling my attention to the relevance of Cleaver's testimony.

46. *Forbes ASAP,* March 25, 2002, 40.

47. For example, the improvement program promised through the Tuskegee Institute, a.k.a. "The Tuskegee Machine," founded 1881; see *Cultural Contexts for Ralph Ellison's* Invisible Man (New York: Bedford, 1995), especially editor Eric Sundquist's introductory note and bibliography on Booker T. Washington, "The Wizard of Tuskegee," 33–35. One may note how these popular monikers associated with vocational training link mechanism, magic, and blackness.

48. "The Paradise of Bachelors and The Tartarus of Maids," *Great Short Works,* 215.

49. http://www.cluetrain.com/.

50. "AT&T Labs Technology Makes Computers Talk in 'Red Planet,' " http://www.re-search.att.com/projects/tts/redplanet.html.

51. "AT&T Labs—Research News—Text-to-Speech (TTS) Synthesis," http://www.re-search.att.com/news/2001/September/TTS.html.

52. "We do the math, so you don't have to," http://www.convertogadget.com; "fills forms," http://www.roboform.com; "search," http://www.searchalot.com; all lo-cated using the Google search engine. The "We do I.T." sponsor ad aired on NPR during the winter of 2001. Evidently the "just do it" ethos, born in the recreational realm, does not extend to "doing" I.T.

53. Michael Dell with Catherine Fredman, *Direct from Dell: Strategies that Revolution-ized an Industry* (New York, HarperBusiness, 1999), 153.

54. Maxine Hong Kingston, *Tripmaster Monkey: His Fake Book* (New York: Knopf, 1989), 100.

55. I allude to Dana Nelson's thesis on the bond of *National Manhood: Capitalist Citi-zenship and the Imagined Fraternity of White Men* (Durham, N.C.: Duke University Press, 1998). In *The Grifters* (1990, dir. Stephen Frears, screenplay by Donald E. Westlake), the Henry Fellowes scam appears in chapter 11 on the DVD.

56. This scene may also be read as a brief parable *avant la lettre* of the recent economic past. During the heyday of the dotcom bubble, many investors poured large sums of cash into ventures they poorly understood. They invested out of ignorance and fear—that is, a greedy fear that they would be left out of a good thing but also a fear that kept them from adequately redressing their technological ignorance. In essence, many of these investment scenarios were pure *confidence* games. When collective confidence began to fail, few investors possessed sufficient knowledge to discrimi-nate between bankrupt technologies and those with genuine merit—so all of the bubbles burst together. Because people had never really looked, they didn't know whether or not they had invested in the illusory hum of an empty room, so to speak.

57. Owen Edwards, "Mores: The Boys in the Bandwidth," *Forbes ASAP,* June 24, 2002, 128. A sketch of Edwards's vaguely Hemingway-esque visage graces the column.

58. *PC World,* March 2002, 25. The ad also appeared in general-interest news maga-zines.

59. For a discussion of John Wayne's calculated mastery of this pose, see Garry Wills's book on that cultural icon, *John Wayne's America: The Politics of Celebrity* (New York: Simon and Schuster, 1997). The pose of the goat expert in the Office Depot ad approximates that of Michelangelo's *David*.

60. I am indebted to Gabriel Lopez for picking up on this Shakespearian echo. My point is not that the advertisers intend any allusion to Shakespeare but rather that Shakespeare accurately names the game that their imagery may serve.

61. *Othello,* act I, scene i. For a full discussion of the presence of blackness in the drama, see Arthur L. Little, " 'An Essence That's Not Seen': The Primal Scene of Racism in *Othello*," *Shakespeare Quarterly* 44, no. 3 (Fall 1993): 304–24.

62. Cleaver, *Soul on Ice,* 209.

63. The offense in question involved the fact that a computer had given the highly touted University of Texas football team a low ranking. Randy Riggs, "In NYC, It's a Long Way to the Top for Longhorns," *Austin American-Statesman,* October 1, 2002, C1. This proposed violence against the machine is not without historical

racial echoes; such sentiments may give new meaning to Clarence Thomas's memorable phrase, "high-tech lynching." In this example, the prospect of irate sports fans brandishing a noose resonates with the collective violence of mob justice. For a theorizaton of race and gender with regard to lynching with an emphasis on the treatment of black masculinity, see Robyn Wiegman, "The Anatomy of Lynching," in *American Anatomies* (Durham, N.C.: Duke University Press, 1995), 81–114.

64. *IBM Annual Report 2001,* 15, emphasis in original. The side-by-side shots of Bishop and Cantu appear at the top of the facing page. I refer to the print edition; it is also available in web format at http://www.ibm.com/annualreport/2001. Bishop and Cantu shots available at http://www.ibm.com/annualreport/2001/decisions/dec_03_a.html, http://www.ibm.com/annualreport/2001/decisions/dec_03_b.html.

65. This notion of 100 percent availability also appears, for example, in an ad for Microsoft Windows 2000 Professional. To represent the absolute dependability of the software, the ad shows a mug shot of a solemn, almost sad, black man, with a text box slapped across his chest: "I'll Be There When You Need Me"; *Forbes,* January 22, 2001, 77. Rather than pitching some other quality of the product, such as its power or versatility, the black man's body bolsters the simple claim that the operating system is always in place and on call. The same can be said for the presentation of IBM's Cantu.

66. *Forbes.com* [title of print edition devoted to online commerce], June 25, 2001: 60–61.

67. *Forbes,* October 8, 2001: 32–33.

68. I refer in particular to the work of René Girard, who proposes that sport derives from religious ritual. Girard thus argues against Huizinga's *Homo Ludens* thesis, which subordinates religion to a form of play. Girard also significantly argues against Frazer and the Cambridge ritualists, who suggest that sacrificial ritual arises as an observance to nature and its succession of seasons. Girard argues that, on the contrary, sacrifice is primary and foundational—the justification of that sacrifice as somehow "natural" enters later through the mythologizing work of culture. See Girard's *Violence and the Sacred,* trans. Patrick Gregory (Baltimore: Johns Hopkins University Press, 1977), 95–96, 154. For a study that employs the anthropological language of sacrifice to describe the black experience in America, see Orlando Patterson's *Rituals of Blood: Consequences of Slavery in Two American Centuries* (Washington, D.C.: Civitas Counterpoint, 1998). In the context of the current antipathy toward technology, a discussion of sport can occasionally revert to overtly sacrificial language, as with the "somebody git a rope" example discussed above.

69. I use the word "decisive" for the violent echoes Girard has noted: to decide is to slit the throat of the sacrificial victim. That action marks the power divide between priest and victim, here replayed in the face-off between the executive and the executee of the technological imperative.

70. *Forbes,* September 2, 2002, 25.

71. The fact that companies are far from oblivious to issues of race is reflected in a frank editorial by Robert L. Woodson Jr.: "Most big companies have an office that, let's face it, is there to make sure there are no waves on racial matters." "Paying Ransom," *Forbes,* April 1, 2001, 48.

72. *Invisible Man* (New York: Vintage Books, 1972), 27.

73. In the context of air safety, the status of the "black box" also surfaces. The recording angel diligently takes down all of the flight data. But, if all goes well, the technology

keeps these numbers to itself, safely stowed away in a dark, confined compartment. Only if something goes terribly wrong will humans ever open the black box and inspect its contents.

74. For the rise of racist discourse in the Enlightenment, see David Theo Goldberg, *Racist Culture: Philosophy and the Politics of Meaning* (Oxford: Blackwell, 1993).

75. See http://www.tenzing.com. See also "Boeing Rival Acquires In-flight Net Service," *Austin American-Statesman,* June 15, 2002, C1. For another online service deploying a similar metaphor of techno-labor, see http://www.marketingsherpa.com.

76. See Jon Krakauer's *Into Thin Air* (New York: Villard, 1997).

77. See http://www.tenzing.com/about/about.html.

78. In *Typee,* these are the two English words that the narrator teaches to his indigenous host.

CHAPTER 4. TECHNO-BLACK LIKE ME

1. For a crushing exposition of a white family's manipulation of the expression to work "like a nigger," see Gilbert Sorrentino's *Red the Fiend* (New York: Fromm International, 1995), a fugue on the phraseology of loathing and its toxic repercussions.

2. Michael North, *The Dialect of Modernism: Race, Language, and Twentieth-Century Literature* (New York: Oxford University Press, 1994), 24.

3. Susan Gubar, *Racechanges: White Skin, Black Face in American Culture* (New York: Oxford University Press, 1997), 136. Gubar acknowledges the influence of Eric Lott's *Love and Theft: Blackface Minstrelsy and the American Working Class* (New York: Oxford University Press, 1993).

4. I adopt the concept of "victimary thinking" from Gil Bailie's *Violence Unveiled: Humanity at the Crossroads* (New York: Crossroad, 1995).

5. The book version of the film *Slacker* reproduces this headline clipping for the inside of the front cover. "Slack Like Me" parodies the (in)famous pose of "Black Like Me"—the sensational 1961 John Howard Griffin book and the subsequent movie. Griffin, a white journalist, posed as a black man in the South but aimed the book at a "universal" and generalizable perspective; "The real story," Griffin claimed, "is the story of the persecuted, the defrauded, the feared and detested." Preface, *Black Like Me* (Boston: Houghton Mifflin, 1961).

6. Melissa Segrest, "Master SLACKER," *Austin American-Statesman,* July 1, 2001, K1.

7. Melissa Petrek and Alan Hines, "Withdrawing in Disgust is Not the Same as Apathy: Cutting Some Slack with Richard Linklater," *Mondo 2000* 9 (1993): 81.

8. *Hotwired* is *Wired* magazine's Web supplement. The "Geek of the Week" profile may be found at http://hotwired.wired.com/members/97/47/index0a.html; the white "slave" geek in the spotlight claimed to have taught a class at MIT and have founded his own company—still profitable—in high school; honorable mention for that week went to a part-time geek who proved his "cool" by finishing all of his sentences with the hip-hop expression "Yo!" For a *Wired* story that discusses *Temp Slave,* see http://hotwired.wired.com/zines/96/19/index0a.html. For a reception of Slave Labor Graphics that tells a story of information age *ressentiment,* see http://hotwired.wired.com/netizen/96/27/katz1a.html.

NOTES TO PAGES 120–124

9. As Ellen Ullman reminds us in *Close to the Machine* (San Francisco: City Lights Books, 1997), the term "hacker" initially referred to a skillful coder, not simply to an electronic vandal. That the predominant popular use of the term now refers to a malicious creator of viruses and worms fits a societal view of coding as itself pathological.

10. Bill Lessard and Steve Baldwin, *NetSlaves: True Tales of Working the Web* (New York: McGraw Hill, 2000). Abolitionists Garrison and Phillips provided the introduction to *The Narrative of the Life of Frederick Douglass* (1845), a true tale of an escaped slave.

11. For a critical account of such dubiously authenticating gestures, see Laura Browder, "Postwar Blackface: How Middle-Class White Americans Became Authentic through Blackness," in her *Slippery Characters: Ethnic Impersonators and American Identities* (Chapel Hill: University of North Carolina Press, 2000).

12. Mel Krantzler and Patricia Biondi Krantzler, *Down and Out in Silicon Valley: The High Cost of the High-Tech Dream* (Amherst, New York: Prometheus Books, 2002).

13. The OED gives the first usage of the derogatory slang expression "get a life" as 1983. The entry cites several examples, including this 1994 instance: "If I'm using e-mail because I can't handle the stress of being in close proximity to other people, then I'm sad and should probably get a life."

14. One may also note that the term "micromanagement" as a term of opprobrium for an overly vigilant corporate style became prominent in the era of the microprocessor. The *micro-* in micromanagement refers to a supervisor's obsessive focus on tiny details. But it is in this undeviating insistence on precise specifications that the manager most grows to resemble a microcomputer—"micromanagement" thus resonates strongly as a pejorative in a workplace that fears the tyranny of cybernetic control. The first usage of a series of related words, as dated by the OED, suggests the historical clustering of these concepts: microcomputer (1968), microprocessor (1969), micromanagement (1975), micromanage (1976, chiefly U.S.).

15. Posted January 30, 2003, to alt.destroy.microsoft and several related boards. Typography as in original.

16. Samuel R. Delany, *Longer Views: Extended Essays* (Hanover, N.H.: Wesleyan University Press/University Press of New England, 1996), 101. Audience horror at Vader's enslavement to technology may be tempered by a "fascination" with his acquired blackness, as witnessed by Kevin Smith in "Darth and Me," *Rolling Stone,* June 2, 2005, 50. Smith writes admiringly about the "baddest brother in the galaxy," reminiscing that, like suburban youth of today, he found himself drawn to "black culture, personified in Darth Vader" (50).

17. Thus Leonard Maltin characterizes Browne, who portrays the technological black Box that blocks the white protagonists' access to nature; see http://www.imdb.com/name/nm0001975/bio. Jeremy Dean, extending an earlier critique of *Logan's Run* by Michael Ryan and Douglas Kellner, introduces race as an added term: "Ryan and Kellner, in their reading of *Logan's Run,* argue that the hero's escape from metropolis to nature in effect advocated traditional values of American individualism, and, we might add, white privilege"; Jeremy Dean, "The Slave Cyborg and Liberation Technology in *The Brother from Another Planet*" (manuscript essay), citing Michael Ryan and Douglas Kellner, "Technophobia," in *Alien Zone: Cultural Theory and Contemporary Science Fiction Narrative,* ed. Annette Kuhn (London: Verso, 1990), 62. For other cultural critics skeptical of knee-jerk humanist techno-

188 NOTES TO PAGES 125-127

phobia, see also Andrew Feenberg, *Questioning Technology* (New York: Routledge, 1999) for an argument contra "essentialist" philosophies of technology that have tended to foreclose serious social analysis (vii–ix); and Mark Poster, *What's the Matter with the Internet?* (Minneapolis: University of Minnesota Press, 2001) for a discussion that avoids both negative and positive technological essentialisms, "technophobic demonization" and "naive celebration" (13, 61).

18. Bill Nichols, "The Work of Culture in the Age of Cybernetic Systems," *The New Media Reader*, ed. Noah Wardrip-Fruin and Nick Montfort (Cambridge, Mass.: MIT Press, 2003), 630. The essay first appeared in 1988.

19. Scott Bukatman, *Terminal Identity* (Durham, N.C.: Duke University Press), 266. Here Bukatman briefly and fruitfully suggests that such anxiety about race pervades science fiction. Also relevant to the analysis of cyberpunk cyberphobia in both this chapter and the next is Bukatman's documentation of *Alien*'s powerful influence on the imagination of William Gibson (363–64). Whereas Gibson highlights the aesthetic of the "dirty kitchen-sink spaceship," *Alien*'s positing of a menacing alien intelligence in parallel with a cybernetically controlled corporate environment seems equally influential for Gibson's plotlines. For critical and fearless "reflections that link the alien to a political context of paranoia and a technological context of complexity, uncertainty, and interconnection," see Jodi Dean's *Aliens in America: Conspiracy Cultures from Outerspace to Cyberspace* (Ithaca, N.Y.: Cornell University Press, 1998), 14. For an assessment of the technophobic strain in Gibson's work, see Rob Kitchen's argument that "techno-utopians" have overlooked Gibson's "irony" about the cyberspace future; *Cyberspace* (New York: Wiley, 1998), 96. I would specifically emphasize Gibson's portrayals of heavy computer use as a practice that consumes white bodies. For example, in his *All Tomorrow's Parties* (New York: Ace Books, 1999), the reflection in a computer "display reveals Laney's hollowed eyes"; Laney, a white keyboarder suffering from a hacker "syndrome" reminiscent of "tuberculosis," wastes away over the course of the novel, plagued by "Information. This flow. This . . . corrosion" (4, 3, 40).

20. This evolution of cyberphobia in the direction of partial identification with the machine may even be read in the final installment of the four-film "Alien Legacy," *Alien: Resurrection* (1997), which concludes with a bio-engineered Ripley/Alien hybrid (Sigourney Weaver) returned to earth, holding hands with a cyborg (Winona Ryder). More recently, *Matrix Revolutions* (2003) and *I, Robot* (2004), for all their apparent cyberphobia, ultimately reflect a desire to make peace with the machine. The latter places a cyberphobic black man in the lead (played by Will Smith)—a variation on Luke and Vader, he struggles with the trauma of a cybernetic limb—who gradually overcomes his anti-robot prejudices to shake hands with the humanoid Sonny.

21. One such reference appears in a news item that observes a crossover between the *Matrix* and *Office Space* universes: the "video game that expands upon the plot of *The Matrix: Reloaded . . .* includes several references to another film with a devoted cult following, Office Space"; Dave Larsen, "Enter the 'Office Space,'" *Dayton Daily News*, June 8, 2003. The *Los Angeles Times* notes that although *Office Space* did little damage at the box office, "the movie is now held up as a deft satire about office drones who work at a faceless, downsizing, high-tech company. Today, *Office Space* often airs on cable and is beloved among video-store clerks"; Paul Brownfield, "'White guys, engines and beers' is credo," *Los Angeles Times* story, reprinted in the

Hamilton Spectator, October 24, 2002, D9. Another *Office Space* phenomenon is the meteoric rise to popularity of the red Swingline stapler fetishized by one of the film's characters: "When it came out on video, it was clear the movie was reaching cubicle-dwelling computer programmers. For months, demands for 'that red stapler' poured in to Swingline." Geoffrey A. Fowler, "Cult Film's Collateral Spinoff: Red Stapler," *Wall Street Journal,* July 26, 2002, 14. Numerous other news stories use the word "cult" to describe the film.

22. Thanks to John Rumrich for remembering this 1983 example of the black male computer expert, with Richard Pryor as light-fingered code cracker Gus Gorman, an kind of idiot savant whose programming skills surface as if by magic.

23. One may consider, for example, the debate on the recent trend to grant more visas to technology workers, typically from South Asian countries. In such cases, third-world outsourcing effectively goes in-house. See Julia Malone, "Techies See New Threat: Foreigners on L-1 Visas: Workers Facing Layoffs in a Slumping Market Are Spurred to Action," *Austin American-Statesman,* June 23, 2003, D1, D3. *Dilbert*'s dutiful Asok fulfills a role similar to Samir's in the popular imagination of cubicle tech work.

24. The form of the gangsta curse suits the occasion. The fax, maker of facsimiles, is the evil replacement for the mother, substituting electronic reproduction for natural. It must die for its technological violation of the mother principle. One could note the famous kiss-off line hurled by Sarah Connor (Linda Hamilton) at the Terminator in the first movie of that name: "You're terminated, fucker!" Bearer of all of mankind's hopes in her womb, she destroys the machine that would end all natural reproduction on earth. Rebel leader Reese refers to the killing machines as "motherfuckers" and to the Terminator sent to kill the "Mother of the Future" as "the motherfucker."

25. He thus imitates a move of the company he hates; as Peter has learned by talking to outside consultants hired to boost efficiency at Initech, management is about to lay off some software engineers and "farm some work out to Singapore—standard operating procedure."

26. *Mondo 2000* 9 (1993): 73.

27. When he first awakens from the world of illusion, the world in which Thomas Anderson is a suit-wearing software engineer trapped in a cubicle, Neo finds that he is in fact naked, bald, curled up helplessly inside a snug oblong vessel filled with fluid, and connected to a tube system that keeps his body alive. What is the Matrix? The word itself supplies an answer. Translating from the Latin: the matrix is a womb. S. Paige Baty's *e-mail trouble: love & addiction & the matrix* (Austin: University of Texas Press, 1999) was written before the film appeared but highlights this etymological significance in its chosen metaphor for the Internet's enveloping embrace. The matrix is a womb, but the most horrible perversion of a womb imaginable. It is an entirely unnatural mechanism of suspended nurture, a purely technological uterus for arresting development, a womb without a mother that holds a fetus that will never be born. This unspeakable spectacle imbues the movie's fantasy of oppression with a compelling nightmare to be overcome.

As *Alien*'s deadly "Mother" of a computer suggests, *The Matrix* does not stand alone in registering this particular form of technohorror. In "Some Thing to Watch Over You: The Surveillance Art of Julia Scher," Constance Penley addresses the artist with a summary diagnosis: "If I can characterize the psychosexual imaginary of the spaces you construct in your installations, I'd say it's that of the murderous womb." Penley puts a feminist query to this image: "What are the consequences of metaphorizing our modern technocultural world as a devouring, abusive mother? How does this differ from the cultural tendency to conflate technology out of control with women out of control?" Julia Scher gives a partial answer, assigning to her art the work of marking "the horror in words, to bring it closer to the surface, to lift the dead weight of repression" (*Mondo 2000,* February 1993, 39). Scher here sees her installations as presenting a cultural fear in an objective form that makes its logic more accessible to critique. How does such a deployment of the murderous womb image differ from garden-variety gynophobia? The horror presented in both Scher's work, as in *Alien* and *The Matrix,* seems at root to have less to do with the fear of women per se, and much more to do with revulsion at what technology has *done to* motherhood. At issue is not a terrifying woman whose womb acts as a killing machine, but rather a deathly machine that has substituted itself for the woman's natural maternal body.

28. Here one could consult Lisa Nakamura's *Cybertypes* (New York: Routledge, 2002), 153n14, on the "open secret" of Keanu's Asian-ness—precisely that which is suppressed in his role as Thomas Anderson but which comes into full flower as an identity accessory in his ascent to replendent Neo-ness. Once he is freed, *The Matrix* has him kung fu fighting, and *Reloaded* resplendently costumes him as a Zen priest. He had been a slave while working for Metacortex, a slavery that was experienced as an extreme whiteness. As an acquaintance says early on, "Something wrong, man? You look a little whiter than usual." His whiteness in "The Matrix" verges on the powdery; his escape allows him to overcome any limitations his pallidness might impose by a virtual bond with blackness that unleashes his potential for exotic heroism.

29. For the everlasting appeal of gear, see Thomas de Zengotita, "The Romance of Empire," *Harper's,* July 2003: 31–39.

30. *Mondo 2000* 9 (1993): 23–24.

31. Played by Marcus Chong, Tank may be read as portraying a Black-Asian identity. As the Operator for a ship that is labeled "Made in the U.S.A.," Tank is responsible for providing the crew with access to the Japanese-coded Matrix (see discussion in this chapter). In this contribution to the team, he recalls Jingo Asakuma in *Rising Sun* as an emblem of America's multiracial superiority in meeting a monocultural Asian threat. His brother Dozer and his other family members (introduced in the sequels) are coded more uniformly as "black."

32. The dreadlocked Link hearkens back to an old cyberpunk standard, one recently called out by Kalí Tal. In her review of Lisa Nakamura's *Cybertypes,* Tal points out the flaw of, for example, viewing Neal Stephenson's half-black Hiro Protagonist in *Snow Crash* as an "outsider" to cyberpunk conventions:

That Nakamura can see Protagonist's blackness only as a symbol of his alienation is disturbing, particularly since black characters in cyberpunk literature and film are (re)presented so consistently. No African Americanist could miss the repetition of the figure of the black techno-primitive in science fiction in general and cyberpunk in particular. From the "Rastas in space" exoticism of *Buckaroo Bonzai* [sic] and the reggae-flavored data havens of Bruce Sterling's *Islands in the Net,* to the gritty street cred of the characters played by gangsta rapper Ice-T in *Johnny Mnemonic* and *Tank Girl,* the magical touch of the titular *Brother From Another*

Planet, and the wise guides of *The Matrix,* the sci-fi/cyberpunk trope of blackness as simultaneously a site of wisdom, danger and unimpeachable hipness is baldly apparent to anyone with an eye to see it.

See http://www.freshmonsters.com/kalital/Text/Reviews/Nakamura.html.

33. The co-presence of both katakana and kanji characters distinguishes the inscription system from Chinese. The "matrix code" thus connects with the fears of *Haiku Tunnel,* discussed earlier, and its diagnosis of death by Japanese numbers.

34. See Bukatman, *Terminal Identity,* 274. Bukatman's discussion of Sterling also astutely notes the confusion between literal and figurative signification that characterizes the Sterling style, 277.

35. Whether *Blade Runner*'s Shimago-Dominguez Corporation that recruits for the colonies or *Alien*'s Weyland-Yutani Corporation, the evil empire likewise arrives in the form of a multinational conglomerate with a distinctly Japanese component. During an era when Japanese investors were snapping up large chunks of downtown Southern California, Japan supplied the default Asian component of the menacing multinational, especially in the Hollywood imagination. With the more recent prospect of China as a major capitalist force—not to mention the widespread illegal electronic reproduction of Hollywood content in China—Sinophobia may begin to supplant Nippophobia. In the 2004 remake of *The Manchurian Candidate,* "Manchurian Global" pulls the cybernetic puppet strings in a conspiracy to control American politics (the movie's tagline turns reassurance into cybernetic menace: "Everything is under Control").

36. Though such techno-blackening aligns with the racial work of other cyberphobic texts, Sterling's narrative does not explicitly racialize Pilot's and Modem's technological transformations into "Lobster's." *Islands in the Net* (New York: Arbor House, 1988) further suggests Sterling's difference from *Matrix*-style racialization in the deployment of techno-blackness. When a globetrotting white techie character boosts the melanin levels of his skin, he becomes blackened—not as a result of monitor burn but rather to prevent sunburn; adoptive blackness functions as a consciously adaptive response to climate rather than simply as a victimary index of occupational oppression.

37. One should note that a Sterling hero does—at first with great reluctance, but finally without fear, as a kind of tough-minded necessary self-sacrifice—become a "Posthuman" reshaped in the "lobster" image of "Modem" in the story "Cicada Queen," reprinted in *Schismatrix Plus* (New York: Ace Books, 1996), 293. Sterling dances much more ambivalently than most at the edge of posthumanism. See Bukatman for the important posthumanist turn signalled by "Cicada Queen" (*Terminal Identity,* 275).

38. See, for example, "'Matrix' Sequel's Multihued Future Flies in the Face of Sci-Fi Tradition," Annette John-Hall, *Philadelphia Inquirer,* reprinted in the *Austin American-Statesman,* June 6, 2003, F7. Cornel West is quoted in praise of the films' treatment of the "fundamental humanity of black people" as a departure from the norm: "Black humanity usually scares (white filmmakers) to death. They don't know what to do with it." While acknowledging the positive nature of many of the roles for black characters in these films, I would suggest that West's words also accurately imply what the *Matrix* films do all *too* effectively: they do find something

"*to do with*" black humanity. They technologize and instrumentalize it, especially in the characters of Tank and Link.

39. Jess Cagle, "*The Matrix* Reloads," *Time,* May 14, 2002, 62.

40. *Digital Delirium,* ed. Arthur and Marilouise Kroker (New York: St. Martin's, 1997), 16.

41. In blurring the boundary between tech worker and black slave, such narration must manage to suppress any thought that such an equation may amount to a trivialization of black history and, moreover, a denial of ongoing racial injustice. The success of such a stratagem depends upon an audience so thoroughly convinced and absorbed by its own sense of oppression that it is willing to accept the narration as sincerely addressing both tech and black oppression.

42. Neal Stephenson, *Cryptonomicon* (New York: Avon, 1999), 78. I can confirm this, in all seriousness: bad things really do happen to good technologists in academia. You who read these words: if you can troubleshoot computers, don't let them find you, unless you want tech support to become your career. In academia, even in the hard sciences, I have seen brilliant grad students and postdocs sucked dry by the importunate demands of willfully helpless technophobes. I want to make clear that in taking a critical position on discourse that speaks of such exploitation, I am not denying that this abuse is real and damaging; my critique pertains rather to the appropriation of specifically *racializing* terms and attitudes in describing technological labor. The technologically competent who complain of being overburdened by the tech work of others as reminiscent of the black slavery of the American past only fuel the racist unconscious of the technophobes whose avoidance and, perhaps more importantly, devaluation of tech work has created those overloads in the first place; such devaluation can be a barrier to the professionalization of information technology positions with adequate compensation.

43. State Farm may well be sincere about minority recruiting. But the *Wired* demographic remains overwhelmingly white. State Farm thus displays to this primary audience its diversity goals as further proof of its benevolence.

44. *Cryptonomicon*'s notion of the tactical impersonation of negroes may borrow from the Schwarzkommando episodes of *Gravity's Rainbow* (New York: Viking, 1973), especially in that the Allies first invent the idea, and stage the spectacle, of black rocket engineers before they discover that this strategic fantasy has a real counterpart on the German side of the incipient global Rocket State (75). For an account of the pervasiveness of Pynchon's presence in the cyberpunk "loop," see Brian McHale's "POSTcyberMODERNpunkISM" in *Storming the Reality Studio,* ed. Larry McCaffery (Durham, N.C.: Duke University Press, 1991), 315. But see also John Johnston, *Information Multiplicity: American Fiction in the Age of Media Saturation* (Baltimore: Johns Hopkins University Press, 1998), 3–7, which, qualifying the literary genealogies presented in the McCaffery casebook, categorically excludes cyberpunk from "the fiction of information multiplicity" pioneered by Pynchon. While acknowledging that Stephenson in particular takes cyberpunk "to a new complexity," Johnston disqualifies the genre in general for its return to "conventional narrative ordering" (268n13, 6).

45. In a review of *Neuromancer,* Iain Rowan refers to "the weakest part of the novel, Gibson's Rastas in space, all righteous dub warriors and quasi-mystical philosophers wreathed in marijuana smoke and references to Babylon. It's a genuine at-

tempt on Gibson's part to show a diverse future, I am sure—but it comes across as a clumsy and patronising near-parody"; see http://www.infinityplus.co.uk/nonfiction/neuromancer.htm. The allusion to "reggae-flavored data havens" appears in Kalí Tal's inventory of cyberpunk's repeated use of "the black techno-primitive" as a source of hipness by association; see http://www.freshmonsters.com/kalital/Text/Reviews/Nakamura.html.

46. Jay Clayton aptly locates Stephenson's contribution in "Convergence of the Two Cultures: A Geek's Guide to Contemporary Literature," *American Literature* 74, no. 4 (December 2002): 807–31. "The lesson I draw from Stephenson and other novelists, poets, and playwrights who focus on science is that a critical engagement with technology, not withdrawal, is the best hope for what were once called humanist values" (825). In a sympathetic vein, D. Quentin Miller's "Deeper Blues, or the Posthuman Prometheus: Cybernetic Renewal and the Late-Twentieth-Century American Novel" fruitfully proceeds from the premise that the "tendency to view computers as powerful and potentially dominant adversaries is an understandable but unfortunate impulse, and it continues to saturate the popular imagination"; *American Literature* 77, no. 2 (June 2005): 379. Miller's article, which appeared while the present book was in press, in many ways anticipates the approach of my final chapter, in that Miller looks to contemporary novelists for alternatives to popular cyberphobic narratives, especially movies: "Perhaps because computers and film share the image-based interface of a screen, films about computers have played into human fearfulness in a way that much print fiction has not" (379).

CHAPTER 5. THINKING INSIDE THE BLACK BOX

1. The quoted phrases belong to the opening track, "P.Funk," and to the commentary of Tom Vickers, former "Minister of Information for Parliament-Funkadelic," in the liner notes for the reissued *Mothership Connection*. George Clinton's adoption of the alien pose perfectly illustrates what Alexander Weheliye writes about black culture's response to a history of dehumanization: "Because New World black subjects were denied access to the position of humanity for so long, 'humanity' refuses to signify any ontological primacy within Afro-diasporic discourses. In black culture this category becomes a designation that shows the finitudes and exclusions very clearly, thereby denaturalizing the 'human' as a universal formation while at the same time laying claim to it"; Alexander Weheliye, " 'Feenin': Posthuman Voices in Contemporary Black Popular Music," *Social Text* 20, no. 2 (Summer 2002): 22, 27. Clinton's revenant alien, broadcasting the Mothership Connection, simultaneously reclaims the pyramids and Afro-diasporic humanity. The phrase "How We Were Never Human" forms Weheliye's own reply to Katherine Hayles's *How We Became Posthuman* (Chicago: University of Chicago Press, 1999). See also Ben Williams, "Black Secret Technology: Detroit Techno and the Information Age" in *Technicolor: Race, Technology, and Everyday Life,* ed. Alondra Nelson and Thuy Linh N. Tu with Alicia Headlam Hines (New York, New York University Press, 2001), 154–76, esp. Williams's discussion of "We Are the Robots": "Becoming robots was, for African American musicians, a subliminally political act, the ramifications of which can be read as both a form of self-empowerment and an identification with

otherness, whether technological or racial" (161). I am indebted to Noah Mass for emphasizing Clinton's empowered stance on technology.

2. Weheliye's " 'Feenin' " unpacks the Zapp recording, identifying the band as "associated with George Clinton" but distinguished "by virtue of heavily mechanized funk and extensive vocoder use" (35; the vocoder is "a speech-synthesizing device that renders the human voice robotic," 22). Weheliye locates the achievement of "Computer Love" in Zapp's overlapping of "vocoderized and human voices to unearth the 'humanity' of machinic affections"; "Here, the 'human' and 'machinic' become mere electric effects that conjoin the human voice and (intelligent) machines" (36, 37).

3. *No Maps for these Territories* (2000), a documentary feature film, dir. Mark Neale.

4. Here we may detect a Victorian anxiety updated for the digital age. One scientific nightmare emphasized by Lord Kelvin foresaw the "heat death" of the universe: the laws of entropy would eventually empty nature's pockets of all usable heat difference, producing a uniformly low, deadly temperature. In Gibson's tagline, the laws of entropy may be seen to go to work not on heat but on information, tending toward a final state of undifferentiated meaninglessness.

5. Jeffrey Howard suggests an analogy to the death and life distinction, in *Gravity's Rainbow* (New York: Viking, 1973), between Blicero's Rocket 00000 and Enzian's Rocket 00001; Enzian refuses the "Final Zero" (525). Howard also emphasizes the importance of the racial dimension of Enzian's trajectory from slave/victim to figure of resistance. Personal correspondence, February 2005.

6. Paul D. Miller, *Rhythm Science* (Cambridge, Mass.: Mediawork/MIT Press, 2004), 17.

7. The de-alienation of "technology" could well begin with a simple reminder of its etymological components and their affinity for art, as in Miller's alertness to the "melding of the Greek words for art, craft and word" (72). As Samuel Weber similarly observes in a close-reading of Heidegger, "*technè* is a form of *poèisis* that in turn is closely related to art"; *Mass Mediauras: Form, Technics, Media,* ed. Alan Cholodenko (Stanford: Stanford University Press, 1996), 60. See also Thomas P. Hughes, *Human-Built World: How to Think about Technology and Culture* (Chicago: University of Chicago Press, 2004), 3.

8. Timothy Melley, *Empire of Conspiracy* (Ithaca, N.Y.: Cornell University Press, 2000), 7–16, 94. For a further development of Pynchonian responses to "agency panic," see Joseph Tabbi, *Cognitive Fictions* (Minneapolis: University of Minnesota Press, 2002), 34.

9. For a fascinating case study of the need to look out for things, to care from an engineering standpoint, see Bruno Latour's *Aramis, or the Love of Technology* (Cambridge: Harvard University Press, 1996).

10. Pynchon, with Cornellian chip casually on shoulder, seems to have anticipated the charge that he may be instrumentalizing the black musician to demonstrate his own coolness through a display of racial openmindedness and jazz appreciation; Sphere mocks the "the old Northern liberal routine" of "white Ivy League" men who do the same (*V.,* 299). With respect to the question of color monitoring, we may note that this black man is not presented as an innate techno-whiz, but as an artist who learns to experiment inventively through the structures of electrical engineering. An inquisitive artificer rather than a natural machine, Sphere resembles Pynchon himself, who, as Joseph Tabbi observes, "tends to *work through* the systems and im-

ages created by engineers to a holistic vision that does not exclude the systems and images." Tabbi, *Postmodern Sublime: Technology and American Writing from Mailer to Cyberpunk* (Ithaca, N.Y.: Cornell University Press, 1995), 90. Along the way, Sphere's own motto comes as close to a definition of Pynchon's tonal stance as any formula I can find within his work: "Keep cool, but care" (393, and again on 394). See also Richard Poirier's account of a Pynchon who "is in fact as partial to technology and to science as he is to Rilke"; "The Importance of Thomas Pynchon," in *Mindful Pleasures: Essays on Thomas Pynchon*, ed. George Levine and David Leverenz (Boston: Little, Brown, 1976), 25. Leverenz's own contribution to this volume, "On Trying to Read *Gravity's Rainbow*," notably begins with the apparent givens of a nature versus technology polarization and then proceeds to read past this dualism and the paradoxes such a reading scheme entails.

11. Bruno Latour, *The Politics of Nature: How to Bring the Sciences into Democracy* (Cambridge, Mass.: Harvard University Press, 2004), 246.

12. The phrase "racial allegory," taken from Walter Kirn's review in *Time*, appears in the front cover blurb for the Anchor paperback edition of *The Intuitionist*, issued January 2000.

13. The final section of *John Henry Days*, "Adding Verses," proposes extending the legend via a continuation of *The Intuitionist*'s renegotiation of relation to objects: "Perhaps a quote from the engine itself might shed some light on the situation, explain the events of that day in the Big Bend Tunnel, lend some perspective. Let the other side speak" (341–42). Also along these lines, Whitehead's novel tracks the most dedicated archivist of the John Henry legacy, who has compiled all extant performances of the Ballad of John Henry, recorded over the years on a variety of media, including 78s, then 33s, then 8-tracks, cassettes, and CDs. In assembling the John Henry museum, the archivist of song becomes an archivist of technology, discovering that "the replacement of one form of technology by a superior form was an exhibit in itself" (381). Whitehead's novel reveals history as a story of and by technologies of memory.

14. For a resonant work in the philosophy of science, see Michel Serres, *The Natural Contract* (Ann Arbor: University of Michigan Press, 1995).

15. Cited in the epigraph to Weheliye's " 'Feenin,' " 21.

16. Carol Cooper's review in *Vibe* is quoted on the jacket to Octavia E. Butler, *Bloodchild and Other Stories* (New York: Four Walls Eight Windows, 1995).

17. Marge Piercy in *He, She, and It* (New York: Fawcett Crest, 1991) similarly places a premium on the survival value of cyber-expertise: her island of hope is the kibbutz-like "free town" of Tikva, whose mastery of computer security ensures its safety and economic independence in a sea of rapacious "multis."

   In Paul Beatty's novel *The White Boy Shuffle* (Boston: Houghton Mifflin, 1996), the main character, "reluctant" poet and black community leader Gunnar Kaufman, likewise expresses the pragmatic attraction of cybercommunity: "After growing accustomed to police officers pulling students out of classes for impromptu interrogations . . . I started to make friends, mostly with the nerdier students. The computer was the only place where we had true freedom of assembly" (64). But he also fears that he may be primed to betray his race on an apocalyptic scale, through a leadership compromised by deterministic hopelessness: "Wherever I travel, a long queue of baby black goslings files behind a plastic wind-up bard spring-driven toward self-destruction, crossing the information superhighway and refusing to look both ways" (1). Yet the true menace of this vision lies not in technologies of information per se—Internet road kill—but in the temptation of despair: "In the struggle for freedom, a reluctant young poet convinces black Americans to give up hope and kill themselves in a climactic crash 'n' burn finale" (1).

18. Cf. Erik Davis, *Techgnosis: Myth, Magic, Mysticism in the Age of Information* (New York: Harmony Books, 1998). Thanks to Chuck Bradford for this citation.

19. Tom LeClair, "Pitch Perfect," *Book,* January/February 2003, 72.

20. Ishmael Reed, introduction to *Black No More* (New York: Modern Library, 1999), xi.

21. Ralph Ellison, *Invisible Man* (New York: Vintage Books, 1972), 304, 307. By the same token, one may worry that *Color Monitors* represents the overzealous voice of a man from the ivory tower, passing judgment on the racial clumsiness of American culture, pounding his fist: "The brother *does not compute!*" Shouldn't there be some way to affirm accomplishment in arte, techne, and logos? The present chapter exists in part to address that concern.

22. Ellison, *Invisible Man,* 9–10.

23. I borrow the term "electropoetics" from a category used by the Electronic Book Review.http://www.electronicbookreview.com/v3/servlet/ebr?command=view_weave &filter=electropoetics.

24. Powers's plight here echoes that of Ronald Frobisher, the tragic novelist-in-a-datacan from David Lodge's *Small World* (New York: Viking Penguin, 1985). Frobisher loses his will to write after a visit to "Centre for Computational Stylistics," which eventuates in his entire corpus being committed to a magnetic tape and analyzed for word frequency (181–82).

25. Tabbi, *Cognitive Fictions,* 72. D. Quentin Miller has recently encouraged readers of *Galatea 2.2* not to "ignore the development of a posthumanist consciousness in Richard, who returns to storytelling not as a retreat from the technology-saturated world but, rather, as a result of what can be learned from technology"; "Deeper Blues, or the Posthuman Prometheus: Cybernetic Renewal and the Late-Twentieth-Century American Novel," *American Literature* 77, no. 2 (June 2005): 398–99.

26. Hayles, *How We Became Posthuman,* 262.

27. Powers's rather vindictive caricature borrows from the venerable hostility of realists to theorists: the frustrated linguistic philosopher attempts to explain that his bomb threat had been delivered in the "moral subjunctive," in reference to a "hypothetical detonation, for which he expected no more than a hypothetical sentence" (273). Powers's jab at misguided academic hairsplitting nevertheless also communicates his strong preference for technology over "theory." Jeffrey Howard further notes that Powers "also parodies the grad student's New Historicist/Post-Structuralist reading of *The Tempest*. Galatea 2.2 (the computer) rejects both humanism and poststructuralism." Personal correspondence, February 2005.

28. John Kelso, crusty Texas columnist and self-described "bubba," supports this meat-versus-microchip hostility: "Are there any barbeque places that have Internet hookups yet? If there are, please let me know so I can go jump off the Congress Avenue bridge." *Austin American-Statesman,* June 15, 2004, B1. See also "Something Foul in the Air at State Parks; Wireless Web," in which Mike Leggett, who covers the hunting beat, gripes that "I'll probably have to look over at the next campsite and see

a couple snuggling to a computer image of a campfire, eating a veggie burger. . . . Used to be that folks would go to a state park and gather around the campfire for a wienie roast." *Austin American-Statesman,* January 6, 2005, D9. These columnists typify a knee-jerk cyberphobic imagination. But Smiley's caricature of the farmer who wouldn't touch a computer with a fork has become increasingly inapplicable to agricultural reality. Dr. Bill Cassady informs me that independent cattle ranchers in Texas are among the most wired of entrepreneurs; computers have helped, for example, with keeping detailed and accurate medical records of each animal. As an academic novel, Smiley's analysis perhaps continues to apply most eloquently to cyberphobic assumptions encountered on campus rather than in the fields. More generally, as discussed in chapter 3 on corporate narratives, cyberphobia may flourish even in a company willing to make large technological investments; concessions to managerial cyberphobia can work well as part of a technology sales pitch, so long as management has the luxury of delegating technological labor. In the case of small independent businesses, that condition is less likely to be in effect.

29. http://whatis.techtarget.com/WhatIs_Definition_Page/0,4152,212589,00.html and http://whatis.techtarget.com/WhatIs_Definition_Page/0,4152,212609,00.html.

30. *PMLA* 114, no. 2 (March 1999): 175.

31. "Two Geeks on Their Way to Byzantium: A Conversation with Richard Powers," *Atlantic Monthly,* June 28, 2000; accessed online via *Atlantic Unbound,* http://www.theatlantic.com/unbound/interviews/ba2000–06–28.htm. On Powers's "discovery that code combined action and meaning," we may recall, as Paul Miller does in *Rhythm Science,* the words of William Carlos Williams: "Poetry is nothing but a machine made of words" (32).

32. Donald Knuth, *The Art of Computer Programming,* vol. 1, *Fundamental Algorithms* (Menlo Park, Calif.: Addison-Wesley, 1968), v.

33. http://www-cs-faculty.stanford.edu/knuth/mmix.html.

34. Donald Knuth, *Literate Programming* (Stanford: Center for the Study of Language and Information, 1992), 99, ix, emphasis in original.

35. Knuth, *Art of Computer Programming,* 1: viii.

36. John Cayley, "Pressing the 'Reveal Code' Key"; published in *EJournal* in 1996, http://www.hanover.edu/philos/ejournal/archive/ej-6–1.txt, republished on *New Media Reader* CD-ROM, in the file found at \1990s\Cayley\Pressing.txt. Neal Stephenson recommends that readers get a "taste" of computer code by selecting the "View/Document Source menu item" while browsing a webpage; *In the Beginning . . . Was the Command Line* (New York: Perennial, 1999), 15. While he holds no particularly high regard for HTML, Stephenson's larger point is the Graphical User Interface revolution, set in motion by the Macintosh OS, resulted in what he metaphorically describes as "attractively styled cars with their innards hermetically sealed, so that how they worked was something of a mystery" (5). His argument here, against an image-based interface that obscures or replaces a word-based command line, resembles Joseph Tabbi's point above, that *Windows* creates opacity.

37. Rita Raley, "Interferences: [Net.Writing] and the Practice of Codework," http://www.electronicbookreview.com/v3/servlet/ebr?command=view_essay&essay_id=rayleyele. See also Katherine Hayles, "Deeper into the Machine: The Future of Electronic Literature," *Culture Machine* 5 (the e-Issue, 2003), http://culturema-

chine.tees.ac.uk/Cmach/Backissues/j005/Articles/Hayles/NHayles.htm; and John Cayley's "The Code Is Not the Text (unless It Is the Text)," http://www.electronic-bookreview.com/v3/servlet/ebr?command=view_essay&essay_id=cayleyele#fnˆ25.

38. Jessica Loseby explains the genesis of "Code Scares Me" at http://www.kanon-media.com/news/nml/code.htm; Raley also discusses this piece in "Codework."

39. Christos H. Papadimitriou, *Turing: A Novel About Computation* (Cambridge, Mass.: MIT Press, 2003), 246. This remark about Alexandros's initial technophobia appears in an afterword of postings "From the Newsgroup."

40. Emphasis added. In opposing information to entropy, Mosley favors Brillouin's definition over Shannon's. See Hayles, "Self-Reflexive Metaphor in Maxwell's Demon and Shannon's Choice," *Literature and Science: Theory and Practice,* ed. Stuart Peterfreund (Boston: Northeastern University Press, 1990), 232. A similar value system informs Matt Ruff's novel, *Set This House in Order* (New York: Perennial, 2003). The story, which deals with multiple personality disorder, is structured on the tension between chaos and order, building to the victory of the latter (volume III, "Order") over the former (volume II, "Chaos"). The novel early on establishes the metaphor of virtual reality for thinking about the psychological coping strategies of a main character, Andy, who has built a house for his multiple personalities in an imagined geography within his mind. Based upon these credentials, he gets hired by the Reality Factory, a tech start-up specializing in "virtual reality," because, says the boss to Andy, "You know more about it than anyone I've ever met. . . . it's a lot like what you've got in your head" (31). On the one hand, the novel tends to equate computer ability with psychopathology; for example, another main character, Mouse, also has multiple personality disorder and is said to be "a natural programmer" (76). But, on the other hand, the association here between computer work and clinical condition is quite different than, say, the one presented in *Haiku Tunnel* (discussed in chapter 4): there, Josh suffered from instability and depression as a *result* of his technological labors; here, Andy and Mouse appear to acquire technological abilities in the process of dealing with their psychological challenges—brain hacking translates into general technical skill. In *Set This House in Order,* virtual reality supplies a metaphor for treating the traumatized mind, a tool for affirming order and life over chaos and death. I am indebted to Susan Barnett for bringing Ruff's engrossing work to my attention.

41. For a discussion of "Informational Infection and Hygiene in *Snow Crash,*" see Hayles, *How We Became Posthuman,* 272.

42. This impression is reinforced by the book's design: the display font used for the cover, title page, and chapter headings is the retro "computer" typeface associated with the early punch-card and tape-drive mainframes alluded to in the novel, such as the legendary IBM System/360 (129). To get a fuller technological context for the years of Mosley's "history" (*Blue Light* covers 1965 to roughly the mid-1980s), see Paul E. Ceruzzi, *A History of Modern Computing* (Cambridge, Mass.: MIT Press, 1998), esp. ch. 5, "The 'Go-Go' Years and the System/360, 1961–1975" and ch. 8, "Augmenting Human Intellect, 1975–1985."

43. M. Mitchell Waldrop, *Washington Post,* June 9, 1999, H6.

44. Ishmael Reed, *Japanese by Spring* (New York: Atheneum, 1993), 211.

INDEX

Items in **bold** indicate major concepts and arguments in this book